The American Academic Profession

The American Academic Profession

A Synthesis of Social Scientific Inquiry Since World War II

MARTIN J. FINKELSTEIN

Ohio State University Press: Columbus

Table 3.2 is reprinted, by permission, from Martin Trow (ed.), *Teachers and Students* (New York: McGraw-Hill, 1975). Copyright © 1975 by The Carnegie Foundation for the Advancement of Teaching.

Figure 1 and Table 3.4 are reprinted, by permission, from Verne A. Stadtman, *Academic Adaptations* (San Francisco: Jossey-Bass, 1980). Copyright © 1980 by The Carnegie Foundation for the Advancement of Teaching and by Jossey-Bass. All rights reserved.

Tables 3.5, 3.6, and 3.7 are reprinted, by permission, from Seymour Lipset and Everett C. Ladd, "The Changing Social Origins of American Academics," in *Qualitative and Quantitative Social Research,* edited by Robert K. Merton, James S. Coleman, and Peter H. Rossi. Copyright © 1979 by The Free Press, a Division of Macmillan Publishing Co., Inc.

Table 4.2 is reprinted, by permission, from Reece McGee, *Academic Janus* (San Francisco: Jossey-Bass, 1971). Copyright © 1971 by Jossey-Bass.

Table 5.3 is reprinted, by permission, from Robert C. Wilson, Jerry Gaff, Evelyn Dienst, Lynn Wood, and James Bavry, *College Professors and Their Impact on Students* (New York: Wiley InterScience Series, 1975). Copyright © 1975 by John Wiley and Sons, Inc.

Table 5.4 is reprinted, by permission, from Kenneth A. Feldman, "The Superior College Teacher from the Students' View," *Research in Higher Education,* Vol. 5, No. 3 (1976).

Table 7.1 is reprinted, by permission, from Allan M. Cartter, *Ph.D.s and the Academic Labor Market* (New York: McGraw-Hill, for The Carnegie Commission on Higher Education, 1976). Copyright © 1976 by The Carnegie Foundation for the Advancement of Teaching. All rights reserved.

Table 7.4 is adapted and reprinted, by permission, from Judith M. Gappa and Barbara S. Uehling, *Women in Academe: Steps to Greater Equality,* AAHE-ERIC/Higher Education Research Report No. 1 (Washington, D.C.: American Association for Higher Education, 1979).

An earlier version of chapter 2, entitled "From Tutor to Specialized Scholar: Academic Professionalism in Eighteenth and Nineteenth Century America," appeared in *History of Higher Education Annual,* 3 (1983).

Parts of chapter 7, entitled "The Status of Academic Women: An Assessment of Five Competing Explanations," are reprinted, by permission, from *The Review of Higher Education,* 7, No. 3 (Spring 1984).

Library of Congress Cataloging in Publication Data
Finkelstein, Martin J., 1949–
The American academic profession
Includes bibliography and index.
    1. Universities and colleges—United States—Faculty—History—20th century. 2. College teachers' socioeconomic status—United States—History—20th century. 3. Educational surveys—United States. I. Title.
LB2331.72.F56 1984   378'.12'0973   84-3613
ISBN 0-8142-0371-X

For Rena, and for what Felipa meant to us both,
and for my parents

Contents

Tables

Acknowledgments

This study was originally undertaken as a doctoral dissertation at the State University of New York at Buffalo between 1976 and 1978, under the direction of J. Bruce Francis. In the years since 1978 I have worked, off and on, at making the dissertation into a book.

Two people have had a singular hand in that process. The idea of making the dissertation into a book belonged to Robert J. Silverman, editor of the *Journal of Higher Education* and a member of the original dissertation committee. He not only raised the prospect but shepherded me through the entire manuscript submission process—alternately encouraging, cajoling, and pushing. And then there is Robert T. Blackburn, professor of higher education at the University of Michigan, and instigator, directly or indirectly, of a disproportionate share of the research on American academics over the past decade and a half. He provided me with copious comments on the original dissertation and indeed suggested the substantive organization that is reflected in the present book. He not only carefully critiqued the original document but he read and reread the revised and entirely new chapters. His pointed comments and his intimate knowledge of sources have saved me from innumerable errors (and those that do remain no doubt represent instances where I have failed to take his advice).

Closer to home, Allan O. Pfnister, my colleague at the University of Denver, read and commented on several chapters and generously shouldered the larger share of our collaborative research responsibilities for several months to allow me the time to complete the manuscript. Moreover, during the extended rush of the final typing, he functioned, in effect, without secretarial support. Final typing was supported by a grant from the University of Denver's Faculty

Senate Research Committee, as was research assistance in developing the chapter on women and minority faculty. Margie Pinnell and Cindy Lynch, graduate students in higher education at the University, both spent many hours in the library tracking down and verifying sources—all too often without compensation. And Linda McCarthy patiently managed to translate my scrawl and scores of dictated tapes into a near perfect final manuscript.

Closer to home still, my wife, Rena, sacrificed more evenings and weekends without a husband than either of us cares to remember and met the peaks and valleys of my enthusiasm with unfailing love and support.

I am pleased to acknowledge my enormous personal debt to all.

MARTIN J. FINKELSTEIN
South Orange, New Jersey

1

Introduction

This volume is about American academics as objects of social scientific inquiry. It highlights the generalizations about academics that have emerged over three and a half decades of increasingly intensive study.

The findings reported here are based largely on doctoral dissertation research begun in 1976. The research was inspired by the observation on the part of eminent leaders in higher education as well as serious students of the academic profession that although the study of academics had been increasing by leaps and bounds, particularly after 1960, the fundamental understandings required for informed academic decision-making yet remained elusive. This gap between what had been "learned" in empirical research and what was "known" or "understood" by administrators and faculty was attributed largely to the character of the research studies themselves. Thus, Blackburn (1971), Hodgkinson (1972), and Light (1972) collectively located the source of the gap in (1) the relative dearth of good theory undergirding research on faculty leading to studies that "reflect either the interests of those financing them or the questions of the day" rather than the truly fundamental issues (Light, 1972) and (2) the relative lack of "cross-fertilization" among research studies, that is, the failure of investigators to recognize the work of others bearing directly on their own, yielding a host of inquiries on the same phenomenon on noncomparable samples and employing noncomparable instruments.

The problem of "cross-fertilization" suggested yet another dimension of the knowledge gap: the relative inaccessibility of research findings both to specialized investigators and to the general academic community. The two preeminent sources of knowledge about faculty were doctoral dissertations and the research reports of academic social scientists. The former's findings were, with few exceptions, irretrievably lost to all but the authors' doctoral committees and ungeneralizable beyond the faculty at a single focal institution. The latter's findings tended to scatter over tens of specialized disciplinary journals in the social sciences and to focus on faculty in a single or small range of disciplines. To be sure, a number of integrative reviews of extant research had been undertaken (Stecklein, 1961; Medalia, 1963; Blackburn, 1971, 1972; Blackburn and Aurand, 1972; Light, 1972; Faia, 1974; Blackburn and Behymer, 1976), but these tended to be highly circumscribed in their scope, both with respect to the topics and the number of studies covered, and not readily accessible.

Beyond these, there were three other sources of knowledge about faculty which, though far smaller in volume, were decidedly more available. Most accessible were the periodic reports in the *Chronicle of Higher Education* of Ladd and Lipset's biennial faculty surveys and Minter and Bowen's biennial surveys of the condition of independent higher education. The former, constrained by a journalistic format, have highlighted faculty responses to a few survey questions related primarily to faculty political roles on and off campus. The latter have focused only peripherally on questions of faculty workload, compensation, and qualifications within the broader contexts of an assessment of the strength of the independent sector. A more inclusive view was provided by a spate of books published over the past decade, some of which received considerable attention even in the academic community (Livesey, 1975; Mandell, 1977). Although these efforts often represent a serious attempt to untangle academic knots, they are at best impressionistic and one-sided in their treatment, at worst, muckraking exposés (can the distinguishing characteristic of professors qua professors be that they are lazy, petty, and self-seeking?). A far more balanced, scholarly treatment of the academic professions is provided by only a handful of volumes: Ladd and Lipset's on academic politics (1975), Wilson and Gaff's on the teaching role (1975), Steinberg's on religion and ethnicity (1974), Tuckman's (1976) and Lewis's (1975) on the academic reward system, Blau's (1973) on productivity, Logan Wilson's (1979) update of his 1942 classic on academics at the major universities, and Bess's (1982) on the organization of the faculty role. These latter inquiries treat aspects of the academic role or the academic role in a limited range of institutions. Valuable as they are, they leave one without a sense of the whole.

It was in the service of promoting a view of the whole and closing the gap between what is known, on the one hand, and what we as academic citizens know, on the other, that the study which resulted in this volume was conceived. Specifically, I had in mind a report that would bring together the scattered, largely inaccessible results of social scientific and dissertation research on faculties and research on different aspects of the faculty role into a single, broadly accessible format.

Quite felicitously, my aim met with the growing development of methodological tools for integrating the results of diverse research studies. In an important 1971 article, Feldman (1971) attempted to codify some of the techniques he and Newcomb had employed in bringing together the vast corpus of research on college impacts (Newcomb and Feldman, 1969)—in particular, procedures for attaining greater comparability across studies. Feldman's initial efforts have since been augmented by the work of Light and Smith (1971), Jackson (1978), and Glass (1976, 1981).

Armed both with my initial purpose and the means for realizing it, I began a comprehensive search of the available literature. Two shaping decisions defined the parameters of that search. Substantively, the decision was taken to limit it to research on full-time academics at four-year colleges and universities. Beyond the obvious desire to avoid "mixing apples and oranges" (part-time faculty and those at two-year institutions differ substantially, as a group, from their four-year counterparts in background, training, and work activities), this decision recognized work already underway specifically focusing on faculty at the two-year college (Cohen and Brawer, 1977) and the varieties of part-time faculty (Tuckman, 1978, 1979; Leslie et al., 1982). Temporally, the focus of the search was expanded to include social scientific inquiry during the entire post–World War II period. While I recognized that the fortunes of American higher education, in general, and the academic professions, in particular, have fluctuated considerably over that period (changes in the academic job market are a case in point), and are indeed at this very moment in a stage of transition probably unprecedented since the Great Depression, I made several key assumptions. First, I assumed that earlier inquiry might uncover certain *general factors,* those larger principles of faculty motivation that would be readily adaptable to my own concern with basic understanding—provided that both their questions and my own shared a common referent, the same species of thoroughly professionalized academics that emerged fully at about the time of World War II. Second, I assumed that earlier inquiry would provide an all important baseline against which the results of inquiry currently underway might be judged in context. I proceeded, then, with the view that what was learned about the academic professions during their earlier ascendance was not irrelevant to understanding them in their current stage of stabilization or decline and might simultaneously provide the baseline context against which current changes might be assessed.

It was within these parameters that I foraged through several bibliographies, published and unpublished, various abstracts and indexes, computerized and not, and followed up assiduously on the references of references. The search yielded a tangible product: over three hundred systematic, empirical studies of postwar faculty.[1]

With a sample of research studies identified, the inquiry proceeded as follows.[2] Each of the research studies was treated as a *subject* or *case* and data were collected on twenty-three characteristics from each, including date of research report, dependent variables/topics examined, research strategy, data analysis procedure, sample composition, as well as the findings (recorded as descriptive statistics or the results of tests of statistical significance). The data on sample characteristics were subjected to a content analysis and examined to discern trends in research topics and strategies over time. Results of these analyses are fully reported in the original doctoral dissertation (Finkelstein, 1978). In order to integrate the findings generated by these inquiries, the research studies were grouped by dependent variable/topic and examined for overall patterns in the findings—that is, patterns in the outcome of tests of the relationship of all independent variables to each dependent variable/topic. In cases where no consistent overall pattern emerged, the groups of studies organized by topic were further broken down by characteristics of the studies themselves (for example, type of faculty studied), and I sought to discern patterns within these subgroups of studies. This procedure assumed that while no consistent findings might emerge for faculty as a whole, it might be possible to discern patterns along the lines of disciplinary affiliation or the type of institution in which faculty taught, or along temporal lines—that is, one kind of relationship may have held in the 1950s and quite another in the 1970s.

The results of the analysis were reported in the original doctoral dissertation. During the 1980–81 academic year, these results were updated by repeating the search and analysis cycles for research studies completed after 1975. In presenting the updated results here, I have striven to maintain a balance between the demands of fellow specialists for scholarly precision and full documentation and the demands of more general academic readers for a sharp substantive presentation cluttered only when necessary with footnotes and tables.[3]

The basic findings are presented in three chapters. Chapter 4 encompasses what we have learned about the choice to enter the professoriate, the dynamics of securing an academic position, advancement through the ranks, job changing between and within institutions, the norms that guide the academic career (academic freedom, professional autonomy, and the merit principle), career satisfaction, and retirement. Chapter 5 focuses explicitly on how faculty spend their time, with special attention to the research and teaching roles. We focus as well on faculty as academic citizens—their role in governance and in implementing educational innovations. The chapter concludes with a look at the stresses and satisfactions faculty experience in the work role. Chapter 6 highlights the "other side" of college and university faculty: their family life, leisure activities, their links to the religious/ethnic and political life of their communities.

The basic findings are preceded by an examination of the historical evolution of the modern academic role, with emphasis on the analysis of primary nineteenth century documents (chapter 2) as well as a demographic portrait of the contemporary academic profession (chapter 3). Chapter 7 is a detailed examination of the special case of women and minority faculty and draws upon the best available evidence to test the major explanations of their marginal status in academe.

Finally, the volume concludes with an attempt to put some conceptual order into the broad array of findings presented earlier (chapter 8).

1. A detailed description of the search and sampling procedures is provided in Appendix A.

2. A detailed description of these procedures is provided in Appendix B.

3. Those seeking fuller documentation on any particular point are urged to consult the original dissertation.

2

The Emergence of the Modern Academic Role

By World War II nearly one hundred and fifty thousand faculty were instructing some one and a half million students—about 15 percent of the eighteen to twenty-one age cohort. American higher education, generally, and the academic profession, in particular, were about to undergo their most explosive growth surge. During the next thirty years, the ranks of the American professoriate were to nearly quadruple. Between 1965 and 1970 alone, they swelled by one hundred and fifty thousand with the number of *new* positions exceeding the entire number of positions in 1940 (Lipset and Ladd, 1979). Now six hundred thousand strong, college and university professors were instructing nearly 50 percent of the college-age population.

This chapter seeks to chronicle the critical stages of that ascent in order to provide the historical context within which subsequent discussion of contemporary academics must be understood. In so doing, it focuses primarily on the early development of the professorial role during the latter half of the eighteenth century, the progressive professionalization of the faculty during the nineteenth century, and the subsequent consolidation of the modern academic role during the post–World War I period.

The generalizations presented here are drawn from a variety of secondary sources, including institutional and general histories of American higher education, several recent statistical studies of college faculties during the nineteenth century by McCaughey (1974) on Harvard, Creutz (1981) on Michigan, and Tobias (1982) on Dartmouth, as well as the author's own unpublished analyses of the nineteenth century faculties of Brown, Bowdoin, Yale, and Michigan.[1] Although the findings, then, cannot be viewed as representative of all of American higher education at any period, they do provide insight into developments at a half dozen or more "leading" institutions, thus avoiding the pitfalls of generalizations based on the peculiar life history of any single institution.

The findings are organized following Donald Light's (1972) conceptualization of the three analytically distinct, yet interrelated, strands of the modern academic career. The first, the disciplinary career, includes those events specifically connected with a discipline and its goals rather than with a particular job (for example, specialized training, work history prior to assumption of an academic career, involvements with disciplinary organizations and research activity). The institutional career includes those events associated with a faculty member's employment at a particular institution (for example, movement in a promotion system). Finally, the external career includes those work related activities undertaken outside the institution but rooted in a faculty member's disciplinary expertise (consulting, government service, public lecturing). Thus, we now turn to an examination of the evolutionary unfolding of these three career strands over the past two centuries.

THE EMERGENCE OF AN INSTITUTIONAL CAREER, 1750–1820

During the seventeenth century and the first half of the eighteenth century, the disciplinary career strand was, of course, virtually nonexistant, and even the institutional strand proved secondary to the external one. American colleges operated on a model not unlike the British universities after the Elizabethan Statutes of the late sixteenth century (Cowley, 1980). It was assumed that any bright graduate was ready to teach all subjects leading to the degree, and thus instructional staffs were composed entirely of *tutors,* young men, often no more than twenty, who had just received their baccalaureate degree and who were preparing for careers in the ministry (Morison, 1936). The responsibilities of tutors were both pedagogical and pastoral-custodial in nature. Ideally, a single tutor was assigned the shepherding of a single class through all four years of their baccalaureate program, both inside and outside the classroom. "Tutors were with their pupils almost every hour of the day [in the classroom recitations, study halls, and at meals], and slept in the same chamber with some of them at night. They were responsible not only for the intellectual, but for the moral and spiritual development of their charges" (Morison, 1936). In less than ideal practice, the tutorship functioned as a "revolving door"; at Harvard, prior to 1685, very seldom did a tutor see a class through all four years (only a half dozen of the forty-one tutors during this period remained at Harvard more than three years). While the next half century saw a progressive lengthening of the tutors' tenure at Harvard, and indeed the ultimate establishment of "permanent" tutorships in the latter half of the eighteenth century,[2] the "revolving door" concept of the tutorship persisted throughout this period at Yale, Brown, Dartmouth, and Bowdoin.

Development of a Small Core of "Permanent" Faculty, 1750–1800

It was not until the last half of the eighteenth century that an institution's short-term tutors were supplemented by a small core of "permanent" faculty—the professors. Carrell (1968) found only ten professors in all of American higher education in 1750, the bulk of whom were at either Harvard or William and Mary. By 1795 the professorial ranks had swelled tenfold to 105 while the number of colleges had only slightly more than doubled. All in all, some two hundred individuals had served as professors in nineteen American colleges during this period.

How did these professorships develop? At Harvard, they developed slowly and as a direct result of philanthropic bequests. During the 1720s two Hollis professorships were endowed, one in divinity, occupied by Edward Wigglesworth for forty-four years, the other in mathematics and natural philosophy, occupied initially by Isaac Greenwood for eleven years, and then by John Winthrop for forty-one years.[3] By 1750 President Holyoke was being supported in his work by three permanent faculty members—the two Hollis professors as well as Henry Flynt, permanent tutor.[4] Throughout the rest of the eighteenth century, four additional professorships were endowed, of which three were actually filled before 1800.[5] By 1800, then, permanent professors had achieved near parity with tutors on the Harvard faculty.

At Yale the first professorship was likewise established as the direct result of a philanthropic bequest. In 1746 the Livingston Professorship of Divinity was established, and nine years later, its first occupant joined President Clap and the tutors in supervising instruction. By 1800 Yale had established only one additional professorship, but two years later, with the promotion of Jeremiah Day and Benjamin Silliman from their tutorships, it counted four professors among its faculty ranks—a situation of near parity between permanent professors and transient tutors (*Historical Register,* 1939).

The pattern that developed at Harvard after over a century and at Yale after a half century was adopted early on by those colleges founded during the second half of the eighteenth century. At Brown, for example, within five years of its founding, a core permanent faculty was already emerging with Howell's promotion from tutor to professor to join forces with President and Professor Manning. By 1800 Brown's five tutors were supplemented by three permanent professors (*Historical Catalog,* 1905). At Princeton, by 1767, two decades after its founding, three permanent professors had joined the three tutors (Wertenbaker, 1946); at Dartmouth, during the administration of John Wheelock (1779–1817), several professors were appointed to supplement the single professor who together with two or three tutors constituted the faculty during the preceding administration of Eleazar Wheelock (Richardson, 1932, p. 820 as cited by Cowley, 1980, p. 80).

What were the characteristics of this early core of permanent faculty? How did they resemble or differ from their more junior colleagues, the tutors? Both professors and tutors were drawn disproportionately from the higher socioeconomic strata of colonial and postrevolutionary society: fully one-quarter came from "professional" families (with fathers engaged in the ministry, law, medicine) at a time when 1–2 percent of the labor force was "professional" and 80–90 percent were engaged in agricultural pursuits (Carrell, 1968). Moreover, both professors and tutors undertook very similar activities as part of their college responsibilities: both supervised recitations and dormitories, and assumed overall responsibility for student discipline and moral, as well as intellectual, development. There the similarity appears to end. In the first place, professors did not take charge of a class for its four years at the institution; they were appointed in a particular subject area such as natural philosophy, divinity, or ancient languages and were, for the most part, engaged in the supervision of instruction within that area. In the second place, professors were generally older and more experienced than the tutors. Professors were, on the average, at least five to ten years older than the tutors. The vast majority, unlike the tutors, had some postbaccalaureate "professional" training in theology, law, or medicine. Among the eight professors at Brown during the eighteenth century, seven had such training (*Historical Catalog,* 1905), and at Harvard all ten professors during this period had such training (Eliot, 1848).

The most fundamental respect, however, in which professors differed from tutors was in the "permanence" of their positions. Carrell's analysis of biographical sketches of 124 professors during the second half of the eighteenth century illuminates the peculiar meaning of a "permanent" faculty appointment during this period. In the first place, a professorship implied an institutional career, most often at one's alma mater. Nearly 40 percent of Carrell's sample professors taught at their alma mater, ranging from just over one-third at the College of Philadelphia (later the University of Pennsylvania) to 83 percent at Harvard. Fully 88 percent taught at only one institution during their academic careers; barely 2.5 percent taught at three or more institutions. Second, a permanent professorship remained a "nonexclusive" career. In analyzing the lifetime occupational commitment of his sample, Carrell found that less than 15 percent ($N = 23$) appeared to identify themselves exclusively as professional teachers, less than 20 percent ($N = 32$) appeared to identify themselves primarily as professional teachers (with a secondary occupation in the ministry, medicine, or law), and over half ($N = 68$) appeared to identify themselves primarily as practioners of one of the traditional professions and only secondarily as professional college teachers (often having come to a professorship following a lengthy stint as a minister or practicing physician).

If college teaching was hardly the exclusive career, or even the first-choice career, of a majority of eighteenth century professors, Carrell's (1968) subsequent analysis suggests that it became a long-term commitment for many once the move was made. In an analysis of indicators of occupational commitment of his sample professors during their teaching tenure, Carrell found strikingly different results: nearly 45 percent ($N = 56$) identified themselves exclusively as college teachers, while about one-quarter identified themselves, respectively, as *primarily* or *secondarily* college teachers. In the latter two categories, clergy were heavily represented in the first, while physicians and lawyers made up the greater portion of the second, suggesting that clergy were more likely than the other learned professions to develop a primary commitment to the professorial role once it was assumed.

That the assumption of a professorship increasingly brought with it a heightened commitment to college teaching is further supported by at least three additional pieces of evidence. (1) The average length of professors' tenures was increasing. Over the second half of the eighteenth century, the average tenure of professors at Yale increased from 21.5 years to 36.8 years, and that of professors at Brown increased from 30.7 years to 36.0 years (by 1750, Harvard's two professors had an average tenure of 42.5 years). (2) There was a negative correlation between age at first appointment and tenure in the professorial role. Carrell reported a zero order correlation of

−0.35 between these two variables, suggesting shorter tenures were, at least in part, attributable to late career entry. (3) The proportion of professors who pursued subsequent careers was relatively small. Just over half of Carrell's sample (N = 64) died in office; over 75 percent (N = 92) died within ten years of leaving teaching; less than 25 percent engaged in another occupation after leaving the professorship, and among this group several either retired because of bad health or were retired by their institutions. It would appear safe to conclude then that the professorial role, once undertaken, was pursued with a considerable degree of permanency, particularly in light of the frequency of dual occupations—medicine and agriculture, law and agriculture, religion and education—characteristic of the late eighteenth century (Carrell, 1968).

One final issue concerning the relationship of the tutor to the professor remains—the relative integration or separation of the two roles in terms of the individual career track. To what extent did the tutorship function as the first step toward a professorship? And to what extent was a professorship the reward of skillful tutoring? The evidence suggests that at least two contrasting patterns had developed by the close of the eighteenth century. The Harvard pattern was one of separate career tracks. Not a single Harvard tutor went on to a Harvard professorship during the eighteenth century. Indeed tutoring became something of a permanent career option in itself (Smith, 1966). The pattern at Yale and Brown, and it would appear at most other institutions, was one of a separate, transient career track, tempered, however, by the use of the tutorship as a very selective feeder for the professorship. Thus, at Brown, only four of eighteen tutors (22.2 percent) went on to professorial appointments at Brown; three of the eight professors appointed during that period had served as Brown tutors. At Yale, tutors were less than half as likely as their Brown counterparts to achieve professorial appointments at Yale, but all six Yale professors during the period had indeed served as Yale tutors.

The Ascent of the Institutional Career, 1800–20

The first quarter of the nineteenth century has been credited by historian Frederick Rudolph (1962) as the beginning of the "college movement"—the large-scale founding of small colleges throughout what was then the West stimulated at once by the "community building" imperative of the period and the increasing competition among religious denominations. It may also be credited as the beginning of the "professor movement." Between 1800 and 1820 the ratio of permanent professors to tutors dramatically reversed itself at many of the leading institutions: by 1820 permanent professors outnumbered tutors at both Harvard and Yale by 10 to 6 whereas but two decades earlier there was a situation of parity at Harvard (5 to 5) and a 3 to 1 majority of tutors at Yale; at Brown, professors outnumbered tutors by a ratio of 3 to 1 where only two decades earlier the tutors had been in ascendance by a 5 to 3 ratio.[6]

The momentum of the professor movement can be seen graphically in developments at Harvard during President Kirkland's administration, 1810–28. During the entire eighteenth century, six professorships were established at Harvard (Eliot, 1848). They were created when funding to support them was obtained from private donors; and indeed if the initial gift was insufficient to support an incumbent, it was allowed to accumulate over one or more decades before the professorship was filled (the Hersey and Boylston professorships, for example, remained vacant for this reason). In the decade preceding the Kirkland presidency, a subscription was launched by Harvard for the creation of a single professorship. During the eighteen years of Kirkland's presidency, the number of Harvard professorships fully doubled. Seven professors were appointed while the funds destined for their support were not always yet available. In his zeal to make appointments, Kirkland frequently had to draw upon tuition revenues to pay the newly hired incumbents (Eliot, 1848, p. 107).

How can this ascendance of the permanent faculty in a brief two decades be explained? While it is impossible to postulate strict cause and effect relationships, several developments during the period would appear to provide necessary, if not sufficient, conditions for that ascendance. The first of these is sheer growth: growth in size of some of the leading institutions—the Yale faculty doubled in size between 1800 and 1820, and those of Harvard and Brown grew by 50 percent (*Historical Register,* 1939; *Historical Catalog,* 1905; Eliot, 1848)—and growth in the number of institutions as a result of the college movement. Allied with growth was the progressive acceptance of the professorship as a long-term, if not an exclusive, career as reflected in progressively longer average tenures throughout the eighteenth century and the indicators of increasing career commitment reported by Carrell. Yet a third factor which may help to account for the rise of the professorship were changes underway during the first quarter of the nineteenth century in the ministerial career. Calhoun, in a case study of the New Hampshire clergy during the late eighteenth and early nineteenth century, reported a radical shift in clerical career patterns at about this time, which he attributes to the increasing secularization and urbanization of the populace (Calhoun, 1965, cited by Tobias, 1982). The average terms of service in local parishes, which throughout most of the eighteenth century had been measured in lifetimes, began to resemble the average tenures of modern college and university presidents. This new found job insecurity, the difficulty of obtaining even so insecure a position, together with the low salaries of clergy in rural and small town churches led many ministers to seek to enhance their careers by building organizations such as colleges and by becoming professors (Tobias, 1982). And the correlation of these developments in the clerical career with the ascent of the professorship is lent further credence by Carrell's findings that clergymen became significantly more likely than their fellow professionals in law and medicine to identify themselves *primarily* as college teachers by the end of the eighteenth century.

THE STATUS OF THE PROFESSORIATE IN 1820

By the end of the first quarter of the nineteenth century, the professor movement had produced a relatively large cohort of career academics. Although still a thoroughly homogeneous group of upper middle class, New England-born Protestants,[7] the confluence of a number of social and intellectual forces during the course of the nineteenth century wrought some fundamental changes in the group career. The progressive secularization of American society was penetrating the classical college, subjugating the demands of piety to the religion of progress and materialism, reflecting the needs of a growing industrial economy (Calhoun, 1965; Brubacher and Rudy, 1968; Hofstadter and Metzger, 1955). At the same time, the rise of science and the tremendous growth of scientific knowledge was breaking apart the classical curriculum and giving rise to the development of academic disciplines (the distinction of professional versus amateur) and of research and graduate education (Oleson and Voss, 1979; Oleson and Brown, 1976; Berelson, 1960; Wolfle, 1972; Veysey, 1965). By mid-century, increasingly large numbers of Americans were studying abroad in Germany and were importing their version of the German university and the German idea of research back to the United States (Hofstadter and Metzger, 1955). Once graduate specialization took hold in earnest in the last quarter of the nineteenth century, it was but a short step to the establishment of the major learned societies and their sponsorship of specialized, disciplinary journals: the American Chemical Society in 1876, the Modern Language Association in 1883, the American Historical Association in 1884, the American Psychological Association in 1892 (Berelson, 1960).

These developments together provided American higher education with the capability of producing graduate trained specialists and created clear career opportunities for the specialists so produced. They provided the impetus for a fundamental restructuring, toward professionalization, of the academic role. Although touted by some as a veritable "academic revolution," an examination of the evolving disciplinary, institutional, and external careers of faculty at our sample institutions suggests that the restructuring process actually proceeded by gradual steps over more than a half century as successive groups of professors were replaced by products of the latest graduate training.

Before turning to the evolution of these three career strands during the nineteenth century, let us review the status of each of them as they manifested themselves among college faculties in 1820.

The Disciplinary Career

By 1820 the outline of a disciplinary career was discernable only in the cases of a few individuals at selected campuses rather than among entire faculties. While a majority of individuals continued to come to the professorship with postbaccalaureate training in the traditional professions of divinity, medicine, and law (mostly divinity), there remained, with the exception of Harvard, a paucity of faculty with postbaccalaureate training in their teaching specialty.[8] For the most part without specialized training, the majority of faculties (50 percent at Brown and Harvard; 100 percent at Bowdoin) continued to be drawn to their initial academic appointments from nonacademic jobs, primarily in school teaching and the ministry, secondarily in law and medicine. Moreover, for a majority of faculty at some institutions, any semblance of a disciplinary career in effect ended with their institutional career. At Brown and Bowdoin, the modal pattern was for the majority of faculty to move into nonacademic careers following their stints as college teachers (50 percent of the full professors at Brown and 60 percent of those at Bowdoin; virtually all the junior faculty at both institutions). It should be noted, however, that those full professors who left teaching averaged nearly two decades in their institutional positions (21.2 years at Brown; 18.5 years at Bowdoin) so that college teaching still constituted a significant chunk of their careers.[9]

At other institutions, most notably Harvard and Yale, patterns of career commitment appeared to be differentiated along senior/junior faculty lines. While no junior faculty at either institution persisted in an academic career beyond their tutorship or instructorship, the majority of permanent professors did (more than 80 percent at Yale and 70 percent at Harvard). Interestingly enough, this suggests that Yale, and also Brown, were shifting toward the late eighteenth century Harvard pattern of separate junior and senior faculty career tracks.

Whatever their career commitments college faculties in 1820 evidenced fairly low disciplinary commitment as measured by their associational involvements and scholarly publications. Only a single faculty member at Brown, Bowdoin, Harvard, and Yale was involved to any significant extent in the activities of the learned societies of the day, namely, Caswell at Brown, Cleaveland at Bowdoin, Peck at Harvard, and Silliman at Yale, who had the year before founded the *American Journal of Science* (*Historical Catalog,* 1905; Packard, 1882; McCaughey, 1974; *Historical Register,* 1939). And, excluding the medical faculty, it was only those same single faculty members who were at all involved in publication in their specialized field. While many professors at these institutions were indeed publishing, their work consisted chiefly in collections of sermons and addresses made at commencements and other public occasions.

The External Career

While many professors were in 1820 actively pursuing external careers, virtually none was rooted in their academic specialization. Beyond the budding careers of a few men such as Silliman and Cleaveland on the academic public lecture circuit, the vast majority of professors consumed their extra-institutional time in clerical and civic activities. Fully three-quarters of the professors at Dartmouth, two-thirds of those at Bowdoin, and half of those at Brown were engaged in itinerant preaching and work with missionary societies. Somewhat lower proportions participated actively in community life, principally by holding political office at the local and national levels, assuming leadership roles in local civic associations unrelated to education or intellectual culture (for example, tree planting societies) or, in fewer cases, holding membership in state historical societies (Tobias, 1982; Packard, 1882; *Historical Catalog,* 1905).

The Institutional Career

In 1820 the now familiar formalized institutional career track of progression through the junior ranks to a full professorship had not yet begun to take hold. Indeed, in many respects, the two-track system largely operative at the end of the eighteenth century remained intact: junior faculty in temporary, dead-end appointments and senior faculty in long-term appointments. At Harvard, fully 80 percent of the senior faculty were initially appointed to their professorships from outside the institution, with 62 percent of these claiming no previous academic experience (McCaughey, 1974).[10] While Harvard was alone in this period in having established the "instructorship" as distinguished from the tutorship and the professorship,[11] instructors almost never went on to Harvard professorships, nor did tutors move up to such instructorships.[12]

While Yale and Brown continued to reflect some departure from the Harvard pattern by promotion from within of tutors to full professorships, the departure appeared to be decreasing. Fully two-thirds of Brown and Yale arts and sciences professors had served as tutors at their employing institutions, but the portion was a significant decrement from the 100 percent who had so served on the faculties of 1800. Moreover, none of the six tutors on the Yale faculty in 1820 advanced to a Yale professorship (compared with two of six in 1800); and only two of the thirty-two tutors on the Yale faculty during the 1820s were so advanced (*Historical Register,* 1939). At Brown, even more dramatically, none of the ten tutors appointed during the decade of the 1820s advanced to a Brown professorship (*Historical Catalog,* 1905). It seems fair to conclude, then, at least on the basis of the increasing convergence of practices at Harvard, Yale, Brown, that by 1820 the dual track academic career, defined along junior-senior faculty lines, was on the ascent rather than the descent.

In sum, it may be said that there were at least two "typical" faculty members by the end of the first quarter of the nineteenth century. The first was quite young and took on a temporary assignment as either a tutor or an instructor before embarking on a nonacademic career, usually the ministry. He typically came to his employing institution from the ranks of its immediate past graduates and probably undertook training in some traditional profession (usually the ministry) either during or just after his short-term appointment. The second typical faculty member, the professor, had had some postbaccalaureate training in one of the traditional professions (albeit not in his teaching specialty) and had come to a professorship at his alma mater perhaps from a tutorship at the same employing institution, or, more likely, from a nonacademic occupation (often a ministerial seat). During the course of his appointment, he was engaged in itinerant preaching and a variety of community activities that were probably noneducational and nonintellectual in nature (except perhaps for membership in the state historical society). Depending on his particular employing institution, he may have been likely to move on to a nonacademic occupation after a fairly lengthy tenure, or he may have continued his teaching activities for the rest of his life, most probably at his original employing institution. Together, these two types approached their role as a teaching/custodial function, oftentimes as an extension of an earlier or concurrent ministerial role (the college as parish).

THE EVOLUTION OF THE ACADEMIC CAREER, 1820–80

The Disciplinary Career

Well before the Civil War, the disciplinary career of the American professoriate as reflected in the incidence of specialized training, publication activity, association involvements, and career commitment was undergoing significant changes. With Harvard at the vanguard in the area of specialized training—by 1821 fully 40 percent of the faculty had received such training—isolated instances of specialty-trained faculty could be discerned during the 1830s and 1840s at Brown, Bowdoin, and Yale. These institutions, however, did not begin replicating the Harvard pattern to any significant degree until the 1850s and 1860s. In 1841 at Brown, for example, John Lincoln was sent to study in Europe prior to assuming his assistant professorship; however, it was not until the mid-1850s that nearly one-quarter of the Brown faculty were to take leaves for European study, two of them returning with European Ph.D.s (*Historical Catalog*, 1905). At Bowdoin, as early as 1835, John Goodwin was appointed professor of modern languages and dispatched to Europe for two years to prepare for his position; Goodwin, however, remained alone during his thirteen-year tenure pending several appointments in the early 1860s (Packard, 1882). At Yale in 1843 Thomas Thatcher took leave to engage in European study, but it was not until 1863 that Yale appointed its first Ph.D. to the faculty (*Historical Register*, 1939).

At Dartmouth and Williams, developments began later but proceeded more rapidly. At Dartmouth, as late as the mid-1850s, nearly all of the faculty in the academical department had received training in the traditional professions and none in a specialized academic discipline. With a half dozen appointments in the late 1860s and early 1870s, however, Dartmouth virtually reversed that trend in a single decade (Tobias, 1982). At Williams the first professionally trained faculty member was not appointed until 1858,[13] and a second did not assume professorial duties until the close of the Civil War. By 1869, however, fully five of the thirteen members of the Williams faculty could boast graduate training in their teaching specialty (Rudolph, 1956).

As the proportion of faculty with discipline-related credentials increased, so did the proportion of those embarking on an academic career immediately following their training. At Harvard, by 1869, the proportion of faculty with no previous nonacademic career had doubled since 1845, 44 percent versus 22 percent (McCaughey, 1974). Even more dramatically, at Bowdoin during the 1870s nearly two-thirds of the faculty were embarking on their academic careers immediately after their graduate training, compared with barely 20 percent during the preceding decade (Packard, 1882).

If the pattern of increased specialized training together with increased assumption of an academic career immediately following that training did not take hold until the 1850s, other aspects of the disciplinary career such as scholarly publication and participation in learned societies were developing earlier. At Bowdoin the largest jump in the faculty's "professional index"[14] during the nineteenth century occurred during the second quarter of the century. By 1845 70 percent of the faculty were publishing in their field (nearly half were publishing primarily textbooks) and some 30 percent were active in scientific associations (Packard, 1882). At Harvard the professoriate's professional index took its largest jump in the early 1840s during the Quincy presidency, nearly doubling in less than two decades (McCaughey, 1974). The most significant jump in the Brown faculty's professional index occurred between 1845 and the end of the Civil War. By 1845 fully half the Brown faculty was publishing in their field of specialization (even if in the more popular media), and by the Civil War, fully one-half were affiliated with the major disciplinary and scientific associations of the day.[15]

By the 1850s, one unmistakable sign of the ascendance of the disciplinary career was evident: institutional commitments, built on inbreeding, were breaking down in the face of professional mobility resulting from disciplinary commitments (better job opportunities at other institutions). At Bowdoin, three faculty left for positions at other institutions where only one had done so in the previous half century—Henry Wadsworth Longfellow went to Harvard (Packard, 1882). At Brown, while only one professor left during the decade preceding the Civil War, several junior faculty were beginning to pursue their career interests by moves to other institutions (*Historical Catalog,* 1905). And during the 1850s and 1860s, the University of Michigan, and to a lesser extent the University of Wisconsin, were both serving as "revolving doors," especially for senior faculty. At Michigan, for example, among forty-three professors appointed between 1845 and 1868, twenty-three left, typically after relatively short tenures. While many were clearly victims of internecine strife, at least ten left for better academic positions.[16] Thus by the eve of the Civil War, interinstitutional mobility was progressively becoming a fact of academic life.

The External Career

Beginning in the 1850s, the bare outline of an external career based more on faculty's disciplinary expertise, expertise as educators, and role as proponents of culture rather than proponents of religion was becoming discernible at some institutions. At Brown, for example, the immediate pre–Civil War period saw the first instance of a faculty member using academic expertise in the service of state government: the appointment of a professor of chemistry to head the Rhode Island board of weights and measures. By the end of the Civil War, the proportion of the Brown faculty involved in itinerant preaching and other clerical activities dropped from over a third at mid-century to only one-eighth. While a large majority (approaching 75 percent) of the faculty remained involved in civic and community affairs, a change in the nature of that involvement had taken place: only a single faculty member was directly involved in elective politics while the majority were involved in distinctively cultural, academic, and education related activities such as membership on boards of education, holding office in national honor societies, art and historical societies, and state and federal government commissions (*Historical Catalog,* 1905). At Bowdoin, by the eve of the Civil War we find a majority of faculty (four of seven) engaged in extra-institutional roles as specialists, educators, and public men of letters. Parker Cleaveland was holding public lectures on mineralogy and Alpheus Packard on education; President Woods and Professor Packard were engaging in commissioned writing for the Maine Historical Society; and Thomas Upham was producing pamphlets for the American Peace Association (Packard, 1882).

Other institutions lagged a decade or more behind in these developments of the external career. At Dartmouth, as late as 1851, three-quarters of the faculty continued to participate actively in the community as preachers, licentiates, or ordained ministers, and as civic boosters. By the late 1870s, however, the proportion of faculty engaged in clerical activities had dropped precipitously to 15 percent while over half were now significantly engaged in scientific associations in their fields of specialization (Tobias, 1982). At Wisconsin, by the early 1870s professors at the university were being called upon to head the state geological survey (Curti and Carstensen, 1949).

The Institutional Career

The disciplinary career and discipline-based external career taking shape in the immediate pre–Civil War period gave rise to two significant, interrelated changes in the institutional career during the 1860s and 1870s. First was the development of new roles (instructor, assistant professor) and the forging of these new roles into a career sequence that at once gave shape to the academic career and regulated the movement through the junior ranks to a full professorship. Concomittantly there was an expansion and professionalization of the junior faculty. Together, these developments served to integrate into a single structure the dual career track system that had characterized the early part of the nineteenth century.

The instructorship and the assistant professorship actually made their appearance quite early in the annals of some institutions. As early as 1821, fully one-third of the Harvard faculty were serving in instructorships (McCaughey, 1974). The first instructors were appointed at Yale in 1824 (during the 1830s in arts and sciences), at Michigan in 1843, and at Brown in 1844. The first assistant professors were appointed at Brown in 1835, at Yale in 1842, and at Michigan in 1857 (*Historical Catalog*, 1905; *Historical Register*, 1939; *General Catalog*, 1912). Despite the early precedents, these new roles did not take hold for several decades, even at these trend-setting institutions (with the exception of Harvard) and for an even longer period at institutions such as Dartmouth, Bowdoin, and Williams. Thus at Yale only four instructors were appointed during the two decades following the first appointment; and only four additional assistant professors were appointed during the three decades following the first appointment (*Historical Register*, 1939). Similarly, at Brown and Michigan the instructorship languished until the 1860s and the 1870s, respectively, and the assistant professorship languished until the 1890s and the 1880s, respectively (*Historical Catalog*, 1905; *General Catalog*, 1912). At some of the more insulated institutions such as Dartmouth, Bowdoin, and Williams, it was not until the 1860s that these roles first appeared and several decades later that they were firmly entrenched (Tobias, 1982; Packard, 1882; Rudolph, 1956).

These new roles represented a significant departure from the "tutorship"—their incumbents were appointed within a specific department of instruction and were likely to be the products of specialized training—and indeed significantly transformed it, leading in some institutions to the effective disappearance of tutors (at Brown in the 1840s and at Williams in the early 1860s) and in others to the effective transformation of the tutor into a junior instructor. At Yale, for example, in the 1830s tutors began to be assigned to departments of instruction (*Historical Register,* 1939). But for at least several decades they were not quite equivalent to their modern counterpart in at least one fundamental respect: they did not serve in a majority of cases as feeders to the full professorship. At both Harvard and Yale it was not until the 1860s that a substantial proportion of junior faculty advanced to a full professorship (25 percent at Harvard and just over a third at Yale), and not until the decade of the 1870s were a bare majority of the junior faculty so advanced (McCaughey, 1974; *Historical Register,* 1939). Similar patterns prevailed both at Brown and at Michigan—albeit in the latter case quite dramatically so. Between 1845 and 1868, only one of eight junior faculty at Michigan had risen to a full professorship; a single decade later fully 80 percent were so advancing (*General Catalog,* 1912).

The junior faculty role, then, had during the decade immediately following the Civil War undergone a fundamental change from a temporary, dead-end appointment to the first step in the academic career ladder. At the very same time, the ranks of the junior faculty were undergoing their most rapid expansion in terms of numbers and their largest increase in professionalization. By 1880 junior faculty outnumbered their more senior colleagues at Harvard by a ratio of 8 to 5, compared with 3 to 2 a decade earlier (McCaughey, 1974); attained full parity with senior faculty at Michigan, compared with a 2 to 8 ratio a decade earlier (*General Catalog,* 1912); and were on their way to parity at Brown, now constituting 40 percent of the faculty versus less than a third a decade earlier (*Historical Catalog,* 1905). Junior faculty were increasingly coming to their academic career directly from graduate training in their specialty or from junior appointments at other institutions. By 1880 the majority of instructors at Michigan, for example, were either working on or had just completed their doctoral degrees; and, at least at

Harvard and Brown, their professional orientation was as highly developed (as measured by McCaughey's professional index) as their senior colleagues'. The modern academic career had come of age.

Its emergence placed strong pressures on the inner life of the traditional liberal arts college still loyal to the aims of discipline and piety. These pressures were reflected in the pre–Civil War period at institutions such as Yale in the emergent, but amicable, struggles between the old and new guard concerning the relative emphasis on student discipline and moral development versus more academic concerns (Dwight, 1903). They were reflected both more dramatically and less amicably in the immediate post–Civil War period in the form of veritable faculty revolts at some of the more traditional institutions. At Williams, Mark Hopkins, the prototypical old-time college president, was faced with a faculty uprising during the later years of his administration (1868–72). While ostensibly rebelling against the president's disciplinary laxity (his attempt at discipline by precept and moral suasion), their desire for enforcing regular class attendance via a marking system was undergirded by a pervasive concern for standards of scholarship and academic performance. Two years earlier the faculty had succeeded in institutionalizing annual written exams; and in 1869, at the faculty's insistence, admissions standards were tightened and the practice initiated of sending lists of class standings to all parents—all this, despite severe enrollment difficulties. By 1872 these conflicts had led to Hopkins's resignation and the inauguration of a new president—who eight years earlier had come to Williams as only the second European-trained specialist on the faculty (Rudolph, 1956, pp. 223–24).

A decade later, at Dartmouth, fifteen of the twenty-two resident members of the faculty petitioned the Board of Trustees for the resignation of President Bartlett, also of the old guard. The petition precipitated a quasi-judicial hearing by the Board of Trustees on the conduct of President Bartlett's administration. The faculty's action came as a result of the president's attempt to secure the appointment of a new professor of Greek whose religious and moral qualifications seemed preeminent but who did not meet peer evaluation standards within the field of classics. While the faculty were not personally bitter towards Bartlett, they nonetheless viewed it as their professional responsibility to insist on the highest standards of faculty appointments, even if public controversy was necessary. While Bartlett survived the trial and lingered on for over a decade, his successor, William Jewett Tucker, recognized in his 1893 inaugural address the development of a "New Dartmouth," a new kind of college staffed by a new kind of faculty (Tobias, 1982).

CONSOLIDATION OF THE ACADEMIC CAREER IN THE TWENTIETH CENTURY

The new academic profession in the first decade of the twentieth century, reflecting Tucker's "New Dartmouth," had clearly broken away from the traditions of the liberal arts college devoted to student discipline and piety; it had not, however, yet fully arrived at its contemporary guise. Its uneven development, the tension between the traditional and the new, was reflected in the founding of the American Association of University Professors in 1915. The coming together of eighteen academic luminaries from seven of the leading universities to charter the first national organization of professors suggests a new-found sense of collective professorial self-consciousness, a sense of colleagueship or fraternity in the service of scientific progress. As E.R.A. Seligman, one of the eighteen, proclaimed:

> Loyalty to our institution is admirable, but if our institution for some unfortunate reason stands athwart the progress of science, or even haltingly follows that path, we must use our best efforts to convince our colleagues and the authorities of the error of their ways. . . . In prosecuting this end, we need both individual and collective efforts. The leisure of the laboratory and of the study accounts for much; but almost equally important is the stimulus derived from contact with our colleagues. (cited by Hofstadter and Metzger, 1955, p. 471)

Yet, this sense of collective consciousness was highly restricted in at least two senses. In the first place, it was circumscribed by the definition of who was to be *included* in the collectivity. In the organization's initial constitution, the membership base was limited to "recognized" scholars with at least ten years of experience in the professoriate. While the base was broadened in 1920 to include faculty with three or more years of experience, nonetheless the *collectivity* that was conscious of itself constituted only a small, exclusive contingent of professionalized scholars within the professoriate. Moreover, the evidence suggests that even among those within the collectivity a sense of professional self-consciousness was not widespread. Despite the prominence of the founding team, including men such as John Dewey, J. M. Cattell, and Arthur Lovejoy, many of those initially invited refused or were wary of joining (Hofstadter and Metzger, 1955).

The initial membership invitations were accepted by 867 research-oriented full professors percent of the professoriate; seven years later, something less than 6 percent of the professoriate could be counted among the AAUP membership (N = 4000). And even among this select group of professors, strictly professional concerns seemed secondary to institutional ones. John Dewey had sought to direct the energies of the new organization towards developing professional standards for the university-based scholar and away from intervention into faculty-administration disputes at the institutional level. But the membership clearly saw the association's primary function as that of a grievance committee assisting individual faculty vis-à-vis institutional administrators, and during its first years, the association was overwhelmed by the grievances brought to its attention. Thus, in response to its members' needs, a new organization of professors kept strictly professional issues largely in abeyance (Hofstadter and Metzger, 1955).

It was during the period between World War I and the end of World War II that the transformation begun a century earlier was consolidated.

Consolidation of the Disciplinary Career

The two decades between the wars witnessed unprecedented growth in graduate study and research. The annual rate of production of doctorates increased five-fold, from 620 in 1920 to nearly 3,300 in 1940. More discourses and pronouncements on graduate education were published than in any previous or subsequent twenty year period, excepting the present. A cycle of intense, second-order specialization was evident in the differentiation of yet more specialized subareas within the disciplines. The social sciences, for example, spawned in quick succession the Econometric Society (1930), the American Association of Physical Anthropologists (1930), the Society for the Psychological Study of Social Issues (1936), the American Society of Criminology (1936), the Rural Sociological Society (1937), the Society for Applied Anthropology (1941), the Economic History Association (1941), and others. And these more esoteric societies sponsored, in turn, yet more specialized scholarly journals, for example, *Econometrica* (1933), *Sociometry* (1937), *Public Administration Review* (1940), *Journal of Personality* (1932). By the mid-1940s, the dominance of the graduate research model as we know it today was clearly established as was the professoriate's claim to that crucial desideratum of professionalization—specialized expertise (Berelson, 1960).

Consolidation of the External Career

This ascent of specialized expertise by World War II brought faculty into public service on a scale heretofore unknown. Although the public service role had been evolving during the pre–Civil War period and, to a larger extent, during the Progressive Era and World War I, the number of faculty remained relatively small and their national exposure limited. During the heyday of the Wisconsin Idea, (1910–11), some thirty-three individuals held official positions both with the state and with the university, mostly as agricultural experts or with the state railroad or tax commission; thirteen others were "on call" at the capital as needed, including political scientists, economists, and lawyers. Less than 10 percent of the university faculty was directly involved, and this group included representatives of only a handful of disciplines (Veysey, 1965).

During World War I, faculty served the nation primarily through two vehicles: the National Board for Historical Service and the Committee on Public Information. The former, linked to the leadership of the American Historical Association, channeled the efforts of several dozen historians into the revision of secondary schools' social studies curricula in the direction of pro-war civics. Under the latter's auspices, over a hundred social scientists were commissioned to write wartime propaganda pamphlets, and others were pressed into service to monitor foreign language newspaper editorial policies to detect disloyalty (Gruber, 1976).

The Brain Trust assembled by Franklin Roosevelt to address the economic and social havoc wrought by the Depression provided a highly visible, public showcase for faculty talent on an unprecedented scale as well as a testament to the practical utility of research and scholarship. Between 1930 and 1935, forty-one private and state-supported universities examined by Orr (1978) granted nearly three hundred leaves to full-time faculty for the express purpose of serving the federal government. A much larger number of faculty, particularly those at the larger universities with graduate departments, served state and local governments "on overload." Again, in the early 1940s, it was to academics that the federal government turned in support of the national defense effort and the prosecution of World War II.

This new found visibility and public support contributed immeasurably to the differentiation and upgrading of the faculty role. The esteem in which members of the academic profession were held increased markedly as did the prestige attached to an academic career. Bowen (1978) has documented the close association of public attitudes toward academe and levels of faculty salaries and pinpointed World War II as marking a major upturn in both the level and rate of real growth in faculty salaries. Not only did the salaries sharply increase but growing attention was focused on the economic security of faculty members. The faculty had initially been excluded from the Social Security program and only a very small group were covered by the Carnegie Corporation's faculty pension program, which was created in 1906 and was by then effectively closed. The 1930s witnessed the widespread establishment of faculty retirement plans, including incorporation of the Teacher's Insurance Annuity Association. In 1934 about 40 percent of faculty were covered, and by the beginning of World War II, the proportion had increased to nearly three-fifths (Orr, 1978).

Consolidation of the Institutional Career

On their own campuses, professors' expertise translated into the bargaining power necessary to markedly improve their lot. It was during this period that the quest for job security was satisfied. Through the nineteenth century and the first quarter of the twentieth century the modal principle of *faculty as mere employees,* though increasingly challenged, remained firmly entrenched. No provisions for job security existed, and tenure as we know it today was simply unheard of. While many full professors were on *indefinite* appointments, that simply meant that no term of appointment had been specified in their contract. Indefinite appointments were never the equivalent of *permanent* appointments, either in intent or law; and individuals on such appointments could be dismissed at any time. Practically and legally speaking, even the most senior faculty served at the pleasure of the board of trustees (Metzger, 1973). Moreover, for junior faculty, neither a recognized set of procedures nor a timetable were yet established for attaining even these *indefinite* appointments that were the reward of a full professorship. An individual faculty member might serve his institution for fifteen or twenty years and be dismissed at any time without reason given and without a hearing. And this possibility was time and again realized, even at those institutions such as Yale and Wisconsin with a tradition of faculty power (Orr, 1978). In its 1940 statement on tenure, culminating fourteen years of discussion, the American Association of University Professors articulated the judicial concept of *permanent* faculty tenure, designed a means for regularizing the flow of tenure decision-making (that is, by stipulating the six-year "probationary period"), and endorsed procedures ensuring due process on nonreappointment. By that time the AAUP had sufficient stature to gain widespread institutional acceptance of its pronouncement.

It was during this period as well that increasing recognition of faculty as professionals was being reflected in their increasing role in institutional decision-making. Cowley (1980) rightly points out that faculty governance structures had existed statutorily at several leading institutions, including Harvard, Princeton, and Pennsylvania, as early as the mid-eighteenth century when many institutions were first developing a small core of "permanent" faculty; and by the latter half of the nineteenth century, faculty bodies had developed considerable authority at institutions such as Yale, Cornell, and Wisconsin. However, although precedent may have clearly placed within their purview such areas as student discipline and admission and degree requirements (Cowley, 1980), faculty prerogatives in matters of curriculum and educational policy, and to an even greater extent in matters of faculty appointments and promotion and selection of academic administrators, were neither clearly nor consistently established. Moreover, in the early twentieth century, powerful presidents such as Nicholas Murray Butler and even William Rainey Harper (Cowley, 1980) were not unknown to ignore them with impunity.

The 1930s saw the blossoming of faculty committee structures at nearly all institutions. By 1939 Haggerty and Works found over two-fifths of their faculty sample employed at institutions accredited by the North Central Association serving on an average of two committees each. Through such committees, faculty came to share increasingly in institutional administration (two-thirds of the then extant committees were primarily administrative in function) and in a more limited way, in the formulation of educational policy (only one fifth of such committees focused on educational policy per se). These developments culminated in the report of Committee T of AAUP in November 1937, which set forth five overarching principles for faculty participation in institutional governance. Taken together, the principles mandate a role for the faculty in the selection of administrators, in the formulation and control of educational policy, and in the appointment and promotion process. While the role assigned to the faculty is largely *consultative,* the document has at its core the conviction that "faculty were not hired employees to be manipulated by president and trustees, but were academic professionals whose role involved teaching and contributing to the direction and major decisions of an institution" (Orr, 1978, pp. 347–48).

The growing recognition of faculty as professionals served not only to elevate the profession but also to broaden entry into it. Professionalization permitted (although it by no means ensured) the introduction of achievement-related criteria of success—the merit principle—and a concommitant reduction in the salience of ascriptive criteria of class origin ("gentlemanliness") and religious orthodoxy. The relaxation of barriers to entry as well as the professions' growing, though by no means great, prestige infused new blood into the academy: by World War II Catholics and Jews constituted nearly one quarter of a heretofore exclusively Protestant profession; the offspring of mid-Atlantic and upper midwestern states were supplanting New Englanders; the sons of farmers and manual laborers were increasingly joining the sons of businessmen and professionals; and *daughters* were now joining the *sons*—fully 13 percent of a sample of faculty from North Central Association accredited institutions (Kunkel, 1938; see also Lipset and Ladd, 1979).

By the end of World War II, the components of the academic role had clearly emerged and crystallized into the highly differentiated model by which we recognize the professor today—teaching, research, student advisement, administration, institutional and public service. Since its initial crystallization, the model has shown remarkable durability; over thirty-five years and enormous fluctuations in the fortunes of American higher education, it has only come to approach more closely its ideal typical expression through greater emphasis on research activity, fuller participation in academic citizenship, and fuller development of the public role.

1. In the cases of Brown, Bowdoin, and Yale, historical catalogues were employed to collect data comparable to McCaughey (1974) and Tobias (1982) on faculty at five points in time: 1800, 1820, 1845, 1869, 1880 (see *Historical Catalog*, 1905; Packard, 1882; *Historical Register*, 1939). The variables for which data were collected included: geographic origin, source of baccalaureate degree, the timing and nature of postbaccalaureate training, the nature of previous nonacademic employment, age and years of teaching experience at the time of initial appointment and at appointment to professorship, academic rank, years at focal institution, nature and timing of any subsequent occupation, nature and extent of publication activity, nature and extent of involvement with extra-institutional organizations (such as historical and literary societies and, later, disciplinary organizations and local and state government), and scores on two indices developed by McCaughey: the outsider index (assessing the relationship of the focal individual to the institution previous to initial appointment)

and the professional index (assessing the extent of professionalization as reflected in postbaccalaureate training, career pattern, publication and research activity, and associational involvements). A similar analysis was also undertaken for the University of Michigan faculty in 1845, 1869, and 1880, based on *General Catalog* (1912).

2. During the period 1685–1701, the tenure of Harvard tutors averaged 6.4 years, increasing to 9.0 years during the first half of the eighteenth century (Smith, 1966).

3. Greenwood no doubt would have stayed on if not for his abrupt dismissal on the grounds of "moral turpitude" (Eliot, 1848).

4. At Harvard, "permanence" was achieved by the appointment of "permanent" tutors as well as professors. The tutorship became institutionalized there in a way it was not at Harvard's sister institutions, largely, it would appear, as a result of the precedent set by the fifty-five year tutorship of Henry Flynt during the first half of the eighteenth century (Smith, 1966).

5. When endowment funds were insufficient for the full maintenance of a professorship, the funds were allowed to accumulate for as much as one or two decades before filling the position (Eliot, 1848).

6. Even at institutions such as Bowdoin, where the ratio of professors to tutors remained the same, appointments during the 1820s gave the permanent professors ascendance (Packard, 1882).

7. Among faculty at the "leading" institutions, over three-fourths were of old New England families; ecclesiastical and business family backgrounds continued to predominate, although the proportion of farm families had begun to increase; and protestantism continued as the professorial religion—although some of the "lower" Protestant denominations, such as Baptists and Methodists, were now rivaling the Presbyterians, the Congregationalists, and Unitarians for hegemony (Veysey, 1965).

8. Four out of ten Harvard professors had studied in Europe, but at least three of these had done so on Harvard stipends provided after their initial appointment as a means of preparation for their professorship (McCaughey, 1974).

9. These mobility patterns represent no significant change from those in 1800.

10. While we use the term "outsiders" here and subsequently to describe these appointees, it should be noted that virtually all of these outsiders at Harvard and elsewhere were in a fundamental sense "insiders" as well, that is, they were returning after a hiatus to their baccalaureate alma mater.

11. Yale did not appoint an instructor until 1824 and that in law. None were appointed in arts and sciences until the 1830s. At Brown, the first instructor was appointed in 1844.

12. Although it is true that two of Harvard's ten professors in 1820 had served as Harvard instructors, this was clearly a notable exception rather than the rule. Indeed, none of the five instructors in 1820 went on to Harvard professorships (McCaughey, 1974).

13. Thomas Clark, who had just received his doctorate in chemistry from the University of Gottingen.

14. See note 1.

15. Included in this latter group were a founder and future president of the American Philological Association; a future vice-president of the American Chemical Soci-

ety; a founder and future vice-president of the American Association for the Advancement of Science; and a founder of the National Academy of Sciences.

16. See Creutz (1981, pp. 55–64) for details on faculty–Board of Regents conflicts. For mobility data, see *General Catalog* (1912, pp. 6–9).

3

A Demographic Portrait of
The Contemporary Academic Profession

The dramatic growth of the academic profession after World War II, which peaked during the boom years of the 1960s, continued throughout the 1970s, though at a reduced pace and less uniformly across the spectrum of higher education. Between 1969 and 1979, the number of individuals at the rank of instructor or above rose by 46.2 percent (Table 3.1)—barely over half the rate of the previous decade (90.7 percent). The number of full-time faculty, however, rose by only 28.9 percent compared to the 107 percent rise in part-timers. The difference between these figures underscores the first significant change in the pattern of post–World War II growth: the relative slowdown during the 1970s of the full-time professoriate's growth together with the dramatic rise of part-time faculty from just over one-fifth of the academic profession in 1969 to nearly one-third of the profession a decade later.[1]

A second change in the growth pattern occurred in the distribution of faculty over the increasingly differentiated institutional structure of higher education. In 1969, nearly one-half of ranked faculty members were at universities, which accounted for about one-seventh of higher education institutions (fully one faculty mem-

TABLE 3.1
NUMBER OF FACULTY AT RANK OF INSTRUCTOR OR ABOVE (in thousands)

Year	Total	Full Time	Part Time
1960	236	154	82
1969	450	350	100
1979	658	451	207

SOURCE: National Center for Education Statistics (1980).

ber in eight was located in the elite, research universities); approximately two out of five were at other four-year colleges, which accounted for just over half of all higher education institutions; about one out of six were at two-year community colleges, which accounted for about a third of all institutions (Table 3.2). By 1979 this distribution had undergone significant changes (Table 3.3). The university sector claimed barely a third of all faculty, while the four-year sector had increased its share to 46 percent and the two-year sector to 22.4 percent. Although the 1969 and 1979 data are not precisely comparable, the former reflecting part-time as well as full-time faculty at the rank of instructor and above and the latter reflecting full-time faculty only, the available evidence appears to confirm this trend of differential growth favoring two-year community colleges and public, four-year colleges. Thus Stadtman (1980) found that the institutions most likely to have reported an increase in the size of their instructional staff during the 1970s were two-year community colleges and public comprehensive institutions—the new growth sector of American higher education. And thus, too, in 1976, Cartter (1976) had predicted that a decline in the academic labor market would tend to disproportionately increase hiring at the bottom end of the institutional prestige hierarchy.

At the same time that the locus of faculty moved from the university to the public four-year college and the community college, the qualifications of faculty, as reflected in the proportion holding the doctorate, appear to have increased in response to labor market supply-demand imbalances. Thus, in 1969, about two out of five

TABLE 3.2
DISTRIBUTION OF INSTITUTIONS AND OF FACULTY, 1968–69

| | Quality Level[a] and Type | | | | | | | |
| | Universities | | | Four-Year Colleges | | | Community Colleges | |
	High	Medium	Low	High	Medium	Low	All	*Total*
Institutions								
Number	43	141	176	110	248	997	893	2,608
Percent	2	5	7	4	10	38	34	100
Faculty, percent	13	18	16	6	11	22	15	101

SOURCE: Trow (1975).

[a]The grouping of universities by quality level is based on institutional ratings in *The Gourman Report* (Gourman, 1967). The quality level grouping of four-year colleges is based on a combination of Gourman rankings and rankings provided by *College-Rater* with precedence given to the higher of the two for each college. All two-year colleges are treated as one grouping (see Trow, 1975, pp. 366–70).

TABLE 3.3
DISTRIBUTION OF FULL-TIME FACULTY OVER INSTITUTIONAL TYPES, 1979

Institutional Type	Number of Faculty	Percent of Faculty
Public		
Universities	90,233	31.6
Other 4-year institutions	112,029	39.3
2-year institutions	83,101	29.1
All	285,280	100.0
Private		
Universities	32,909	31.3
Other 4-year institutions	67,750	64.5
2-year institutions	4,402	4.2
All	105,061	100.0
Public and private		
Universities	123,142	31.5
Other 4-year institutions	179,779	46.0
2-year institutions	87,503	22.4
All	390,424	100.0

SOURCE: U.S. Department of Health, Education, and Welfare, National Center for Education Statistics (1980).

NOTE: Faculty count excludes students who assist in instruction, faculty in religious orders if their salaries are not determined and paid by the same common principles as those which apply to lay faculty, faculty for clinical medicine, administrative officers even though they may devote part of their time to classroom instruction, faculty in the ROTC program if their salaries are determined on a different basis from civilian faculty, and faculty on contracts other than 9-10 or 11-12 month duration.

faculty overall had earned the doctorate, ranging from about 60 percent in research universities and elite liberal arts colleges to about one-quarter at less selective liberal arts colleges and 5 percent at two-year community colleges (Trow, 1975). By 1979 a survey completed by the National Education Association showed about 60 percent of higher education faculty holding the doctorate (the proportion holding the degree from major research universities may have dropped, however, from the 35 percent figure reported for faculty in 1969 by Trow, 1975). Although the NEA estimates may be somewhat inflated owing to a sample that slightly overrepresented senior faculty, the general trend toward an increasing proportion of doctoral degree holders in the academic profession has recently received several independent confirmations. Atelsek and Gomberg (1978) in their study of hiring patterns of new full-time faculty in 1976–77 found that 52.9 percent of these new faculty had either received the degree or were expecting to within the next year. And Stadtman (1980) found that among the two-thirds of college and university presidents reporting that faculty quality at their institutions had been enhanced during the 1970s, an increased proportion of faculty holding the doctorate was among the top three reasons for their favorable judgment.

More modest change is evident in the disciplinary background of teaching faculty, although the direction of these changes, too, is in line with recent developments in higher education. The data in Figure 1 below show that in 1969, just over three-fifths of American academics were teaching in the traditional arts and sciences fields, and nearly one-third were teaching in the professions (including business and health sciences as well as the traditional professions of law and medicine). By 1976 there had been a modest, but perceptible, shift toward the professions and away from the traditional arts and sciences. The shift appears particularly modest in light of the more dramatic shift in student enrollments and majors reported by Levine (1978). One suspects, however, that more recent data would reveal continued, if still modest, shifts in this direction.

Apart from the major changes described above, perhaps the most notable legacy of the 1970s is the growing "seniorization" or "graying" of the faculty. The large cohort of new faculty who were hired during the mid and late 1960s to meet fast-growing student enrollments and subsequently promoted or tenured at the turn of the decade has, in the wake of the enrollment steady state, produced both an older and more senior faculty. This is graphically reflected in Table 3.4 by the decreasing proportion of faculty under thirty-five, the increasing proportion of those over fifty, and the increasing bulge in the thirty-six to fifty year age cohort. It is reflected as well in the increased proportion of faculty who have achieved senior rank

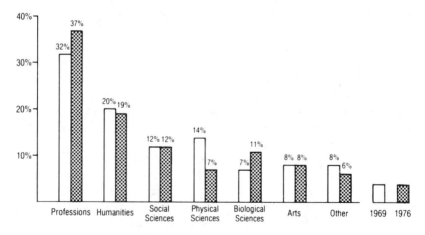

FIG. 1. Percent of faculty members teaching major subject fields, 1969 and 1976. (Numbers may not add to 100 because of rounding errors.) Reprinted, by permission, from Stadtman (1980)

TABLE 3.4
AGE DISTRIBUTION OF AMERICAN ACADEMICS, 1969 AND 1975

Range in Years	Percent in 1969	Range in Years	Percent in 1975
61 or more	8	60 or more	10
51–60	16	50–59	19
46–50	13	45–49	13
41–45	15	40–44	14
36–40	17	35–39	18
31–35	17	30–34	14
30 and under	13	29 and under	11

SOURCE: Stadtman (1980).

and tenure: 46.7 percent were tenured in 1969 (Bayer, 1973) versus 56.1 percent in 1979 (NCES, 1980). These data suggest, however, that the change may have been less dramatic than is commonly supposed.

In at least one respect, the American professoriate has changed little in the post–World War II years. It continues to fill its ranks with individuals from predominantely well-educated, middle-class backgrounds. Professors are twice as likely as the general population to have fathers who were college graduates (nearly one-fourth do) and nine times as likely to have fathers who did graduate work (nearly one-fifth). The data in Table 3.5 show that in terms of fathers' occupation, two-fifths of faculty come from professional, semi-professional, and managerial families, and another one-fifth from small business backgrounds. Only one-fourth are of working class origin, despite the fact that fully 70 percent of the male labor force were in manual or white collar and sales positions in 1950, when the fathers of most of today's faculty were occupationally active (Lipset and Ladd, 1979). While breaking the data down by age cohort does reveal some differences in paternal occupational backgrounds— younger faculty are less likely to be the offspring of farmers or small businessmen and more likely to be the offspring of professionals— faculty under thirty-five are no more likely to have fathers in semi-skilled or unskilled trades, or in white collar jobs, than are their older colleagues. Moreover, there is evidence to suggest that younger faculty are actually drawn from wealthier family backgrounds. In their 1975 survey, Lipset and Ladd (1979) asked faculty to describe their family economic status on a scale ranging from "wealthy" to "above average," "average," "below average," and "poor." Disaggregating the data by age groups, they found that the proportion of

TABLE 3.5

OCCUPATIONS OF FATHERS OF AMERICAN ACADEMICS, 1969 AND 1975, AND
OCCUPATIONS OF MALE LABOR FORCE IN 1950 (as percent of N)

	1969 Survey Distribution (N = 60,028)	1975 Survey Distribution (N = 3,536)	Males in Labor Force 1950 (N = 42,722,000)
College, university teacher/administrator	4	4	0.5
Elementary, secondary school teacher/administrator	3	3	0.6
Other professional	15	16	2.6
Managerial and semi-professional	16	17	10.2
Owner, large business	2	1	0.4
Owner, small business	18	18	3.3
White collar	8	7	12.6
Farmer	10	8	9.8
Skilled worker	16	17	23.6
Semiskilled and unskilled workers	8	9	33.6
Armed services	1	1	0.9

SOURCE: Lipset and Ladd (1979).

faculty reporting poor origins ranged from 14 percent of those over fifty to 6 percent of those under thirty. While 41 percent of the oldest cohort reported below average or poor backgrounds, only 23 percent of the youngest did. Conversely, the proportion reporting wealthy or above average backgrounds was highest among the youngest (29 percent) and smallest among the oldest (19 percent).

If the post–World War II professoriate has not broadened its social class origins, it has "democratized" to some extent its religious, ethnic, and gender base—a function initially of the dropping of barriers to Jews and Catholics after the war, and more recently of federal affirmative action regulations. Although the data in Tables 3.6 and 3.7 indicate the persistent modality of the white Protestant of British origin, they also suggest the increasing inroads of Jews, those of non-British national origin, and some ethnic minorities (especially Asian-Americans). The proportion of Jews in the professoriate was three times that of their representation in the general population and fully one-third of these were teaching at major research universities. While the proportionate representation of Jews appears to be leveling off, that of Catholics appears to be increasing (see chapter 6).

In the case of blacks and Hispanics, however, no such proportionate increases are discernible. The proportion of black faculty has held relatively constant at about 3 percent (about one-quarter of

TABLE 3.6

DISTRIBUTION OF RELIGIOUS BACKGROUND OF FACULTY AND OF THE GENERAL
PUBLIC (as percents)

Religious Background	All Faculty		General Public	College-educated Population
	1969	1975		
Jewish	9	10	3	5
Catholic	19	18	27	28
Other	4	5	1	1
None	3	5	3	3
Protestant				
Baptist	NA	9	23	17
Methodist	NA	14	14	16
Lutheran	NA	7	8	7
Presbyterian/Congregationalist	NA	17	6	11
Episcopalian	NA	6	2	4
Morman	NA	2	(a)	(a)
Quaker Unitarian	NA	1	(a)	(a)
Other	NA	6	10	8

SOURCE: Lipset and Ladd (1979).
NA: Data not available. (a): Less than 1 percent.

their proportionate representation in the general population); and
blacks are no more heavily represented in younger faculty age cohorts than in older age cohorts.[2] And, not coincidentally, fully three-
fifths of black faculty tend to come disproportionately from that
segment of the profession reporting "poor" or "below average" family income (Lipset and Ladd, 1979). Among Hispanics, proportionate
representation in the profession has also held constant at about 1
percent (compared to a proportionate representation of 4 percent of
the general population), although it appears to be slightly increasing among younger faculty age cohorts. This latter fact, however,
may be a function of the inclusion under this rubric of a significant
minority of well-educated middle-class immigrants from Cuba and
South America (Lipset and Ladd, 1979).

Perhaps no group has benefited more from this democratization
than academic women, at least over the past decade. As late as 1960,
women constituted barely one-fifth of the professoriate, a 13.1 percent decline from their peak representation in the pre–World War II
period (Table 3.8). Their proportionate representation increased
only 1.9 percent in the ensuing decade and a half but increased fully
4.3 percent between 1976 and 1979—a function largely of the disproportionate representation of women among "new hires" in the
late 1970s. And while academic women have historically tended to

TABLE 3.7
Ethnic Origins of Faculty and of the General Public, 1975 (as percents)

	Faculty	General Public (a)
British Protestant	33	16
British Catholic	2	1
Irish Protestant	6	7
Irish Catholic	5	4
German/Austrian Protestant	17	14
German/Austrian Catholic	4	4
Scandinavian	5	7
Italian	4	6
East European, non-Jewish	5	5
East European, Jewish	8	2
Other European, non-Jewish	5	3
Other European, Jewish	1	(b)
Hispanic	1	4
Black	3	11
Asian	1.5	(c)

Source: Lipset and Ladd (1979).
(a): The percentages for the general public do not add to 100; some respondents refused to classify themselves as to ethnic background, whereas others were of sufficiently diverse backgrounds that they cannot be located in the table's fifteen categories.
(b): Less than 1 percent.
(c): No reliable estimate is possible from these data, but the census estimate for Asians is 0.6 percent.

be disproportionately located at community colleges, the less selective four-year colleges, and underrepresented in the university sector, the trend particularly among "new hires" appears to be toward a more equitable distribution over institutional types (see chapter 7 for a fuller discussion).

In sum, the post–World War II period has been one of overall growth for the academic profession, with the past decade showing both a moderation and differentiation of that growth pattern. The

TABLE 3.8
Proportionate Representation of Female Faculty, 1930–78

Year	Percent Female Faculty
1929–30	32.5
1959–60	19.4
1963–64	19.6
1972–73	20.6
1975–76	21.3
1978–79	25.6

Source: Based on data in Lipset and Ladd (1979).

growth of the full-time professoriate has moderated, while the proportion of part-timer faculty has increased dramatically, although that expansion may be leveling off in the 1980s. The locus of growth has shifted decidedly to the two-year community college sector and the public four-year collegiate sector from the university sector, and less markedly from the traditional arts and sciences to the professions. Supply-demand imbalances in the academic labor market appear to be raising the educational qualifications of the profession at the same time that they are raising its mean age and redistributing faculty members toward the senior end of the academic rank structure. While maintaining a certain homogeneity with respect to socioeconomic background, the profession has expanded its religious and ethnic base, and, more recently, its gender base to the extent that market conditions allow.

All of this suggests that the past decade, in particular, has been one of some historic moment for the academic profession. To what extent the changes we have chronicled will affect the collective traditions, values, behavior, and career patterns that we identify with academics is an empirical question that current and future research must answer. Indeed, the chapters that follow provide the requisite benchmark against which currently reported and future findings can be assessed and interpreted.

1. Stadtman (1980) presents evidence, however, to suggest that the expansion of the part-time academic labor force may be "leveling off" during the 1980s—at least according to the perceptions of college and university presidents.

2. It is true, however, that during this period the location, if not the representation, of black faculty in the profession has improved. The proportion located in the more prestigious colleges and universities has nearly tripled from 5 percent in the late 1960s to fully 17 percent in the late 1970s (see chapter 7).

4

The Academic Career

The term "career" derives from the French *carrière*—literally a "race course." As a *carrière,* the modern academic career has a starting gate (the choice to enter) and a finish line (retirement). A faculty member's institution of employment and, to a lesser extent, his or her discipline define the shape of the course to be run. Together, they form the normative context within which faculty jockey for their place in the academic sun—that is, the conditions of academic work, such as professional autonomy, and the norms that guide it, such as academic freedom and the merit principle. At the same time, the institution and the discipline establish benchmarks against which faculty may assess their position in the race—the institution providing a system of academic ranks and the prospect of permanent tenure, the discipline providing opportunities for colleague recognition that may ultimately translate into institutional status.

This chapter focuses on the structural aspects defining the academic career course—career entry, movement through the disciplinary and institutional tracks, job changing and career switches—and then on the normative context within which the course is pursued— the conditions of work and norms that govern individual orientations to the race. Finally, issues of career satisfaction (is the race worth it?) and career exit (retirement) are addressed.

CAREER ENTRY

Who chooses an academic career? When? Why? The sociological portrait of entering faculty sketched in chapter 3 is based on socioeconomic, religious, and ethnic family background. The available evidence allows us to construct another retrospective portrait that is primarily psychological, including early family relationships, psychosocial development, and enduring psychological traits. The evidence also suggests inferences about the career choice process itself, with respect to both its timing and the formative influences bearing upon it.

The Psychological/Developmental Portrait

There appears to be a number of common threads in the psychosocial development of college and university faculty members.

1. As a group, the professoriate is more likely to count first-born and only children among its ranks than would be predicted by chance (Roe, 1953; West, 1971; Brown and Shukraft, 1974).
2. As a group, professors tend to come from families that stressed intellectual pursuits and school achievement (not surprising in view of the correlation between educational and occupational attainments of social groups and their proportionate representation in the professoriate).
3. Beginning in their childhood, professors, as a group, displayed a noticeable sense of "apartness," together with a preference for solitary, autonomous activities (a predisposition apparently obviating the formation of close personal relationships). Both Roe (1951a) and West (1971), however, noted variations in this solitary characteristic by discipline, with social scientists showing themselves to have been considerably more "social" during childhood and adolescence.
4. As a group, professors appear to show high need for achievement, autonomy (Roe, 1953; Gustad, 1960), and a preference for intellectual modes of satisfaction (Roe, 1951a) as well as intellectual (as opposed to action-oriented) modes of mastering experience (Bloom and Freedman, 1973).
5. Not surprisingly, professors are, as a group, highly intelligent.

This psychosocial portrait of the professoriate is more blurred, however, with respect to parental relationships and school experience. In the case of the former, investigations range from reporting good parental relationships (Bloom and Freedman, 1973) to reporting distant ones (West, 1971) and overprotective, overcontrolling ones (Roe, 1953). But some consensus does emerge: both Roe (1953) and West (1971) found that variation in the degree of warmth characterizing parental relationships did bear a relationship to the individual's orientation to the academic role, with researchers more likely to have known warm parental relationships and teachers less likely. In the latter case, one study reported faculty to have found the school experience rewarding (Gustad, 1960), whereas another reported a majority sentiment that it was boring (West, 1971).

Although the above portrait of the professoriate is relatively clearly drawn, its interpretation is problematic owing to the absence of control groups. Without comparative data on other professionals, it is impossible to determine the extent to which any, or all, of these background factors makes an "essential" contribution to entry into the academic professions as opposed to a whole variety of other intellectual professions. It is likely, or so popular mythology would have it, that a large proportion of writers and literati experienced a sense of apartness during childhood just as a majority of physicians displayed considerable achievement motivation. The crucial question is what makes some solitary, achievement-oriented individuals choose an academic career rather than a literary or medical one. While the findings of the inquiries reported thus far do not allow such inferences, Martin's (1969) comparative study of occupational choice among college teaching, law, and medicine does provide some suggestive clues. At least three factors seem to distinguish among prospective teachers, attorneys, and physicians: academic achievement in college, family socioeconomic status, and parental involvement in, and support of, career choice. Prospective college faculty had significantly higher grade-point averages as undergraduates than either prospective physicians or attorneys. They tended to come from families that showed considerable parental educational and occupational attainments but considerably lower family income and status orientation than either attorneys or physicians. Finally, prospective faculty show a distinctive pattern of relatively low parental involvement in occupational and educational decisions and considerably lower parental support for occupational training. It would appear, then, that prospective entrants to the academic profession differ from prospective entrants to other professions in intellectual achievement, family values, and parental ability to support training, as well as relative independence from parents in educational and occupational decisions.

The Timing of Career Choice

Unlike the prospective physician or attorney, the prospective faculty member has two relatively independent career decisions to make: the choice of a discipline or graduate major and the choice of the academic setting as the peculiarly appropriate context in which to practice that graduate discipline or major (and this is especially true for those disciplines in the social and natural sciences and the professions whose advanced practitioners have considerable opportunity outside the academic community). These decisions typically come later for the prospective academic than for the prospective physician or attorney (Martin, 1969). The evidence arrayed in Table 4.1 clearly shows that the choice of a discipline usually precedes the choice of an academic career. There is some disagreement, however, as to the precise timing of the decisions, particularly of the one to enter the professoriate. All agree that a discipline is most frequently chosen before completing college, though there is some question as to whether the modal period is at the beginning or at the later stages of the undergraduate years (or even earlier); and each study discloses rather wide variation among its sample. The decision to

TABLE 4.1
MODAL TIMING OF DISCIPLINARY AND ACADEMIC CAREER CHOICE

			MODAL TIMING OF CHOICE		
Case	Sample Composition	Sample Size	Pre-College	During College	Post Baccalaureate
			Choice of a Discipline		
Roe (1951b)	"Eminent" physical scientists	≈20		x	
Roe (1953)	"Eminent" psychologists and anthropologists	22		x	
Gustad (1960)	Present and former male faculty in English, chemistry, and psychology at 155 colleges and universities in the South	558		x	
Parsons and Platt (1968)	Arts and sciences faculty at 8 colleges and universities	450		x	
			Choice of an Academic Career		
Roe (1951b)				x	
Roe (1953)				x	
Stecklein and Eckert (1958)	Faculty at Minnesota colleges and universities	752			x
Gustad (1960)					x
Espy (1963)	Faculty at 72 black colleges	823			x
Parsons and Platt (1968)				x	
Eckert and Williams (1972)	Faculty at Minnesota colleges and universities	1383			x

enter the professoriate, on the other hand, comes most frequently, in the majority opinion, during the post-baccalaureate years, although a minority locate it during the baccalaureate years (Roe, 1951b, 1953; Parson and Platt, 1968). In weighing the dissent of Roe and Parsons and Platt from the majority findings, several situational factors need to be considered.

1. Roe questioned her sample about the choice of "science" as a career, and thus it may be that her findings are more closely related to the choice of a discipline rather than to the decision to enter the professoriate per se.
2. Roe studied "eminent" scientists, and Parsons and Platt disproportionately sampled faculty from more prestigious colleges and universities; Parsons and Platt reported that faculty at the most prestigious institutions tended to choose their careers earlier than others.
3. Parsons and Platt sampled disproportionately younger faculty at the lower ranks. Eckert and Williams (1972) reported that faculty in the younger age cohorts tended to have considered an academic career earlier than their older colleagues.

Taking these definitional and sampling factors into account, it would appear most reasonable to accept the majority opinion as descriptive of the professoriate at large.

It should be noted that the findings we have cited are based on aggregated data and thus represent modal responses around which there is considerable variation. Beyond that variation associated with prestige of institutional affiliation and age cohort, Parsons and Platt reported variation among disciplinary areas, although with neither a test of statistical nor practical significance. In their study, natural science professors proved more likely than others to decide on an academic career either quite early (pre-baccalaureate) or quite late (post-baccalaureate); social scientists appeared to make their career decisions slightly later than either humanists or natural scientists as a group.

Sources of Influence on Career Choice

Two prominent investigations that examine the sources of influence on disciplinary choice reach different conclusions: Roe (1953) reported intellectual factors (most notably the discovery of the possibility of doing research) as the modal source of influence, whereas Parsons and Platt (1968) reported another professor (an inspiring teacher) as the modal influence agent. This apparent discrepancy, however, may again be attributed to differences in sample characteristics between the two studies, the "eminent" natural and social scientists in Roe's study differing essentially from Parsons and Platt's more, although not altogether, representative sample from among the liberal arts disciplines. Parsons and Platt indeed reported variations among their sample in modal-influence source by level of institutional prestige and research orientation and by discipline. Faculty at more prestigious institutions were less likely, as a group, to report "affective" influences such as an inspiring teacher and more likely to report intellectual influences such as an appetite whetted by courses and reading, whereas the reverse was true of faculty at the least prestigious institutions. In a similar fashion, humanists were more likely to cite the primary influence of a teacher than natural and social scientists, with the latter most frequently citing intellectual factors. If we assume that Roe's "eminents" were affiliated with the more prestigious/research-oriented institutions (and Roe provides the data to support that assumption), the discrepancy becomes readily explicable: it reflects the variation between the studied samples in intellectual orientation and achievement and academic discipline.

As to the sources of influence on the decision to enter the professoriate, an examination of the findings discloses apparent clusters or patterns of influence over time. Studies completed prior to 1968 reported three primary sources of influence: the individual's intrinsic interest in his or her discipline or in teaching and research; happenstance, that is, a process of "drift" or the simple fact of getting a job offer; and an influential professor who, though important, is clearly less so than the first pair. Among studies completed in the post-1968 period, several shifts in the modality of influence sources can be discerned: the role of an influential professor assumes greater importance, while that of "drift" lessens; intrinsic interest in disciplinary research and intellectual stimulation increases in modal influence at the expense of a desire to teach; and a slightly higher proportion of professors report the "attraction of the academic lifestyle" as influential.

To what extent are these apparent shifts fortuitous artifacts or representative of actual change over time? The best evidence bearing on this question is provided by Eckert's replication of her original survey of faculty in Minnesota's colleges and universities during the late 1950s (Eckert and Williams, 1972). In juxtaposing data obtained from comparable samples over a ten-year interval, Eckert did indeed find changes. Among faculty surveyed in the late 1960s, former professors were frequently mentioned as highly influential in the choice of an academic career; the over-fifty age cohorts reported a higher incidence of drift, while the under-thirty-five age cohorts more frequently cited the influence of other academics and were more often concerned with possibilities for research and intellectual challenge. On the extent to which these differences are attributable to the consummation of the "academic revolution" (Jencks and Riesman, 1968) and the ascendance of research or an increasing preoccupation with career decisions at an ever earlier age, we can only speculate.

Interpretation of the findings is further muddied by the procedures that investigators have employed to identify influence sources. In all cases, respondents were provided with a checklist of predetermined influence items and asked to indicate whether or not each influence source had indeed played a role in their choice of an academic career. This strategy precludes any reliable determination of the relative import of influence sources across individuals; indeed, relative import can only be inferred at the aggregate level of analysis in terms of model frequencies for the sample as a whole. We are thus left no clues as to how the potential sources of influence interact to affect the individual.

Within these limitations, however, a greater measure of clarity may be achieved by examining subgroup variations in sources of influence. In addition to shifts among age cohorts, Eckert (1959, 1972) found patterned differences along sex lines. Women, in both the late fifties and the late sixties, reported themselves more highly influenced by circumstance or drift, and males reported themselves more frequently influenced by scholarly interests. Parsons and Platt (1968) reported variation by level of institutional prestige and discipline. Faculty at the most prestigious institutions more frequently mentioned the allure of the academic environment and the shaping influence of research experience than those at less prestigious institutions (and this coincides with the reports of Roe's sample of eminent natural and social scientists). Among disciplinary groups, social scientists reported a lower incidence of influence on the part of a teacher than did natural scientists or humanists and a much higher incidence than the latter groups of influence by extra-academic experiences and persons; and this may reflect the greater sociability and interpersonal orientation that both Roe (1953) and West (1971) discerned among social scientists.

Summary

As a group, individuals who have entered the professoriate share a number of common background characteristics (family relationships and psychosocial development, intellectual orientation and achievement), and appear to distinguish themselves from entrants to other intellectual professions primarily in terms of level of their intellectual achievement in college, the relative independence of their career decisions from parental influence, and family values that are more attuned to education than to a concern for income and social status. The majority of these individuals committed themselves to a discipline during their undergraduate years, prior to deciding to enter a career in academic work. But the precise timing of these choices varied substantially across individuals from different types of institutions and disciplines, and appears to have generally been earlier for more recent entrants to academe. In choosing a discipline, the prospective professor was stimulated primarily by the allure of intellectual challenge and the model provided by former professors with whom he or she had come into contact. Those who entered fields in the humanities and became affiliated with less prestigious, less research-oriented institutions tended to cite the influence of a teacher more often, whereas "intellectual stimulation" was more often cited by those who entered the natural and social sciences and became affiliated with more prestigious institutions. The pattern of influence sources on the decision to enter the professoriate appears to have shifted over time, with more recent entrants less likely to have drifted into academic life and more likely to have been attracted by the intellectual and knowledge production aspects of the academic role. In addition, variation in sources of influence was reported by sex, discipline, and level of institutional prestige. The interpretation of these findings was, however, muddied insofar as they were based on aggregate distributions of the frequency with which influence items on a prefabricated list were checked. It is therefore impossible to draw inferences about the relative import of influence sources across individuals and to understand the process of how influence sources interact, at the individual level, to lead the prospective recruit into the academic profession. Moreover, it is not clear how this capsule description may be changing in response to the current "drying up" of the academic job market. Breneman (1981) and others have expressed concern that the high level of intellectual achievement that has characterized recruits to the profession in the past may be declining as the "best and brightest" undergraduates turn away from graduate study in the traditional arts and science fields toward the more promising financial rewards of the intellectual professions, such as law and medicine, and the applied sciences, such as engineering and computer science. The issue of recruitment, whose salience emerged in the late 1950s as a response to the prospective short-term under-supply of college teachers, has reemerged, then, in the early 1980s, in response to long-term concerns about the character and quality of the profession over the next one and a half decades of likely depression.

ADVANCING IN THE PROFESSION AND THE ORGANIZATION

Having settled on academic life, the entrant must take up the task of fashioning that choice into a career. Securing a good position at the right institution, moving up the organizational ladder in terms of rank and salary, and for the ambitious few, achieving recognition from one's disciplinary colleagues for contributions to the advancement of knowledge—such are the components of an academic career. How is it fashioned?

Securing a Good Position

Most of what we know about the determinants of securing a good position are the products of sociological studies aimed at establishing the bases of the academic stratification system. The largest share of effort has been directed toward assessing the relative salience of accomplishment (as evidenced by the number and quality of one's publications, measured in part by citation frequency) versus more *particularistic* criteria, such as academic and social ancestry (as evidenced by the prestige of one's doctoral degree-granting institution, one's graduate sponsor, and the socioeconomic status of one's family) in determining who manages to secure academic appointments at the most prestigious departments and institutions.[1]

Two clearly distinctive sets of findings emerge from these investigations: one set of studies (Cole and Cole, 1973; Hargens and Hagstrom, 1967; Allison, 1976; Cole and Cole, 1967; Danziger, 1978) found that one's publications and the prestige of one's terminal degree were equally important factors in securing a prestigious academic appointment; the second set of studies (Crane, 1965 and 1970; Lightfield, 1971; Long, 1978; Reskin, 1979; Youn, 1981), on the other hand, reported that the prestige of one's terminal degree and of one's graduate sponsor were significantly more likely to bring a good job than either the number or critical acclaim of one's research publications.

On what basis are we to evaluate these conflicting findings? The major distinction between the two groups of studies appears to reside in how they assess scholarly productivity; the first examines publication at the time of the investigation, the second at the time of appointment. As Hargens and Hagstrom (1967) suggest, in assessing the limitations of their own work, measuring publication at the time of the study rather than at the time of appointment tends to overemphasize the importance of scholarly productivity insofar as the prestige of one's institutional location has an independent effect on publication activity between the time of appointment and the time of the study. Indeed, Long (1978) has neatly demonstrated the magnitude of such overestimation by separately regressing the prestige of one's terminal degree and graduate sponsor on publication productivity at the time of initial appointment *and* six years after the initial appointment. In this analysis, the import of publication productivity nearly doubled over the six-year period (beta = 0.15 to beta = 0.27) while that of doctorate prestige and sponsorship were slightly reduced. In light of these findings, it would appear that *at the time of initial appointment,* it is much more the prestige of one's terminal degree and one's graduate sponsor than one's scholarly productivity which will lead to a good academic appointment. Moreover, insofar as one's scholarly productivity counts at all, it is the quality, or frequency of citation, of one's publications rather than their sheer number that makes the difference (Lightfield, 1971; Cole and Cole, 1973; Long, 1978; Reskin, 1979). Even the effect of publication quality, however, is not direct but is mediated by "visibility" and "the perceived quality of one's work"; and these are, to a considerable extent, a function of previous institutional affiliation (Cole and Cole, 1973).

The finding that academic ancestry more than scholarly accomplishment is the key to a desirable academic position is subject to two critical qualifications. The first of these concerns the large "residual" variance that emerges across all studies—that is, productivity and academic ancestry together account for only a small percentage of the variance in prestige of institutional affiliation, from a low of 14 percent reported by Cole and Cole (1973) to a high of 46 percent reported by Lightfield (1971), and averaging in the 30 to 35 percent range (Long, 1978; Reskin, 1979). Thus, from 54 percent to 86 percent—and on average about two-thirds—of the variance in prestige of institutional affiliation remains unaccounted for. Put less technically, the allocation of academic positions is still a rather mysterious process with a large unexplained factor. And that residual factor looms particularly large at the beginning of an academic career. Across most studies, the predictability of first-job prestige tends to be considerably lower than for subsequent moves (15–20 percent versus approximately 30–35 percent for second and later jobs).

This leads to the second critical qualification. The relative salience of scholarly productivity and ancestry for securing the right position seems to vary over the course of the academic career. In securing the first position, prestige of the terminal degree and the graduate sponsor clearly overshadow training and productivity.[2] For second and later jobs, the residual effect of doctorate prestige and sponsorship remain but are attenuated. Their salience is almost entirely mediated by their effect on the first academic appointment, which in turn is a powerful determinant of subsequent ones—both independently and via the effects of prestige of institutional location on early career scholarly productivity (Cole and Cole, 1973; Danziger, 1978; Reskin, 1979; Long, 1978; Crane, 1970; Hargens and Hagstrom, 1967). Once having secured the right initial appointment, which is more a function of prestige than demonstrated competence, and more a function of residual, unexplained factors than anything else, subsequent appointments are determined by the prestige of that first appointment and the quality of scholarly work, which is itself, to a considerable extent, a function of the prestige of the initial institutional appointment. In many respects, then, Caplow and McGee (1958) said it best over two decades ago when, after examining the process of filling academic vacancies, they concluded: "Hiring decisions are not based on the actual evaluation of the applicant's work, but rather on the prestige of the candidate's graduate department, the eminence of his sponsors, and chance"—or, at least, unknown factors.

On the face of it, the dynamics of the sponsorship effect seem readily comprehensible. It is a function primarily of the sponsor's scholarly "eminence" as this presumably affects contacts and placement capability (Reskin, 1979) and, to a lesser extent, of the sponsor's own scholarly productivity insofar as it provides a model for the fledgling academic and instills in him or her the habit of productivity (Long, 1978; Reskin, 1979; Cameron and Blackburn, 1981).[3]

The role of doctorate prestige in the academic hiring process as a factor independent of the prestige of the graduate sponsor is both larger and more obscure (Long, 1978; Reskin, 1979). A number of potential competing explanations present themselves. The relative prestige of the graduate department may merely mirror the relative ability levels of its graduate students, thus indirectly translating higher native ability into appointments at better academic institutions. The prestige of the doctoral department may be associated with the quality of training offered and hence with subsequent scholarly productivity so that the academic hiring process is merely discriminating on the basis of good training. The prestige of one's doctoral institution may have a "halo effect," that is, it may endow the job candidate with the aura of prestige that surrounds the doctoral department, thus framing the appointment process as an opportunity for the hiring institution to maximize its own prestige (Wilson, 1942 and 1979; Caplow and McGee, 1958). The available evidence suggests that neither native ability nor quality of training are mirrored in the operation of degree prestige. Both Bayer and Folger (1966) and Cole (1974) found that the relationship between rank of doctoral department and prestige of institutional affiliation remained even after controlling for I.Q. And Reskin (1979) explicitly tested and found no support for the "quality of training" hypothesis; neither student pre-doctoral research experience and publication nor the overall level of scholarly activity of graduate department faculty were systematically related to later institutional affiliation of faculty. There is no direct test of the operation of the "halo effect" in faculty hiring; however Cole and Cole (1973) found in examining the relationship of prestige of institutional affiliation to colleague recognition that the lion's share of the institutional prestige effect was indeed mediated by "the perceived quality" of a faculty member's research contributions—suggesting the operation of a "halo effect" in the evaluation of academic work. It would appear reasonable to assume that a halo effect would operate as well in the evaluation of job candidates.

Quite beyond ability, training, and the halo effect, it appears that doctorate prestige also reflects social class origin—suggesting that in faculty hiring, the academic stratification system may merely serve as a kind of proxy for the operation of the larger social stratification system. Crane (1969) reported that faculty members with lower social class origins (based on father's education and occupation) were less likely to receive their doctorate from a prestigious university and subsequently less likely to hold positions at prestigious universities. Moreover, she found that among recent doctoral recipients, those with lower social class origins were less likely than their middle-class counterparts to get positions at prestigious universities, even after controlling for prestige of doctoral institution. This "social class" effect seemed to be attenuated in the case of a cohort of experienced graduate faculty with whom the group of recent doctoral recipients was compared. The cross-sectional nature of the data, however, did not permit her to determine whether the attenuation indicated that the disadvantages of lower social class had increased over time or were ultimately overcome over the course of an academic career. Recent data reported by Lipset and Ladd (1979), however, appear to support the first explanation. They found that irrespective of age, the most prestigious universities tend to draw their faculty disproportionately from the higher social strata. In light of the available evidence, then, the prestige of one's doctoral institution operates both as a "halo" and a perhaps unconscious social class selector in the academic hiring process.

It should be noted that these conclusions emerge from data more than a decade old when the academic job market was just beginning to contract. How will these prestige dynamics operate in the academic job market of the 1980s? Youn's recent analysis (1981) suggests that they will indeed maintain themselves in the current buyer's market, although the incidence of "trickling down" the institutional prestige hierarchy is likely to increase overall—a trend corroborated by Muffo and Robinson (1981).[4] And as future mobility opportunities decrease, we can expect that where one initially locates oneself (now more than ever a matter of prestige and mystery) will likely have even higher importance in determining the trajectory of the individual academic career.

Advancing in One's Discipline

How does the fashioning of a disciplinary career compare with the process of securing a good academic appointment? Investigators have examined three yardsticks of disciplinary achievement and recognition: receipt of honors and awards, visibility of one's scholarly work to colleagues (recognition as "familiarity"), and actual use of one's scholarly work by colleagues in their own research (as evidenced by citations). The findings permit two broad generalizations. In the first place, disciplinary recognition is more predictable than the prestige of one's institutional affiliation; and among the yardsticks of recognition, visibility or familiarity to one's colleagues is the most predictable of all (Cole and Cole [1973] were able to explain just over 60 percent of the variance in visibility and about one-third of the variance in receipt of honors and awards; Reskin [1977 and 1979] and Long [1978] were able to explain between one-quarter and one-half of the variance in citations to scholarly work). In the second place, scholarly research performance overall emerges as a more important and academic ancestry as a less important arbiter of disciplinary recognition than of securing a good position (indeed, the effects of prestige of graduate sponsor and of doctoral department are largely indirect, mediated by their influence on initial job placement and early scholarly productivity as these affect disciplinary recognition).

Several studies suggest, however, that prestige of institutional affiliation may be nearly as important as (Cole and Cole, 1973; Long, 1978), or even more important (Crane, 1965) than, research performance in determining recognition by each yardstick under certain conditions.

Awards and Honors. While Cole and Cole (1973) found that research performance (the number and quality of publications) explained just over one-third of the variance in receipt of awards and honors, they noted a high zero-order correlation between institutional prestige and receipt of such awards and honors. In the absence of longitudinal data on the timing of awards and academic appointments, they were unable to test for the independent effect of institutional prestige. Crane (1965) was able to do so, however, and found that institutional prestige plays the more critical determining role. Major university faculty were one-and-a-half times as likely to be recognized as faculty at minor universities, and highly productive faculty at minor universities were about as likely to be recognized as less productive faculty at the major research institutions.

Visibility. Visibility, in the sense of colleagues' familiarity with one's scholarly work, is at once the most predictable yardstick of recognition and the most subject to "ascriptive" influences. Even Cole and Cole (1973), who tend to report the lowest estimates of the power of institutional prestige, found that where one produced one's scholarly work rivaled the citation measure of the quality of that work in commanding visibility among colleagues. Moreover, Cole and Cole found that previous formal recognition in the form of awards and honors had a strong independent effect on visibility, even after controlling for the quality of research performance. Thus the fact of previous formal recognition, itself closely associated with the prestige of institutional affiliation, appears to heighten one's visibility significantly, quite beyond the quality of one's research efforts.

Citations of Scholarly Work. The importance of research productivity vis-à-vis institutional prestige in achieving disciplinary recognition emerges most clearly in the frequency of citation of one's scholarly work. Across all studies, research performance emerges as the most important predictor of the use of one's scholarly work by colleagues. Even here, however, two critical qualifications are in order. First, the relatively important role of research performance must be viewed in the context of the large residual, or unexplained, variance in frequency of citation (fully half to three-quarters of the variance in frequency of citation remains unexplained, depending on the particular study). Second, there is evidence to suggest that the influence of scholarly performance declines over time and may be attenuated by other "ascriptive" influences. Long (1978) reported that the formative role of institutional prestige increased as the term of a scholar's appointment at the institution increased, controlling for previous productivity. Thus institutional prestige proved only half as important as scholarly performance to frequency of citation during the third year of appointment but fully equalled scholarly productivity by the sixth year of appointment (and, indeed, this increased independent effect of prestige seemed to be largely responsible for the increased predictability of frequency of citation during the later years of appointment). Cole and Cole (1973) found that the quality of a single paper in physics tended to stand on its own, that is, to receive as much recognition at publication as five years later wherever the author was located, but that citation of the entire corpus of a physicist's work was subject to the influence of institutional prestige and the physicist's professional *eminence* (based on their previous citations or scientific repute and their previous receipt of awards and honors). Moreover, the influence of institutional prestige and professional eminence proved transferable from one collaborator to another; co-authorship with a well-placed and highly reputable colleague led to a higher likelihood of citation. Incursion of ascribed characteristics seemed, however, to be mediated by the quality of the work itself. The very best papers (those most heavily cited five years after publication) tended to be recognized (cited) early *irrespective* of author's location and eminence. It may therefore be that the power of ascribed characteristics operates primarily for those scholarly contributions that are not clearly major ones.

That ascribed characteristics intrude to a significant extent in what is properly the province of disinterested judgments on scholarly merit demands explanation. A number of hypotheses have been advanced by Cole and Cole (1973) to that end.

1. Since most doctoral degree holders receive their degree from the top departments, they tend to keep up with developments at alma mater (the "center" of the discipline for them) whatever their subsequent institutional location—hence the "location" effect. Despite its credibility, this explanation remains untested.

2. The specialities emphasized by top departments may be more visible; hence, the work of their professors commands wide attention. Cole and Cole (1973), however, tested this explanation and found that the impact of institutional prestige remained after controlling for emphasized fields of specialization.

3. Affiliation with a major university may provide a "halo" around its faculty's work, making it look better than it is. In an effort to test this hypothesis, Cole and Cole (1973) computed the correlation of institutional prestige and frequency of citation, partialing out the effects of research productivity and the subjective perception of research quality (the "halo"). In so doing, the zero-order correlation of 0.45 was reduced to a partial correlation of 0.14—suggesting the operation of a powerful halo.

Beyond any halo effect, a more encompassing explanation might proceed as follows. Recognition in the form of citation depends on visibility to one's colleagues; and visibility may be enhanced by either quality research performance, a position at a major university, by previous formal recognition (reputation), or, most completely, by some combination of all three. Although no studies currently provide data on visibility at multiple points in time, which would permit an adequate test of this hypothesis, its relatively high predictability and its close association with institutional prestige and past reputation lends this latter explanation considerable credibility.

In sum, achieving disciplinary recognition is both more predictable than achieving a good academic position and less subject to the influence of institutional reputation or one's past personal reputation. The intrusive presence of ascription, however, athough attenuated, remains.

Advancing in the Organization

Two preliminary observations on the determinants of organizational advancement (that is, promotion through the ranks and salary increases) are in order. First, organizational recognition is much more predictable than disciplinary recognition. Studies over the past decade of the determinants of academic compensation manage to explain between 55 and 85 percent of the variance in salary increments and absolute salary levels, depending on the number and nature of independent variables considered (Tuckman, 1976). Second, unlike the various forms of disciplinary recognition, the determinants of organizational advancement are relatively stable or consistent across forms of recognition; the most important determinants of salary are also the most important determinants of promotion.

What are these most important arbiters of organizational advancement? The vast majority of studies suggest that they are performance factors—research productivity, attainment of the terminal degree, and relative emphasis on components of the academic role (especially time spent in administration and, to a lesser extent, institutional service). Faculty who publish, who assume administrative responsibilities, and who serve on committees are rewarded for their efforts with promotion and salary increments.[5]

Rewards for an individual faculty member's performance are shaped, however, by institutional affiliation, disciplinary field, and academic rank. At more prestigious institutions, faculty are more likely to receive higher salaries, especially at the higher ranks (Muffo, 1979), but are at the same time less likely to be promoted or, at the least, likely to be promoted more slowly (Astin and Bayer, 1973; Cohn, 1973; Tuckman and Hagemann, 1976; Muffo, 1979). Faculty salary scales tend to be lower at church-related institutions (Cohn, 1973) and, to a lesser extent, at private colleges and universities generally (Astin and Bayer, 1973; Tuckman and Tuckman, 1976), and tend to vary across geographical regions, reflecting cost-of-living adjustments (Tuckman and Hagemann, 1976; Lewis, 1979). Individual academic disciplines boast very different supply-demand situations, reflecting differential opportunity structures and salary scales outside academe. Both promotion rates and salary levels tend to be slower and lower, respectively, for faculty in the humanities (Katz, 1973; Tuckman and Hagemann, 1976; Tuckman and Tuckman, 1976; Cartter, 1976).[6] Finally, academic rank importantly affects salary insofar as most institutions operate with a system of salary grades defined by rank, thus effectively rewarding differential performance primarily *within* ranks (Astin and Bayer, 1973; Koch and Chizmer, 1973; Cohn, 1973; Lewis, 1979).

The findings of Astin and Bayer (1973), Katz (1973), Hargens and Farr (1973), Siegfried and White (1973), Tuckman (1976), and Lewis (1979) collectively suggest, however, that longevity of service, both at the employing institution and in the professoriate generally, whatever its quality, may be nearly as important a determinant of advancement as performance. Institutions of higher education are apparently similar to other types of bureaucratic organizations in not being impervious to the claims of *seniority*. The longer a professor remains on the scene, the more likely he or she is to attain higher rank and salary (although this may be less true for those who have remained at the institution from which they received their terminal degree). However productive a faculty member may be, he or she must generally wait a minimum time before being eligible for promotion to a higher rank (in the case of assistant to associate professor, typically a six or seven year probationary period), and during this waiting period must remain subject to the limitations of salary grades. Faculty members who have "put in their time" in rank, on the other hand, irrespective of productivity, are "eligible" for promotion to a higher rank and salary grade. In the past, such eligibility has apparently been met, more often than not, with promotion (although, of course, this has varied considerably across institutional types and disciplines). In the absence of actual current data, it is impossible to determine the effect of the recent tenure and promotion squeeze on the relative strength of the claims of seniority. It would seem likely, however, that as tenure and promotion rates decrease (El-Khawas and Furniss, 1974), the claims of seniority alone will lose much of their past power.

Quite beyond performance or seniority, advancing in the organization is subject to ascriptive influences—most notably those of gender. Both Stewart (1972) and Astin and Bayer (1973) found that gender affected salary and promotion prospects for the most part indirectly via its association with research productivity, institutional location, disciplinary affiliation, and seniority; both Katz (1973) and Tuckman (1976), on the other hand, reported a strong, independent gender effect on salary level, which later studies appear to confirm (see chap. 7).[7] It would appear, then, that sex may operate both directly and indirectly—via its association with the major determinants of organizational status—to bias the allocation of organizational rewards.

Career Advancement: Some Concluding Remarks

On the basis of our discussion of disciplinary and organizational recognition, it seems useful to conceptualize the academic reward system as two interacting subsystems: the somewhat mysterious, loosely organized stratification system of the academic professions, that allocates peer recognition, professional honors, and appointments to prestigious positions; and the more rationalized, predictable stratification system of institutions of higher education that differentially allocates salary and promotion through the ranks to more or less "deserving" faculty. Both subsystems operate on the basis of meritocratic and particularistic criteria. They both attribute importance to academic accomplishment as a criterion of advancement—although, ironically, the evidence suggests that institutions of higher education may adhere more conscientiously to the criterion of scholarly merit than the academic professions. The major difference between the two subsystems hinges on the nature of the particularistic criteria applied. For the academic professions, prestige, as reflected in one's academic ancestry, current institutional affiliation, and formal receipt of awards, rivals scholarly merit as a prime determinant of recognition; for institutions of higher education, seniority proves second in importance only to scholarly merit and administrative work as a determinant of promotion and salary. Neither of these particularistic criteria has much exchange value in the other subsystem. Mere longevity in the absence of continued productivity and visibility does not bring with it disciplinary recognition (Cole and Cole, 1973), nor do disciplinary prestige and visibility unaccompanied by research production, institutional service, and waiting translate into institutional status.

In a very real sense, the individual faculty member's disciplinary and institutional affiliation serve as the points of intersection between the two subsystems. The disciplinary market situation (supply relative to demand and opportunities for meaningful and profitable extra-academic work) shapes the promotion opportunities and salary scale at an institution; the status of the institution shapes the opportunities for visibility and recognition within the discipline. The two subsystems, nonetheless, remain distinct in their contradictory pulls and pushes on the individual faculty member. Managing an appointment at a prestigious institution promises the increased probability of visibility within one's discipline at the same time it promises lower probabilities of promotion or higher probabilities of slow promotion and no real salary advantage until one reaches the senior ranks. Conversely, moving to a less prestigious institution decreases the likelihood of disciplinary visibility while raising the probability of promotion and ultimate salary disadvantage.

JOB CHANGING

Opportunities for changing jobs (moving to a faculty position at another institution) or for changing careers (moving outside academe to a position in industry or government) have both declined precipitously in the last decade. In the mid 1960s, 8 percent of doctorate-holding faculty changed their institutional affiliation annually; by 1972, this percentage had decreased to 1.4 percent (Cartter, 1976). And the latest National Science Foundation Survey of Scientists at Doctoral Universities (*Chronicle of Higher Education,* 1981), traditionally among the most mobile segments of the academic profession, shows that only 1.7 percent of doctorate-granting university scientists changed jobs in the 1978–79 academic year (suggesting a considerably lower overall rate for academic humanists and nonuniversity faculty).[8] In the mid-1960s, nearly 3.5 percent of the professoriate left academic employment annually. The latest National Science Foundation survey shows that that out-migration has dropped to about 1 percent annually; and even among engineering faculty, the highest outflow group, the proportion leaving academe in 1978–79 was only 1.7 percent—half of the aggregate figure fifteen years earlier. While the proportion leaving academe approximately equaled the proportion moving to other academic positions among engineers and physical scientists, among other natural scientists, institution changes outnumbered career changes by a ratio of 2 to 1; and among social scientists, by a ratio of 3 to 1. Moreover, this decreasing rate of career change has occurred despite evidence that the currently dismal prospects for an academic career have led substantial proportions of faculty to think about career change. Palmer and Patton (1981), in their secondary analysis of the 1977 Ladd and Lipset faculty survey, reported that nearly one-third of responding faculty "felt that they would be equally or more satisfied outside academe"; and over one-quarter "had seriously considered leaving academe during the past two years." While fully 17 percent had both considered leaving and believed they would be equally happy or happier outside academe, only about 1 percent, even among the traditionally most mobile segments of the profession, are leaving annually. And this has occurred despite the growing number of academic career transition programs at the national level (for example, Scholars in Transition, the careers in business programs at Harvard, U.C.L.A., the Universities of Pennsylvania, Virginia, and Texas) as well as the nascent career transition programs developed at more than a dozen individual institutions and multicampus systems (Baldwin et al., 1981).

Beyond job and career change are the more limited opportunities offered faculty for changing their job responsibilities while remaining at the same institution or state system. Several institutions and university systems have developed faculty respecialization or retraining programs, aimed primarily at moving underutilized faculty into areas of greater institutional need as well as broadening individual faculty skills and competencies (Neff and Nyquist, 1979). At this point, however, programs are confined to a very small number of institutions and state systems, and their outreach is limited to a very small number of faculty (Baldwin et al., 1981). Finally, there is always the possibility of moving into institutional administration; but this option is limited by the "pyramid" nature of college and university administration, with only a limited number of top jobs to go around. The option is for only a few (Kanter, 1979).

While these options for changing jobs responsibilities, institutions, and career are limited in their availability, research suggests that there is considerable variation in their use. While the lion's share of studies of job changing were the product of concern during the late 1950s and early 1960s with ensuring an adequate supply of qualified faculty and focused principally on interinstitutional mobility within faculty ranks, the results of these studies together with the few more broadly conceived recent studies of job changing suggest some basic common denominators that underlie faculty choice patterns. For faculty, changing jobs or careers appears to be a function primarily of (1) the structure of the academic career, that is, rank structure and tenure system, especially as they operate in a declining job market, and (2) of faculty interests and values, especially as they change over the course of an academic career.

Career Structure Determinants of Job Changing

Baldwin (1979a, 1979b) and Baldwin and Blackburn (1981) in a study of faculty at twelve liberal arts colleges identified three career stages at which faculty were most likely to consider job changes.

1. *Just before coming up for tenure.* The assistant professor with more than three years of experience, while seeking the recognition and security symbolized by tenure, may be dissatisfied with his or her career insofar as it does not measure up to original expectations or insofar as he or she fears a negative tenure decision. This leaves such faculty, quite naturally, to question their future in higher education and to seek out alternative career options should their bid for tenure fail.

2. *Just after promotion to a full professorship.* Having secured the top promotion, the new full professor has reached a career plateau from which there is nowhere else to go professionally. Full professors can look forward to more than two decades with no change in responsibilities.

3. *Just before coming up for promotion to full professor.* Experienced associate professors find themselves in much the same position as the experienced assistant professors. They are com-

ing up for promotion to the final career plateau, which they may or may not reach. Should they fail to be promoted at the expected time, they may feel that they have reached a dead end to which they are locked in by age and economic security needs.[9]

These structural choice points in the academic career reappear again and again. Neff (1978) and Neff and Nyquist (1979) found that among faculty seeking opportunities for respecialization or retraining at the State University of New York, the largest proportion were in the advanced associate professor and continuing full professor categories. Lovett (1980) found that among forty-three senior faculty (advanced associate and continuing full professors with a median age of forty-two) leaving academic employment, the major motivators were a sense that they had "reached the top of the heap and had nowhere else to go professionally in terms of advancement." Palmer and Patton (1981) found that younger faculty who were not yet granted tenure were most likely to report having considered leaving academe. Caplow and McGee (1958) found experienced assistant professors to be the most mobile subgroup among faculty, followed by recently promoted full professors; and indeed virtually all available evidence confirms that the tendency to change academic positions is highest among experienced assistant professors (Marshall, 1964; Brown, 1967; Fincher, 1969; Aurand and Blackburn, 1973; Clark and Larson, 1972). Although these studies also suggest that interinstitutional mobility within the professoriate decreases with age and higher rank or the attainment of tenure, the hypothesis of structurally related career choice points still seems sound. Indeed, McGee (1971) found that the attainment of higher rank and tenure affected the tendency to move but did not affect the involvement of faculty in job market activity. That more senior faculty are actively involved in the job market but are less likely to move reflects less the nonoperation of career reassessment than the operation of other structural constraints at the more senior levels. One is institutional promotion practices (for example, the preference for hiring at lower ranks and promoting from within) such that all but the most exceptional older faculty effectively price themselves out of the market (Caplow and McGee, 1958), and another is the phenomenon of being locked into one's position by virtue of age and economic security needs.

The Normative Determinants of Job Changing

If the structure of the academic career determines the timing of job changes, then ingrained faculty values and interests determine the nature of those job changes. Blackburn and Havighurst (1979), in a study of career patterns of distinguished male social scientists, found that the most active researchers tended to find a suitably stimulating and autonomous institutional environment and stay, and those who least valued scholarly activity tended to be the ones who moved into administration and engaged in more frequent job changes. Similarly, Snyder et al. (1978), in a study of midcareer university faculty, found that basic values distinguished between those who moved or intended to move into administration and those who chose to remain in their faculty roles. Those who had moved into administration, or were about to, placed a significantly higher value on power and authority; those who chose to remain in the faculty role placed significantly higher value on *autonomy* and saw the administrative role as leading to decreased autonomy, achievement, social support, and security. Studies of faculty attrition, retention, and job choice further attest to the formative role of work related values. Stecklein and Lathrop (1960), Brown (1967), Fincher (1969), Nicholson and Miljus (1972), Aurand and Blackburn (1973), McGee (1971), and Ladd and Lipset (1976) all reported that the nature of prospective job duties, the competency and congeniality of colleagues, and the opportunity for research and professional development emerged as the most important factors in job changing decisions—and this held most true for those faculty at the highest levels of professional achievement and at the most prestigious institutions (Ladd and Lipset, 1976).

The studies noted above report only on those faculty who actually changed jobs—a very small group indeed compared with those who were active in the job market (McGee, 1971). When this select group is compared with those who are active in the market, receive offers, but do not move, the critical role of values in job changing is placed in even sharper relief. McGee (1971) examined the sources of dissatisfaction of those faculty who changed jobs and those who stayed despite attractive outside offers. His findings are displayed in Table 4.2 below. What appeared to separate movers from those who decided to stay despite attractive offers were considerations related to institutional philosophy and educational policy and mundane factors such as geography, location, and climate. Oddly enough, faculty-administration relations and working conditions were considerably less important, and ironically, among those dissatisfied with salary, rank, and promotion prospects, no one moved. These findings led McGee to conclude that a faculty member will leave his or her current institution only for a much, much better opportunity to realize his or her professional aspirations.

TABLE 4.2

Sources of Faculty Dissatisfaction in Relation to
the Outcomes of Job Market Activity

Complaint or Problem	Outcome of Market Activity (Percent)				
	Undeveloped	Mobility	Fixed	In Process	Total Sample
Salary, rank, prospects of promotion	11	0	26	27	14
Conditions of personal work	25	20	13	7	20
Institutional philosophy or educational policy	7	40	13	13	13
Administrators or administrative relations or methods	6	20	13	7	9
Geography, climate, location	8	20	4	7	9
Quality of students	3	0	4	0	2
Personal and idiosyncratic matters	6	0	9	20	7
No complaints	33	0	17	20	25
Uncodable	1	0	0	0	1
Total	100	100	100	100	100
	(72)	(15)	(23)	(15)	(125)

Source: McGee (1971), p. 185.

And when interests and values change, faculty tend to seek out changes in their responsibilities. Baldwin (1979a, 1979b) found that over the course of the academic career, faculty experienced decreasing interest in research and decreasing enthusiasm for teaching. This led many faculty to "branch out" within the academic role by, for example, taking on administrative assignments, developing new areas of expertise, taking a more active role in professional organizations and consulting. And indeed Lovett (1980) found that progressive disenchantment with teaching—resulting from neither load nor student quality but from the repetitive nature of offering relatively general and popular courses in preference to courses closer to their research and intellectual interests—was a major reason for leaving academe among nearly one-half of her small faculty sample.

Beyond general academic values and interests, two value factors that affect job changing merit special treatment: salary and prestige.

The Salary Factor. We have no data available on the extent to which higher salaries function as a lure into academic administration independent of normative factors such as the desire for greater power and status. And Lovett's (1980) small scale study of senior faculty leaving academic employment found "the financial squeeze/ income erosion" to be one, although not the most important, motivating factor for just over half of her forty-three faculty respondents. Thus, most of what we know about salary as a motive for job changing among academics comes from studies of interinstitutional mobility within the professoriate. And among these studies, the findings are nearly evenly split between those studies that report salary as a relatively major or relatively minor factor.

The major difficulty here may well be the failure to examine the rated importance of salary in relation to a faculty member's current salary level as well as the net difference between the current and proffered salary. Brown (1967) alone examined the relationship between the rated importance of salary and current salary level and found them to be inversely related, that is, the salience of the salary factor decreased as respondents' current salary level increased. Thus, beyond a certain "critical" level, the promise of a higher salary ceased to function as a real inducement to move. Similarly, McGee (1971) reported that those liberal arts college faculty who commanded the highest salaries showed the lowest level of market activity and further tended to reject outside offers twice as often as the sample as a whole; the lowest salaried faculty together with higher (but not the highest) salaried faculty tended to be most mobile. It would seem reasonable to conclude, then, that for the highest salaried faculty, salary level may be either important or unimportant in retention: important in a negative fashion insofar as the level of their salaries may "price them out of the market", unimportant insofar as the performance which presumably led to a high salary level would enable these faculty members to command high salaries anywhere (so that factors other than salary become more important). As one descends the salary scale, however, salary level would appear to function as a "pushing" force. In their study of faculty at the University of Minnesota, Stecklein and Lathrop (1960) qualify their findings of the relative insignificance of the salary factor with the proviso that "their University of Minnesota salary was comparable to salaries offered for other positions." In this case, then, the relative import of the salary factor was low because of the net difference between current and prospective salaries. In sum, the salary factor would not appear to operate uniformlly; rather its importance would appear to vary by the current salary level of an individual as well as the net difference between the individual's current salary and that of other prospective positions.

There is some evidence, however, that as the relative economic position of the professoriate deteriorates vis-à-vis other intellectual professions, salary is becoming a more important factor. In their 1975 survey of the American professoriate, Ladd and Lipset (1976) reported that "higher salary" would be the single most important factor to faculty if they "were to seek another position elsewhere," for all age cohorts and at all levels of professional achievement—in effect, irrespective of current salary level. To what extent this finding may represent real change, the resurrection of "economic man" among the professoriate, or to what extent it may be an artifact of the hypothetical nature of the question is not, however, clear.

The Prestige Factor. Prestige (at least in the sense of perceived power and status) appears to be a significant motive force behind the decision to move into administration (Snyder et al., 1978); the significance of prestige as a motivator for job changing has been most thoroughly tested, however, in the realm of interinstitutional mobility. These inquiries suggest two broad generalizations: (1) the quest for prestige is clearly secondary to the quest for satisfying work and stimulating colleagues (Stecklein and Lathrop, 1960; Brown, 1967; Nicholson, and Miljus, 1972; Ladd and Lipset, 1976) and (2) much like the salary factor, prestige operates as a "non-uniform" motivator. Its salience appears to vary, in the first place, by career stage. Thus, for example, Caplow and McGee (1958) found younger faculty to be significantly more prestige conscious, while older faculty were more likely to trade off prestige for autonomy or security.[10] In the second place, the nature of the motivating power of prestige appears to be contingent on the relationship between the professional prestige of the individual faculty member and the prestige of his or her employing institution. McGee (1971) found that prestige proved a powerful stimulus to faculty as both a retention factor and an attrition factor. If the level of institutional prestige was on a par with, or higher than, the level of the individual professor's professional prestige, it tended to function retentively; however, if the individual faculty member's professional prestige was higher than the level of institutional prestige, then it appeared to function in quite the opposite fashion.

Insofar as faculty do pursue prestige to varying degrees, to what extent is their quest successfully consummated in moving to another faculty position? The evidence presented in Table 4.3 suggests considerable movement among institutional prestige strata— though primarily downward—whatever the measure employed for assessing institutional prestige. In all studies, except Caplow and

TABLE 4.3

DIRECTION OF INTERINSTITUTIONAL MOBILITY

Case	Total Sample Size	Sample Group(s)	Number of Prestige Strata/ Categories	Findings (Percent)		
				Changing Prestige Strata	Moving Downward	Staying within Same Prestige Strata
Caplow and McGee (1958)	?	Faculty at major universities	?	"Overwhelming majority"[a]	?	Small[a]
		Faculty at major vs. minor vs. "bush league" universities	3	Small[a]	Small[a]	Large[a]
Goldblatt (1967)	438	Social scientists with high-prestige Ph.D.s	3	53.0	53.0	47.0
		Social scientists with low-prestige Ph.D.s	3	50.0	0	50.0
D.G. Brown (1967)	7630	New Ph.D.s	6	74.0	64.0	26.0
		Faculty moving from a previous position	6	72.0	40.0	28.0
Hargens (1969)	682	New Ph.D.s accepting a position at a university	6	50.0[b]		50.0[c]
		New Ph.D.s in natural sciences	6	44.0[b]		56.0[c]
		New Ph.D.s in humanities and social sciences	6	56.0[b]		44.0[c]
		New Ph.D.s from "most" prestigious universities	6	72.0[b]		28.0[c]
		New Ph.D.s from "least" prestigious universities	6	25.0[b]		75.0[c]

(*continued*)

TABLE 4.3 (*Continued*)

Case	Total Sample Size	Sample Group(s)	Number of Prestige Strata/ Categories	Findings (Percent) Changing Prestige Strata	Findings (Percent) Moving Downward	Findings (Percent) Staying within Same Prestige Strata
Cartter (1976)	17,413	New Ph.D.s, 1968[d]	7	78.3	73.2	21.7
		New Ph.D.s, 1973[d]	7	83.3	78.7	16.7

[a]No actual data reported.
[b]Moving up or down at least 2 quality levels.
[c]Staying within one quality level above or below that of doctoral institution.
[d]Based on National Research Council data on new Ph.D. recipients.

McGee (1958), at least one-half of all job changes resulted in concomitant changes in location on the institutional prestige ladder. The direction of one's movement on that ladder appeared to depend, in the first place, on where one started. A faculty member who left a position at a highly prestigious institution was more likely to move downward, if he or she changed prestige strata at all—there is nowhere else to go.[11] In the case of new doctorates, descent was especially likely since the plurality of doctorates are produced by a relatively small group of research universities that cannot absorb all of their own graduates. Conversely, it would appear that the lower the point in the prestige hierarchy at which one began, the greater the likelihood of moving upward—once again, to the extent one moves at all.

In addition to the absolute and relative prestige of the institution from which one moves, determinants of the prestige level of the new institution include variable conditions of the academic labor market, generally, and of the disciplinary labor market, in particular. Cartter (1976) compared the hiring pattern of new doctorate-holding faculty in 1968 and 1973, two years distinguished by relative looseness and tightness, respectively, in the academic labor market. Although Cartter found no significant differences in institutional hiring patterns—departments continued to tap much the same sources for their new faculty—he did find significant differences in institutional hiring rates: in the "bad" year of 1973, lower-prestige departments tended to do a disproportionately high share of the hiring. In that year, then, there tended to be a general downward movement in prestige for newly hired faculty. Similarly, Brown

(1967) reported that idiosyncratic conditions in disciplinary labor markets can influence the direction of migration. The higher the rate of a discipline's expansion, that is, the greater the demand for its practitioners, the higher the probability of an individual's moving up the ladder; the lower the demand, the higher the probability of moving downward.

Finally, there is some evidence that scholarly achievement may have a role to play in ascent or descent. Brown (1967) found that the higher the scholarly credentials of his movers, the greater their probability of moving upward, and vice versa. The findings emerging from studies of disciplinary advancement and recognition, however, suggest that the productivity effect may indeed be both quite small and indirect, mediated primarily by the effect of previous institutional location on productivity.

The Job Search Process

In searching out another position, faculty employ two broad types of approaches. "Informal" methods involve the use of contacts not specifically developed for the job search effort, such as graduate professors and colleagues. "Formal" methods involve the use of agencies and procedures specifically geared to job seeking (institutional and professional association placement offices, blind letters, and so forth). Informal methods are far and away the norm; indeed, formal methods are usually resorted to when informal means do not get results or when the individual has no contacts on which to capitalize. There does appear to be systematic, and not altogether unexpected, variation in the use of informal versus formal methods of job search. (1) Faculty at the higher ranks tend to use informal methods most frequently, although as career age increases, reliance shifts from former teachers to professional colleagues. (2) New doctoral degree holders, non-doctorates, and aspirants to lower-rank appointments, generally, tend to use formal methods (particularly blind letters) more frequently. (3) The more "desirable" the position, the more likely that it will be obtained by informal contacts (Brown, 1967). In sum, the findings may be encapsulated by the observation that the higher the individual's qualifications, the greater the likelihood that he or she will resort to informal measures, and these are more likely than formal measures to prove effective in securing the best positions.

It seems reasonable to assume that faculty pursuing initial positions in academic administration, particularly at the department chairperson and deanship levels, or faculty seeking to change their department affiliation may capitalize on informal contacts in their search.[12] This appears not to be the case for those faculty initially pursuing nonacademic employment. Some faculty may be able to employ informal contacts in moving into research or administrative positions in their field of specialization in government, industry, or foundations; however, Lovett's (1980) modest study of senior faculty making the transition to nonacademic employment suggests a rather "trying" journey, marked by a tendency to resort to formal methods, such as career counseling services and blind contacts with individual employers, a progressive need for reorientation to the peculiar demands of the nonacademic world (such as for a competency-oriented résumé instead of the typical curriculum vitae), and the virtual absence of collegial socioemotional or substantive support. The variety of formal career planning and placement services springing up both nationally and at individual institutions (Baldwin et al., 1981) appears to underscore the need for faculty orientation to a distinctively different job search process in the nonacademic world.

Brown (1967), alone, has sought to go beyond an examination of the methods used for securing academic employment to a more generalizable theory of job search. According to Brown, an individual will continue a job search and use those search methods for which "expected gain" is largest as long as the expected benefits (in terms of the value of the job that might be landed) exceeds the expected costs of the search. Thus, the less desirable one's current position, the longer one is likely to search. A recent doctoral graduate with no job is likely to search long and hard and to use as many methods, both formal and informal, as possible. On the other hand, the individual with high visibility is likely to have a considerably shorter search although the person may spend more time "looking at" than "looking for" a job. Brown's theory appears to explain variation in the academic job search pattern reported by his sample of "movers," but the theory remains untested with that larger group of faculty who, though active in the job market, never move and with that group of faculty in search of nonacademic employment.

Summary

The first general proposition about job changing to which the data point is that faculty are subject to the laws of inertia and do not change their jobs impulsively. Even in the seller's market of the early and mid-1960s, only a minuscule proportion of faculty who received outside job offers actually moved to another position. In the late 1970s, when just over one-sixth of doctorate-granting university scientists were seriously considering leaving academe (Palmer and Patton, 1981) and the vast majority of college and university faculty were expressing alarm at the economic decline of the profession (Ladd and Lipset, 1976), only about 1 percent were actually leaving—even in those fields such as engineering where non-academic opportunities were readily available. While this decreased job changing is no doubt a function of the limited opportunities within the academy as well as the uncertain state of the economy, it is also a function of faculty's historic inertia (McGee, 1971).

When faculty do change jobs, they do not conform to the rational economic labor market model; that is, they do not seek to optimize prestige and income. Indeed, more often than not, faculty reject academic job offers that promise more money, prestige, and advancement opportunities (McGee, 1971; Snyder et al., 1978). Rather, their job changing decisions seem to be determined by the principle of optimizing interests and values, that is, seeking opportunities for professional growth through compatible work activities and colleagues. This is not to suggest that prestige and remuneration are not important motivators—and indeed for some groups of faculty, especially non-tenured faculty at the lower end of the salary scale, they may be of primary importance at a given career stage; but overall their import is secondary to intrinsic motives. Faculty, in their essential work life are normative creatures—a theme we shall be returning to again and again.

One final point. To the extent that the nature of job and career change decisions are predicated on matters of value, their timing is shaped by the structure of the academic career. Thus, interests and values appear to vary predictably over the course of that career. Moreover, that structure appears to give rise to predictable periods of career reassessment when consideration of job changes, if not actual moves, are most likely to occur. In working with college and university faculty on career planning, both the structural and normative bases of career decisions will need to be taken into account.

THE NORMATIVE CONTEXT OF THE ACADEMIC CAREER

There are at least three particular values that have historically shaped the definition of an academic and set the parameters within which an academic career is pursued.

1. *Professional autonomy:* The belief that individual faculty, and by extension, academic departments, are by virtue of their expertise in the best position to determine and organize their own

work, accountable only to their professional peers (Berdahl, 1971; Baldridge et al., 1978; Scott, 1970).

2. *Academic freedom:* Adopted from the German concept of *Lehrfreiheit* (Metzger, 1955), the belief that faculty should have the freedom to pursue issues and problems *in their field of specialization* and communicate their findings in their teaching, research, and extramural utterances (Berdahl, 1971; Metzger, 1955).

3. *Universalism* or *the merit principle:* The belief that faculty should be evaluated and subsequently rewarded solely on the basis of their merits as scholars/teachers and without reference to irrelevant social characteristics (sex, political ideology, religion, race). This belief is based on the premise that the advancement of the scientific enterprise as a whole depends on a social system that promotes the free competition of ideas and promises recognition based on achievement (Merton, 1968; Parsons and Platt, 1973).

To what extent, and in what ways, are professional autonomy, academic freedom, and universalism the mark of contemporary academic man?

Professional Autonomy

Despite its centrality to the very concept of academic man, and despite evidence that faculty's sense of control over their external work environment is an important source of career satisfaction (Cares and Blackburn, 1978), there has been precious little attention to the importance that faculty attach to professional autonomy and the extent to which the norm actually operates within the academic system.

Baldridge et al. (1978) examined six dimensions of faculty professional autonomy: (1) the extent to which faculty employment contracts explicitly specify work to be performed or are relatively open ended, (2) the extent to which professional travel is tightly regulated, (3) locus of control over faculty teaching assignments, (4) the extent to which faculty are evaluated by their professional colleagues rather than by administrators, (5) locus of control over faculty hiring—departmental versus administrative, (6) locus of control over tenure decisions—departmental versus administrative. They found, in the first place, that the extent of professional autonomy varied considerably across the six dimensions. The majority of faculty experienced considerable individual freedom in their teaching assignments and their contractual obligations, and considerable departmental autonomy in hiring colleagues. However, a majority also reported a lack of individual autonomy in professional travel and of departmental autonomy in faculty evaluation and promotion. Moreover, faculty at different types of institutions showed very different levels of professional autonomy. Autonomy tended to be highest at research universities, followed in descending order by private liberal arts colleges[13] and public comprehensive colleges and universities. In a subsequent analysis, institutional size and complexity, defined in terms of the highest degree offered, together with level of faculty expertise, defined by the proportion of faculty with the doctorate, emerged as the most decisive determinants of level of professional autonomy. Those larger, more differentiated institutions boasting a higher percentage of doctorally trained faculty in a large number and variety of departments tended to most fully recognize faculty prerogatives for independence.

If the ideals of professional autonomy, at least in the areas of teaching assignment, faculty hiring, and peer evaluation, are most fully realized at the research university, there is some evidence that faculty themselves do not wholeheartedly cherish these ideals. Lewis (1966), in a study of faculty at a public research university, found that while nearly three-quarters asserted the primary responsibility of faculty for setting academic standards, less than half (46.6 percent) did so for establishing criteria for promotion. Moreover, there was wide variation in attitudinal support of professional autonomy across disciplinary areas. Over 60 percent of the faculty in the social sciences and humanities endorsed faculty prerogatives in promotion but only about 40 percent in the natural sciences and only about one-third in the professional schools did. This suggests that although professional autonomy may be most fully operationalized at the research-oriented university, it may not be the cherished professional norm of all but the traditional arts and sciences faculty.[14]

Academic Freedom

In recent national surveys, the vast majority of college and university faculty lent at least qualified support to the principle of academic freedom in the conduct of research and in classroom teaching. Over four-fifths of respondents to the 1969 American Council on Education Faculty Survey agreed strongly or with reservation that "faculty members should be free to present in class any idea that they consider relevant." And nearly three-quarters of respondents to the 1975 Ladd and Lipset Survey of the American Professoriate agreed strongly (45 percent) or with reservations (29 percent) that research on controversial issues, in this case the "inheritability of intelligence," should have no restrictions (Ladd and Lipset, 1976).

Beyond these general expressions of support, however, faculty views about academic freedom show considerable complexity. Lewis's (1966) study of faculty at a northeastern public university found that faculty support for academic freedom varied across different areas of faculty activity. It was highest for freedom in the conduct and communication of research (fully two-thirds strongly endorsing such freedom) and lowest for freedom to take controversial positions in the classroom (between one-third and two-fifths felt that faculty should use the classroom to take controversial economic and political positions). It suggests as well that faculty are nearly twice as likely to lend support to general statements of the principle of academic freedom than they are to believe in, or defend, its practice. Moreover, even within a single area of faculty activity, such as research, faculty vary in their support for academic freedom. In their 1975 faculty survey, Ladd and Lipset found that while the vast majority of faculty supported no limitations on research on the heritability of intelligence, the majority did support restrictions on classified weapons research.

How can this variation in support across activity areas and specific issues be explained? Ladd and Lipset (1976) suggest that at least issue-specific variation may be attributable to faculty members' differing conceptions of academic freedom—their relative latitude/restrictiveness in defining its proper boundaries. In support of that explanation, they point to the contrasting influences on attitudinal support for classified weapons research and research on the heritability of intelligence. Support for the former breaks down largely along the lines of political ideology (conservatives, for; liberals, against), but support for the latter is virtually immune from ideological influences. Indeed, sociologists, who as a group tend to be most liberal and most likely to find universities guilty of racism, tend to support most highly unrestricted research on the heritability of intelligence. It appears, then, that weapons research is not perceived as posing an academic freedom issue and faculty responses to it are largely shaped by political inclinations. But insofar as an issue is viewed as falling within the boundaries of the guarantee of academic freedom, professional norms appear to override other factors, including political ideology.

Beyond these differing conceptions of the proper boundaries of academic freedom, there appear nonetheless to be systematic differences within academe in support of the basic principles of academic freedom itself. Two principal axes of attitudinal differentiation emerge: level of research involvement and productivity, and disciplinary affiliation. Those faculty who are more involved in research and writing tend to be more supportive of intellectual permissiveness in research and teaching (Lazarfeld and Thielens, 1958; Wences and Abramson, 1971; Ladd and Lipset, 1976); and those faculty members working in academic fields that treat a variety of sensitive public policy issues (social scientists, followed by life scientists and humanists) tend as a group to be more supportive of academic freedom principles than faculty in the natural and applied sciences and the professions (Lewis, 1966; Wences and Abramson, 1971; Ladd and Lipset, 1976).

Even among social scientists, however, support for academic freedom is subject to situational contingencies. Just as colleague attitudes and values can uphold academic freedom as a professional norm, they can undermine it. Goldblatt (1967), in a continuation of Lazarsfeld and Thielens' (1958) study of academic social scientists' responses to McCarthyism, examined the relationship of postdoctoral patterns of interinstitutional mobility to intellectual permissiveness (tolerance of deviance and controversy). He found that levels of intellectual permissiveness were likely to change with concomitant changes in colleague climates as faculty moved among institutional prestige strata. Faculty who moved down the prestige hierarchy from graduate school to their current position were less likely to favor academic freedom than their colleagues whose movement had been horizontal; those faculty who had moved up the prestige hierarchy since leaving graduate school were more likely to favor academic freedom than their colleagues who had remained in the nether strata. Moreover, colleague climate appeared to mediate the effect of other variables on academic freedom attitudes. Lazarsfeld and Thielens (1958) reported that while intellectual permissiveness tended to decline with age (a trend corroborated by Wences and Abramson, 1971), that trend was lowest in institutions characterized by highly "permissive" faculty (based on the aggregation of individual data for each institution in the sample) and highest in institutions with relatively nonpermissive faculties. Thus, like any social norm, academic freedom depends for its support on the character and values of colleagues.

The Merit Principle

American academics come down decisively in support of the merit principle and intellectual competition. In their 1975 survey, Ladd and Lipset (1976) reported that fully seven in ten faculty respondents argued that "before awarding tenure, members of a department should satisfy themselves that the candidate is the most deserving by the most demanding national standards which can be applied"; and about half take the position that salary increases should be determined strictly by merit, even though in a time of scarce resources this requires "denying increases to many faculty of lower scholarly attainment." Fully three-fifths express strong support for scholarly competition as an appropriate part of academic life. This ringing endorsement is, however, tempered by a clear recognition of the imperfect application of the merit principle in academic life. Thus, only 49 percent believe that the merit principle is actually practiced in the academic social system; and nearly two of five faculty who normatively support the principle believe that it has not prevailed in practice (Ladd and Lipset, 1976).[15]

What is perhaps most striking about this considerable overall level of support is that it tends to hold across the board. While faculty at research universities and those who boast the highest professional achievements in research are slightly more likely to be counted among the adherents of merit, the majority of faculty at all types of institutions, at all levels of professional achievement, across all racial and gender subgroups, come down on the side of merit (Ladd and Lipset, 1976). All this would appear to suggest that while the merit principle may be most fully ensconced in the culture of the ideal typical academic (the prolific publisher at the research university), it has a strong ideological foothold in the minds of all college and university faculty—even those who may have historically been the victims of discrimination.

Summary

The above analyses suggest three broad generalizations on the normative aspects of the academic career. In the first place, the norms of professional autonomy and academic freedom and to a lesser extent, the merit principle, are most fully institutionalized at the top of the academic stratification system, among research oriented faculty at research universities. Therefore, they may be most appropriately viewed as "ideal typical" rather than purely "descriptive" of the academic professions. Second, faculty vary in their conceptions and definitions of these norms;[16] academic freedom for one is academic license for another. Finally, there is the obvious, but no less important, conclusion that academics though normative, principled creatures, are nonetheless human—and therefore imperfect. Like anyone else, they are subject to the social pressure of colleagues in changing their attitudes (especially concerning academic freedom) and in translating those attitudes into behavior (for example, the discrepancy between normative support of the theory and practice of academic freedom and the merit principle).

CAREER SATISFACTION—APPRAISALS OF THE ACADEMIC CAREER

Faculty appraisals of their careers present an intriguing paradox. On the one hand, recent survey results document a prevailing pessimism in the faculty mood (Ladd and Lipset, 1977): nearly two-thirds say that the status of the academic profession has declined over the past decade; an overwhelming majority say that their economic status is eroding in comparison with that of practitioners in the nonacademic professions (a marked turnaround from a clear majority perception of relative improvement evidenced in the 1975 Ladd and Lipset survey); seven out of ten would now vote for a collective bargaining agent at their own institution; and about four out of five are seriously concerned about the erosion of standards and of the integrity of the higher education enterprise as a whole. At the same time, faculty report demonstrable satisfaction with their personal lot: between 83 and 88 percent report overall satisfaction with college teaching as a career (Willie and Stecklein, 1982; Ladd and Lipset, 1976), a figure representing only a 7 percent decline from overall levels of career satisfaction in the late 1950s (Eckert and Williams, 1972), and corresponding almost precisely to proportions reporting overall career satisfaction in the mid-1960s (Parsons and Platt, 1968; Eckert and Williams, 1972), and the early 1970s (Bayer, 1973); nine out of ten say that their employing institution is a "fairly" or "very good" place for them; and feel they have been "fairly" or "very" successful in their careers (Ladd and Lipset, 1976).

How are we to reconcile this apparent pessimism concerning the profession and this relative optimism with their personal lot (optimism except in regard to economic status)? It may be that this reflects the by now familiar phenomenon of "Pessimism re: The national situation" and "Optimism re: The personal situation" reported in national surveys of the American mood in the late 1970s (for example, Yankelovich, 1981; Watts, 1981). That faculty are, however, pessimistic about their own personal economic circumstances suggests that something more than a perceptual separation of national and individual circumstance may be operating. A more likely explanation would view this paradox as expressive of the clash between personal needs and expectations, on the one hand, and the actualities of decline in American higher education in the late 1970s, on the other. In the context of our earlier discussion of faculty career choice, the academic career may be viewed as a choice responsive to the innermost needs and personal histories of individuals entering the profession—the need for autonomy and the use of intellect as a mode of mastering experience (Freedman et al., 1979). To the extent that an academic career relative to other pursuits provides a vehicle for the satisfaction of fundamental needs,[17] it is not surprising that faculty should stand by their choice and feel that they have done relatively well for themselves. To the extent that faculty perceive external forces as either undermining their needs satisfaction—by limiting available positions or by detracting from the intellectual character of the enterprise—or adversely affecting the economic viability of its pursuit, it is not surprising that they should be deeply concerned.

This "fundamental satisfaction–situational dissatisfaction" phenomenon appears to intrude on all levels of the professoriate, but there is some indication that it strikes the younger generation most forcefully. In a study of three cohorts of Danforth Fellows, Rice (1980) reported very high levels of satisfaction among the older cohorts with their career choice, a choice marked by close correspondence of preprofessional aspirations with actual career patterns—first teaching appointment in accord with expectations, tenure in due course, and the appropriate promotions. A very different mood, however, prevailed among the youngest cohort, a mood that cannot be attributed merely to the "normally" lower levels of career satisfaction at the earliest stages of the academic career reported by Baldwin (1979a,b). "The immediate overriding concern of the 1964–1967 Danforths and Kents—some not yet tenured—is the impact of institutional retrenchment on their lives." In a summary of one of the workshops, Eldon Jacobson, a 1957 Danforth Fellow, captured the mood of the younger group in an account of their reaction to a comment made by Daniel Levinson in his address to the gathering:

> In his soft, often hesitant, manner, Levinson casually noted in his own autobiographical statement the fact that he had moved, in 1964 or 5, from Harvard to a tenured position at Yale; too, he observed a genuine sense of the human tragedy did not seem really possible to him until one had lived through (and survived) the crisis of mid-life; that is to say, the early 40s. "That is simply absurd," said one young academic who, in his mid 30s, had just been denied tenure at a mediocre state college." Harvard to Yale, for Christ's sake!" decried another. With varying degrees of intensity, younger faculty insisted on describing their situations with

the language of hopelessness . . . about to become unwilling elements in a floating card game where one grabs whatever is dealt.

RETIREMENT

In at least one respect, the exit from full-time professional work resembles entry to it: the role of late decision and drift. While a variety of factors affect the timing of an individual faculty member's decision to retire from academic work—financial situation, relative career success (namely, attainment of a full professorship), attitudes toward retirement—the majority of faculty (about three out of five) retire primarily when, and because, they reach the mandatory age. Less than one in seven retires primarily in order to pursue an interest developed outside the university; and only 7 percent or less decide to retire as a result of poor health, a lack of job satisfaction, or colleague pressure (Patton, 1977).

What do faculty do once they have retired? The available evidence suggests that university faculty typically continue their professional activity well beyond retirement. Dorfman (1978), in a study of emeritus professors at the University of Iowa, found that fully 90 percent had engaged in some form of teaching, research, or service during some period after their retirement. And Roman and Taietz (1967), Atchley (1971), and Rowe (1976) reported between half and three-quarters of their retired faculty samples had been professionally engaged during the year preceding their studies. Although they variously define "continued professional activity,"[18] the studies collectively yield remarkably similar findings. Those faculty who before retirement were most heavily involved in research (Roman and Taietz, 1967; Dorfman, 1978; Blackburn and Havighurst, 1979) and were most active (Dorfman, 1978) and visible (Rowe, 1976) in their professions, tend at all age levels (excluding the chronically ill) to maintain their professional ties, to keep up with their fields (Dorfman, 1978; List, 1956), and to continue their research and writing (Rowe, 1976) after retirement.

This singular perseverance appears attributable to both structural and behavioral sources. Structurally, the research/scholarship role provides a vehicle for continued activity outside any particular institutional context or job and without the need of adopting any new roles (Roman and Taietz, 1967). Behaviorally, research involvement and publication seem to constitute a constellation of behavioral predispositions or habits that once begun tend to persist; once a productive researcher, always a productive researcher (Blackburn, Behymer, and Hall, 1978; Blackburn and Havighurst, 1979). Thus, it is not surprising that retired faculty from those disciplines characterized by relatively high research orientation and productivity, such as those in the natural sciences (Fulton and Trow, 1974), are more likely than those from less research-oriented disciplines, such as the humanities and the newer professions—nursing, education, social work—(Fulton and Trow, 1974) to maintain their professional activities (Fillenbaum and Maddox, 1974), as are those from the more traditional professions, such as medicine and law, that provide an opportunity structure for clinical practice and research outside the academy.

The portrait that emerges here of the professionally engaged retiree is, however, a portrait primarily of the research-oriented university professor. What of the situation of the teaching-oriented, four-year-college professor who has not developed throughout a career the habit of productive research and whose institution does not provide the opportunity for continued engagement in nonteaching roles? The available evidence suggests that while retirement may be a different sort of experience for these faculty, it is no less fundamentally satisfying. Skrabench (1969) found that among a cross-section of college as well as university retirees in thirty-six states, fully 86 percent reported being "happy" or "very happy" in retirement—a figure that corresponds almost precisely to those reported by Patton (1977) and Dorfman (1978) for research-university professors.[19]

Several sources of retirement satisfaction as powerful as continued professional engagement emerged as well. One was the extent to which positive planning preceded retirement. Both Skrabench (1969) and Patton (1977) reported that those faculty who had planned a great deal for retirement tended to be significantly more satisfied than those who had not. Thus mandatory retirees, who tended as a group to do less planning, were half as likely to be very satisfied as discretionary retirees (Patton, 1977). Another was the existence of a social support network independent of professional ties. Acuff and Gorman (1968) and Acuff and Allen (1970) reported that religious and family ties (specifically, a high degree of familial affection and an orientation to an extended rather than nuclear family) contributed as significantly as continued professional engagement to a sense of "anchorage" and a sense of "life purpose."

The interweaving themes of continued professional engagement, orientation to life planning, and the role of social/familial support are drawn together in List's (1956) holistic study of postretirement adjustment. List compared the life histories of a group of professionally active and inactive retirees in an effort to discern those preretirement personality factors and modes of adaptation that would permit the prediction of an individual professor's postretirement adjustment. List reported that professionally active retirees tended to come from families that fostered emotional security and stability, had never abandoned professional practice, tended to have a spouse who continued to collaborate with them, and tended to remain enthusiastic about their work and looked toward the future with confidence. Inactive professors, on the other hand, tended to come from family atmospheres characterized by ambivalence/inconsistency and developed low emotional security; tended to have fewer professional contacts, ongoing professional ventures, and were not collaborating with their spouses; and were resigned to living "one day at a time" with no plans for the future. List concluded that postretirement behavior was an expression of the total personality as fashioned by the individual's life history, and that unsatisfactory adjustment to retirement, therefore, followed from an unsatifactory structure of previous adjustment to important areas of life.

1. Insofar as the origins of several of these investigations can be traced to the nascent Research Program in the Sociology of Science at Columbia in the late 1960s, it is not surprising that they tend to focus on natural and social scientists, and to neglect faculty in the humanities and professional/applied areas. By and large, the findings they generate are based on secondary analyses of survey data or documentary sources such as the Science Citation Index.

2. The beta weights or partial correlations for scholarly productivity range from 0.05 (Reskin, 1979) to 0.18 (Lightfield, 1971), whereas those for doctorate prestige range from 0.31 (Reskin, 1979) to 0.43 (Lightfield, 1971) and those for graduate sponsor prestige from 0.20 (Long, 1978) to 0.25 (Reskin, 1979).

3. As Reskin (1979) rightly points out, however, the absence of data on the extent to which selection processes may match graduate students and faculty on their respective abilities, reputations, or performance precludes elimination of the possibility that any association between sponsorship and subsequent academic appointments could be spurious, with the candidate's caliber the true causal factor.

4. The extent of "trickling down," however, appears to vary substantially among disciplinary markets (Youn, 1981).

5. Only one study (Koch and Chizmar, 1973) reported significant recognition for teaching effectiveness. Since the major extant studies make use of data collected in the early 1970s or earlier, it is not clear to what extent, if any, the increasing rhetorical attention to teaching of the last half decade has actually had an effect on the institutional reward system.

6. These disciplinary markets, it should be noted, operate primarily in research universities. As one moves to four-year and two-year institutions, discipline-related salary differences diminish rapidly and virtually disappear in unionized campuses or in state systems with fixed salary schedules (Blackburn, 1982).

7. Ferber and Loeb (1973) reported that female, but not male, unmarried faculty were more likely to attain high rank and higher compensation than their married colleagues. This finding may, however, be an artifact of the researchers' failure to control for age—the older, more established female faculty cohorts are only half as likely to be married as the younger ones (see chap. 7).

8. This drop is a function not only of the limited availability of academic positions, but also of the new-found professorial reluctance to move, given uncertain economic conditions, including high interest rates and the high cost of housing (Scully, 1978) and given the trend to two-job families. Ladd and Lipset (1976), for example, report that nearly 60 percent of faculty under forty, traditionally the most mobile group in the profession, considered a good job for their spouse as essential or very important in considering a move to another institution.

9. Prospective job changers were least likely to be found among new assistant professors and imminent retirees.

10. As the academic marketplace tightens and as the rate at which tenure is granted decreases, younger academics may begin to think twice about pursuing prestige at the expense of security. Thus, for example, promising young scholars may decide to forego an opportunity for beginning their career at Harvard, where the prospects of tenure are slim, and choose instead a less auspicious employer where prospects for advancement are higher (Scully, 1978).

11. The question of whether one changes prestige strata at all is critical here, for studies of the academic stratification system (see above) show that one's *absolute* position in the institutional prestige hierarchy is at least as significant a determining factor in movement as one's relative position, especially for experienced faculty. That is, those who are sitting at the top to begin with are more likely than other groups of faculty to find themselves at the top following an institutional move.

12. In the absence of any hard data on the actual search process for first administrative positions, one can only guess. However, insofar, as candidates for department chairpersonships and deanships are typically drawn from among faculty ranks, it seems reasonable to assume the operation of such informal networks (Cyphert and Zimpher, 1980; Waltzer, 1975).

13. There appears to be a considerable division, however, between elite and other private liberal arts colleges, particularly in the areas of teaching assignment and peer evaluation, where elite liberal arts colleges more closely resemble research universities and their less elite counterparts more closely resemble comprehensive public colleges and universities.

14. The distribution of attitudinal support across disciplinary areas here parallels the distribution of political liberalism-conservatism across disciplinary areas, suggesting that attitudinal support of at least some aspects of professional autonomy may be determined more by a faculty member's political orientation than by closely held professional norms, with more liberal faculty being more supportive of professional autonomy (see chap. 6).

15. These findings suggest that faculty are realistic evaluators of the operation of the social system of which they are a part (see our earlier discussion of the bases of the academic reward system).

16. This is less clear in the case of the merit principle.

17. Indeed Cares and Blackburn (1978) report that faculty perception of control over their environment (that is, their perception of participation and influence in

institutional and departmental decision-making) is significantly positively corre- lated with their level of career satisfaction.

18. It is defined as maintaining a campus office and continuing to participate in departmental affairs (Roman and Taietz, 1967), as being engaged in paid professional work (Fillenbaum and Maddox, 1974), as spending time in research and writing (Rowe, 1976), and, more generally, "as continuing a high level of professional ac- tivity" (List, 1956; Dorfman, 1978).

19. Although faculty retirees reported high overall levels of satisfaction, this does not imply that they did not also frequently report some concerns over such things as finances and loss of professional roles and contacts (Dorfman, 1978). These concerns did not, however, appear to detract from a feeling of reasonable contentment and acceptance of this new stage in the life cycle.

5

Faculty at Work

The nature of the work performed by academics in their daily routine and its immediate stresses and satisfactions are the subjects of this chapter. Following a brief overview of the general contours of the work role, two aspects of that role are examined: (1) orientation to, and performance of, the "core" academic functions of teaching and research (including interaction with students and discipline-based consulting) and (2) orientation to, and performance of, the obligations of academic citizenship (that is, participation in the political life of an institution). Performance in these areas yields a number of general propositions concerning faculty work motivation, and these will provide the backdrop for a consideration of the stresses and satisfactions that faculty experience in their work.

GENERAL CONTOURS OF THE ACADEMIC ROLE

The American academic profession is essentially a teaching as opposed to a scholarly profession. By a three-to-one majority, American professors have consistently reported their interests as focusing more on the teaching than on the research component of their role,[1] and as the data in Table 5.1 suggest, these interests have translated themselves quite directly into faculty work activities.

Faculty spend most of their work time teaching (Baldridge et al., 1978). Although precise estimates vary, 60 to 66 percent of the professoriate spend nine or more hours a week in the classroom and as much time again in preparation for classroom teaching. Concomitantly, they spend proportionately very little time engaged in research.[2] At least half the professoriate spend four hours or less per week engaged in research, and at least one in five (Ladd, 1979) or as many as one in three (Bayer, 1973) spends no time at all engaged in research activity. Almost equally small portions of faculty time are

TABLE 5.1
ALLOCATION OF FACULTY EFFORT ACROSS COMPONENTS OF THE ACADEMIC ROLE
BY INSTITUTIONAL TYPE

	Teaching			Research and	
Study	% Time in Teaching Undergraduate/Graduate	% ≥9 hrs./ Week in Teaching	% ≥9 hrs./ Week in Teaching Preparation	% Time in Research	% ≥9 hrs./ Week in Research
Bayer (1973)					
Universities		42.4	53.8		43.2
4-Year colleges		67.2	62.1		23.1
All[a]		59.7	58.7		28.6
Baldridge et al. (1978)					
Multiversities (public & private)	33.0 22.0			23.5	
Elite liberal arts colleges	59.0 6.0			14.0	
Public 4-year colleges and comprehensives	58.5 9.5			10.0	
Other liberal arts colleges	66.0 2.0			9.0	
All[a]	52.0 12.0			14.0	
Ladd (1979)					
Research universities		34.0	50.0		60.0
Ph.D.-granting universities		56.0	60.0		45.0
Comprehensive colleges and universities		78.0	61.0		21.0
Liberal arts colleges		82.0	74.0		10.0
All[a]		66.0	58.0		33.0

[a]Includes data for faculty at 2-year institutions.

devoted to administrative service and to contact with students. About two-thirds spend four hours per week or less in administration, and just over half spend four hours per week or less in advising and counseling students outside of class (Bayer, 1973). Community service activities are a barely perceptible portion of faculty work load (Baldridge et al., 1978), although approximately two of every five faculty are engaged during the academic year in at least one traditional form of community service—professional consulting, paid or unpaid (Bayer, 1973).

In at least one sense, the aggregate picture we have painted of

Publication		Administration		Student Contact		Community Service		
% Not Publishing in Last 2 Years	Mean # Articles in Last 4 Years	% Time in Administration and Committees	% ≤4 hrs./Week in Administration	% ≤4 hrs. in Student Contact	% ≥9 hrs. in Student Contact	% Time in Community Service	% Non-Paid Consulting Last Year	% Paid Consulting Last Year
			60.5	54.7	17.2		50.5	47.6
			64.7	54.9	15.8		36.4	32.8
			65.0	55.2	15.8		41.8	37.7
	7.1	17.0				4.5		
	3.2	18.0				3.0		
	2.6	17.5				4.5		
	2.3	18.0				5.0		
	4.3	18.0				4.0		
18.0								
32.0								
46.0								
57.0								
43.0								

professorial work activities demands serious qualification. The salience of individual role components and their interrelationship (especially as regards the balance between teaching and research) vary substantially across different types of institutions. That variation can be captured most readily as the difference between research universities (research universities and, to a lesser extent, doctorate-granting universities, according to the Carnegie classification[3]), on the one hand, and all other types of institutions (liberal arts colleges and comprehensive colleges and universities), on the other.[4] Faculty at universities, especially research universities, have consistently been shown to teach less (Wilson, 1942; Parsons and Platt, 1968; Bayer, 1973; Baldridge et al., 1978; Ladd, 1979), and they are especially less likely to be found at the high end of the teaching load continuum (nine or more hours of classroom teaching per week) and are especially more likely to be engaged in the training of graduate students (Bayer, 1973). Faculty at universities, especially research universities, spend a great deal more time on research and publication. The majority of faculty at research universities spend nine or more hours a week on research (Ladd, 1979) and more time in graduate training and research (about 45 percent) than in undergraduate teaching (Baldridge et al., 1978). The majority of faculty at universities, especially research universities, publish. The majority of faculty at other types of institutions do not. Not only are the former more likely to publish, but they publish more. Baldridge et al. (1978) found that faculty at public and private multiversities published nearly three times as many journal articles over a four-year period as their colleagues in other types of institutions; Ladd (1979) found that faculty at research universities were four times as likely as liberal arts college faculty and twice as likely as faculty at comprehensive colleges and universities to be moderate or heavy publishers. Indeed, it would be fairly accurate to conclude that research and publication are more or less concentrated in this very limited university sector of academe.

Institutional context shapes not only the salience of individual role components but also their interrelationship. Fulton and Trow (1974) examined the interrelationship among the central components of the academic role (teaching, research, and administration) and found that it varied across institutional prestige strata.[5] At elite institutions, those faculty active in research (that is, those who had published within the past year) also tended to be involved in administration.[6] Furthermore, no significant differences were discernible between those actively engaged in research and those who were not in the amount of time devoted to teaching. At other types of institutions, on the other hand, faculty who were inactive in research were significantly more likely to be involved in administration, and active researchers were found to spend much less time teaching than their inactive colleagues. These findings led Fulton and Trow to conclude that at research universities, the academic role tends to be "integrated," that is, researchers tend to be involved as well in administration and to teach just as much as non-researchers; whereas at other types of institutions, the academic role tends to be "fragmented"—research and teaching are distinct and alternative activities, often carried out by different individuals.

The above data suggest at least two fairly distinctive enactments of the academic role. Why do we find this variation in faculty allocation of effort by institutional prestige stratum? Why is the academic role itself apparently operationalized differently at different sorts of institutions? At least three plausible explanations suggest themselves.

1. *Differential reward systems.* At elite institutions, the reward system is more monolithic and emphasizes research, while at other institutions, it is more flexible and oriented toward teaching. Faculty tend to expend their effort in those areas perceived to "pay off."
2. *Differential work load assignment.* At elite institutions, the teaching load is uniformly lower, while at other institutions, it is uniformly higher, albeit flexible.
3. *Differential faculty selection.* Different allocation patterns may be a function of selecting faculty with a particular sense of their professional responsibilities and internalized standards for effort.

In order to determine the viability of any one explanation or mix of explanations, we turn to the available evidence on the determinants of individual faculty distribution of effort. Two studies explicitly focus on the relationship of institutional reward structures to faculty activity preferences. Hinds et al. (1974) examined faculty activity patterns at Stanford University in an effort to test Scott and Dornbusch's theory of the "controlling" influence of organizational reward systems on employee activity patterns in an academic setting. Although nearly four-fifths of the faculty sample viewed research as having supreme influence on the distribution of organizational rewards, they still reported spending more of their time on teaching-related activities (which only 20 percent viewed as likely to pay off). Hinds does, however, provide evidence suggesting that faculty were aware of the imbalance and sought to redress it.

1. Fifty-three percent of the sample expressed a desire to increase the influence of teaching in the allocation of organizational rewards as a means of narrowing the gap between the reward system and their own activity patterns.
2. A slight tendency was discernible among faculty to spend more

time on those activities they believed to pay off (among those perceiving teaching as a rewarded activity, 65 percent were above the median in time spent teaching undergraduates, and 77 percent were above the median in time spent teaching graduate students, compared to 43 percent and 47 percent, respectively, of those who did not see teaching as a rewarded activity).

Despite these indications, it is apparent from the data that nearly one-half of those faculty who did not see teaching as paying off, nonetheless spent more time than most of their colleagues engaged in it. Hinds is thus led to conclude that while faculty activity patterns may, to some extent, be a function of "perceived payoff," they are also subject to the individual's "sense of professional responsibility and internalized standards for effort." Apparently, then, faculty feel an obligation to teach irrespective of the value placed on teaching by others.

The interpretation of Hinds's findings is, however, muddied by two characteristics of the study. In the first place, he neglects to consider faculty work load assignment as an intervening variable, mediating the reward system/activity pattern relationship. Clearly, the limited impact of the reward system on faculty activities may be attributable to institutional work load assignments that are themselves incongruous with the reward system and which directly channel faculty effort across role activities. In the second place, Hinds assumes a causal sequence from reward system to activity pattern. It is at least as plausible to assume that faculty perceptions of their own activity patterns influence their perceptions of the reward system. Indeed, Hinds's own colleague at Stanford, social psychologist Daryl Bem, has seriously questioned the view that attitudes and beliefs determine behavior and presented considerable evidence to suggest that beliefs and attitudes are adduced by individuals from perceptions of their own behavior—"self perception theory" (see Bem, 1970). Thus, it may be that the limited congruence observed between the reward system and faculty activity patterns is attributable rather to the influence of perceptions of activity patterns on perceptions of the reward system.

These two obstacles are, to some extent, treated by Borland (1970) in a study of faculty at Indiana University. Borland found that the perceived payoff of various faculty work activities was largely *independent* of the time and effort allocated to them. Among those faculty who viewed research as a rewarded activity, just as many spent a minor as a major portion of their time on it. If not the reward system, what emerged as the central locus of control of faculty activity patterns? Not work load assignment. Borland found that faculty themselves had the most influence over the allocation of their own professional duties, so that work load assignments, to a great extent, reflected their own individual predilections. Nor did institutional goals prove a controlling influence. Faculty perception of a goal as "primary" was not associated with their spending a major portion of their time on it. Moreover, those faculty who spent the major portion of their time on any given activity (teaching, research, service) were no more likely to perceive it as a primary institutional goal than those who spent a minor portion of their time on it.[7] Faculty, Borland is led to conclude, basically do what they want. Their personal and professional goals become the operational goals of the university, and are reflected both in work load assignment and activity patterns.

These conclusions are by and large supported by DeVries's (1975) exploration of the impact of expectations of the faculty member's role set (colleagues, chairperson, institution, and self) on his or her allocation of effort. DeVries reported that an individual faculty member's "self-expectations" were by far the best predictor of the individual's activity patterns, *uniquely* explaining between 30 percent and 43 percent of the variance in time allocation among the three core role components of teaching, research, administration. Organizational expectations, as reflected in full-time equivalent (FTE) work load assignment, ran a distant second, uniquely explaining between 9 percent and 23 percent of the activity variance. Colleague and chairperson expectations had virtually no independent effect, explaining from 0 to 3 percent of the variance. These findings suggest that, contrary to Borland, assigned work load does indeed play a role independent of self-expectations in determining faculty activity patterns (although a less important one). Why the discrepancy? It may well be a function of the extent of faculty control over work load assignment. The faculty in Borland's sample showed a high degree of control over their work load assignment, thus effectively subjugating it to their "self-expectations." DeVries, on the other hand, found that the common variance explained by the pair was minimal (ranging from 3 percent to 8 percent), suggesting that among his sample of faculty, FTE assignment did not largely reflect faculty self-expectations. Thus, it may be that the import of work load assignment relative to faculty self expectations varies by "extent of faculty control over work load assignment." In those cases where control over work load is high, self-expectations dominate; in those situations where it is lower (for example, among junior faculty), activity patterns are more likely to be subject to the independent effect of work load assignment.

This conclusion not only appears to have some "face" validity, but is supported by additional evidence. DeVries (1975) found that the predictive power of self-expectations and work load assignment varied over the three central components of the academic role. FTE work load assignment showed the strongest relative impact on allocation of effort to administrative tasks and the lowest relative impact on the allocation of effort in the teaching and research areas. The latter are, of course, the core activities of the professor, and it is in these areas that self-expectations are most fully put into practice. Administrative responsibilities would appear to be less central and less flexible, once the individual faculty member has contracted to take them on.

The generalizations we have drawn are based exclusively on the study of faculty at research-oriented universities. For these faculty, at least, it appears that internalized standards of professional performance are the primary determinants of what they do with their time. The impact of work assignment would appear to vary with the degree of faculty control over it and would presumably be greater for junior faculty. The institutional reward system and the perceptions of payoff that it engenders do not appear to have a substantial effect on faculty activity patterns.

We can now return, somewhat better prepared, to our original question. The distinctiveness of faculty activity patterns and the relative "integration" of the academic role at research universities would appear to be a function more of the selection of faculty with a particular set of internalized standards for the proper execution of the academic role. Work assignment would, for the most part, reflect those internal standards (with the possible exception of junior faculty). The incentive structure operationalized in the institutional reward system would appear to play little, if any, *direct* formative role.

To what extent are these generalizations applicable as well to faculty at nonresearch institutions? Baldridge et al. (1978) found that faculty professional autonomy, in general, and control over their work load assignment, in particular, decreased as one descended the institutional prestige hierarchy. Presumably, then, internalized professional standards of performance are less likely to be directly reflected in activity patterns. Fulton and Trow (1974), however, presented evidence which suggests that faculty at non-research institutions did have a choice between teaching and research; and presumably, those who are research oriented do indeed manage to "act out" their orientation, apparently persuading their institution to accommodate their individual self-expectations. Moreover, there is evidence to suggest that all academic institutions recognize systematic differences in orientation among their faculty members—defined, at the very least, along the lines of disciplinary affiliation and career stage. Wilson (1942), Donovan (1964), Biglan (1971, 1973), Kelly and Hart (1971), Blau (1973), and Fulton and Trow (1974) all reported significant differences in faculty role orientation by disciplinary affiliation. While varying in the range of disciplines they encompass and in the precision of their rankings, there appears to be a consensus that natural and social scientists are more oriented to research than professors in the humanities, education, and the semiprofessions. And, at least in university settings, the former tend to teach less, spend more time in research, and publish more (Blau, 1973; Morgan, 1970). Differences attributable to discipline appear to persist, even after controlling for institutional type and prestige (Fulton and Trow, 1974; Blau, 1973), although the latter variables appear to have a considerably stronger independent effect (Blau, 1973). New entrants to the professoriate, in liberal arts college settings (Klapper, 1969; Baldwin, 1979; Baldwin and Blackburn 1981) as well as university settings (Warriner and Murai, 1974; Hesseldenz, 1976), were found to rank research higher as a priority than their more experienced colleagues and to spend more time in it (Hesseldenz, 1976; Baldwin, 1979), although they were no more productive in terms of publication (Ladd, 1979).

All of this suggests that within a similar institutional context, be it a liberal arts college or a university, faculty in different disciplines and at different stages of their careers tend to enact their roles on a daily basis in slightly different ways.[8] Why this patterned intra-institutional diversity? Explanations are few. Using a factor analytic approach, Biglan (1971, 1973) was able to attribute differences among disciplines in research orientation to variation in the structural characteristics of academic tasks. Practitioners of those disciplines that were "harder" (that is, more objective and precise in research methodology) and more "theoretical" than "applied" were more oriented toward research and more socially connected with their colleagues in the research process than practitioners of "soft" and "applied" fields. Drawing upon theories of adult and career development, Baldwin (1979, 1981) was able to identify distinct periods in the career of liberal arts college faculty characterized by an ebb and flow of interests that were directly reflected in activity patterns. Over the course of an academic career, faculty tend to gradually lose interest in teaching and research and to turn their sights to institutional and professional service. Whatever the explanation, it appears quite clear that all academic institutions provide their faculties with at least some "room to maneuver" in accommodating different and changing individual needs and orientations with organizational expectations—although the magnitude and nature of that "room" may vary considerably.

THE RESEARCH ROLE

Publication Activity

We have noted that institutional type determines to a great extent the balance between teaching and research. The data suggested that university, and especially research university, faculty could be distinguished from the rest of the profession in that they support a majority culture that is more interested in research than teaching, that devotes nearly as much time to the former as to the latter, and that engages in publication. The preeminent power of institutional context is resoundingly confirmed by some three dozen studies of the publication activity of American academics. Institutional type (university versus college) and prestige (usually assessed via reputational ratings of graduate departments or faculty qualifications and student selectivity) consistently emerge as preeminent predictors of publication activity. University faculty tend to publish more than college faculty, and faculty at more prestigious institutions tend to publish more than faculty at less prestigious institutions (Wilson, 1942; Manis, 1950; Crane, 1964 and 1965; Blau, 1973; Fulton and Trow, 1974; Kenen, 1974; Reskin, 1977 and 1979), quite independent of their earlier pattern of publication activity (Long, 1978; Blackburn et al., 1978).[9] Indeed, Long (1978) in a longitudinal study of the publication patterns of natural scientists over the first ten years of their careers found that their publication activity actually changed with each move to a new institution—and that change was along the lines of the new institution's publication norms.

The available evidence, moreover, appears to confirm our hypothesis on the sources of the institutional context effect: the operation of selection and environmental stimulus factors as opposed to institutional incentive structures. Blau (1973) explored the relationship of the weight of research in promotion to professors' "felt obligation to do research" and their actual involvement in research activity. He found that the weight of research in promotion and faculty felt obligations to engage in research affected actual research involvment only *indirectly,* not directly as would be expected if incentives were operative. The weight of research in promotion appeared rather to influence actual research involvement via selection—that is, it directly affected the research qualifications of individual faculty hired and furnished them with highly research-oriented colleagues. Similarly, Behymer (1974) reported that perceived pressure to publish had no independent effect on faculty research productivity when individual interest in research was controlled. On the whole, he found that "intrinsic" factors (for example, interest in research and interaction with research-oriented colleagues) rather than "extrinsic" factors (for example, perceived pressure to publish) were the most salient predictors of productivity. Together Blau and Behymer suggest that the dependence of promotion on research productivity does not motivate individuals who are not already inclined to do research; rather it raises research productivity by the selection of individuals with research qualifications and orientation and by providing them with stimulating colleagues. Indeed, the two variables of colleague climate (proportion of faculty colleagues holding the doctorate) and individual research qualifications (possession of the doctorate) accounted for 30 percent of the observed variance in research involvement among Blau's sample of faculty. Behymer, adding to the regression analysis several individual characteristics indicative of research orientation/qualification, was able to explain fully 60 percent of the variance in productivity among faculty. Thus, based on these two studies, it would appear that colleague climate as reflected in institutional prestige together with an individual's own orientation toward research are the prime determinants of publication activity.

These conclusions are strongly supported by the findings of virtually all the remaining three dozen studies. When tested in conjunction with other factors, institutional type and prestige (reflected in colleague climate) and individual professional characteristics associated with a research orientation uniformly emerge as the most powerful predictors of publication activity. Thus, among departmental characteristics, prestige or reputation (in terms of Cartter's ratings) emerges as the only important determinant across studies (although not as important as overall institutional prestige—Manis, 1950; Hargens and Farr, 1973; Long, 1978). The character of administrative leadership, although significant in three of the four studies in which it was tested, emerges as only weakly related to variation in research productivity (Hill and French 1967; McCord, 1970; Glueck and Thorp, 1974; Coltrin and Glueck 1977). Similarly, department size assumes a minor role, although it appears to diminish in significance only when a critical mass of ten to fifteen faculty members is reached (Wispe, 1969; Behymer, 1974).

Among faculty professional characteristics, seven related normative and behavioral variables emerge as the most important predictors of publication: research orientation, highest degree, early publication, previous publication activity, communication with disciplinary colleagues, number of journal subscriptions, and time allocation among academic role components. Indeed, from this constellation of variables there emerges a composite portrait of the productive faculty member. The professorial publisher:

1. Holds the doctorate
2. Is strongly oriented toward research
3. Began publishing early, perhaps prior to receipt of the doctorate and received "recognition" for scholarly contributions (Cole and Cole, 1973; Reskin, 1977)
4. Is in close contact with developments in his or her field via interaction with colleagues and keeping abreast of the literature
5. Spends more time in research, less time in teaching, and is not overly committed to administrative chores (although this may vary over institutional prestige strata; see Fulton and Trow, 1974).

This pattern of individual predispositions can, then, be reinforced by colleague climate both at the institutional and at the departmental levels, but is relatively impervious to the influence of other extrinsic factors.

What formative influences are responsible for producing this particular kind of individual? At the most fundamental level, it would appear that the characteristics are rooted in basic personality patterns that surface quite early in life. All of Roe's (1951a, 1951b, 1953) "eminent" natural and social scientists had become fascinated with the possibility of doing research as college students, and had shown strong proclivities for following up on their intellectual curiosity even as pre-adolescents. More immediately, these fundamental dispositions appear to express themselves and take shape during the years of graduate training. Three aspects of graduate training appear to relate directly and significantly to early career publication activity: close professional involvement with a graduate professor who serves as "sponsor" for the apprentice scholar; pre-doctorate publication; and, most generally, receiving one's doctoral training in a prestigious graduate department (Crane, 1964 and 1965; Behymer, 1974; Cameron, 1978; Cameron and Blackburn, 1981; Long, 1978). The most prolific faculty were those who during their graduate years had collaborated with a productive, prestigious sponsor on one or more research projects resulting in early publication. In directly affecting early publication, sponsorship indirectly contributes to subsequent career productivity: early publication has a strong independent effect on later career publication activity (Reskin, 1977; Long, 1978). More directly, sponsorship contributes to an initial placement at a research university, and that initial placement contributes immensely to subsequent career publication activity in at least three reinforcing ways: (1) via the enhancing effect of a research-oriented colleague climate, (2) via its enhancing effect on subsequent mobility to research-oriented, prestigious institutions, thus assuring continuity in a supportive colleague climate, and (3) via its enhancing effect on the visibility of one's work and the concomitant recognition by one's peers (Reskin, 1977; Cole, 1979), which further tends to reinforce publication activity (Cole and Cole, 1973).

If the direct effect of sponsorship is initially clear and strong, it becomes progressively attenuated over the course of an academic career—yielding to the direct formative influence of early publication and initial institutional placement. The effect of Ph.D. prestige is both initially less clear and less direct. Clemente (1973), Clemente and Sturgis (1974), and Behymer (1974) found reputational ranking of the doctoral institution to be a statistically significant, though very weak, predictor of current publication activity. Crane (1964, 1965), Reskin (1977), and Long (1978), on the other hand, found it to be among the most powerful. The discrepancy may be attributable at least in part to sampling variation. The latter investigators focused on natural scientists, the former on sociologists (Clemente; and Clemente and Sturgis) and, more generally, on arts and sciences faculty (Behymer). It may also, however, be attributable to the varying effects of Ph.D. prestige over the course of an academic career. Both Long (1978) and Reskin (1977), in their study of natural scientists during the first decade of their careers, found that the Ph.D. prestige effect showed up in the second but not in the first half of that decade—even after controlling for early publication productivity. It would appear to operate, if indirectly, in at least two ways. It affects publication activity via its effect on (1) access to prestigious, productive graduate professors who can serve as sponsors and early collaborators (Reskin, 1977) and (2) the prestige of the young Ph.D.'s initial placement (Long, 1978). The nature of any direct effect, however, remains unclear. It may be that more prestigious institutions promote better informal network contacts for their graduates or greater access to "effective" socialization.

The generalizability of the picture we have sketched of the productive researcher as a particular kind of person whose predispositions, given shape in graduate school, are reinforced by a stimulating research environment is qualified, however, by the effects of several other variables: disciplinary affiliation, rank, and age.

Discipline. Disciplinary affiliation is associated with productivity across a half dozen studies (Wilson, 1942; Donovan, 1964; Blau, 1973; Coltrin and Glueck 1977; Fulton and Trow, 1974; Blackburn et al. 1978). Natural scientists, as a group, emerge as the most productive; faculty in the humanities, education, and the fine arts, as the least productive; and social scientists fall somewhere in between. There is, then, perfect consensus on the existence of such a relationship, but there is some question as to its magnitude. Half the studies report large significant differences among disciplinary groupings, explaining as much as 5 percent of the variance in productivity (for example, Blackburn et al., 1978), and the other half detect small, barely significant differences (for example, Fulton and Trow, 1974). This discrepancy may, however, simply be an artifact of the measures of productivity employed. Among those studies documenting large significant differences, all fail to distinguish among different forms of publication and among single versus multiple authorship. They generally examine either the total number of publications or the total number of journal articles. Biglan (1971, 1973) and Roe (1972) have reported significant differences among disciplines in the dominant forms of publication. As one moves from the humanities to the natural sciences, the proportionate frequency of journal articles and technical reports increases and that of books decreases; multiple authorship, almost unheard of in the humanities, is more common in the social sciences and the norm in the natural sciences. Counting all publications equally or articles only tends to favor shorter forms and multiple authorships and thus would work to inflate the production of natural scientists at the expense of the production of humanists and some social scientists. Indeed, among those studies documenting small, barely significant differences by discipline, two employed "weighted" publication indices that accord higher weight to books and single authorship, and one examines research involvement, whether or not that may lead to publication (Blau, 1973). It would therefore seem most reasonable to conclude that when disciplinary differences in form of publication are taken into account, differences in real productivity are relatively small and of limited practical significance.

Academic Rank. It further appears that an individual's academic rank has some bearing on publication productivity. It is hardly surprising that among those inquiries focusing on *cumulative* research productivity, rank emerges as a significant predictor: cumulative productivity is presumably related to longevity, and longevity to higher rank. But rank emerges as a significant predictor of the *rate* of publication as well, explaining about twice as much variance as disciplinary affiliation (at its most inflated). Faculty in the higher ranks tend to publish at a higher rate (Hill and Franch 1967; Fulton and Trow, 1974; Blackburn et al., 1978).

How can we explain the association of rank with publication rate? Selection factors may account for a large part of the relationship—that is, promotion to a higher rank may be a function of an already demonstrated publication rate, which persists in the new status. Fulton and Trow (1974) proposed another hypothesis, that the effect of rank may be a function of differential control over work load assignment. While no significant differences emerged among ranks in research orientation, Fulton and Trow uncovered large significant differences among ranks in actual publication activity. Thus, at lower ranks, a high orientation to research was significantly less likely to be translated directly into publications. Fulton and Trow suggest that junior faculty may be constrained by job requirements over which they have less control from fully "acting out" their predispositions. Their findings, however, admit a number of possible explanations. Faculty at higher ranks may publish more because of the greater *opportunity* for publication afforded them by a higher degree of visibility and greater knowledge of the "ins and outs" of getting a manuscript published. Furthermore, older faculty generally have more colleagues who can function as potential collaborators and are in a position to build up a collection of graduate student disciples for co-publication (Blackburn, 1982). The extent to which each of these factors contributes to a higher rate of publication at the higher ranks is a matter about which we can only speculate. One thing is, however, patently clear: publication does not stop when the incentive provided by the prospect of promotion is no longer operative, but rather seems to increase, and this supports, once again, the preeminent role of "intrinsic" as opposed to "extrinsic" motives for research involvement.

Age. If the rate of publication appears to increase with rank, it decreases with age (Roe, 1972; Behymer, 1974; Fulton and Trow, 1974; Bayer and Dutton, 1977; Blackburn et al., 1978), though the decrement is small, obtaining statistical significance in but a single study (Behymer, 1974). The predominant lack of significance may reflect the fact that the pattern of publication over time is not linear. In the single most comprehensive inquiry into the relationship of age and productivity, Bayer and Dutton (1977) simultaneously tested a half dozen hypotheses by seeking the curve that "best fits" the publication activity over time of three age cohorts of natural and social scientists. They found that the curve of overall best fit was bimodal or saddle shaped, with the first peak occurring about ten years following receipt of the doctorate, and the second peak occurring just before retirement.[10] Moreover, while a saddle-shaped curve best fits the sample as a whole, Bayer and Dutton discovered differences among disciplinary groupings in both the shape of the curve and the actual values of research productivity at different career points (a finding corroborated by Roe, 1972). Other evidence would suggest that the curve also varies by institutional prestige and level of individual academic achievement. Roe (1972), Behymer (1974), and Cole (1979) all reported a high degree of persistence in productivity among faculty with a track record of high publication in their earlier years, and Fulton and Trow (1974) reported that at elite, research universities, no decline whatever in publication rate was discernible with advancing age. It would thus appear that athough aging brings with it a slight decline in overall publication activity, the particular kind of individual possessing the research-oriented characteristics we have described maintains the same high level of performance.

Why do faculty, as a group, publish less as they grow older? The reasons are not at all clear. Behymer (1974), Fulton and Trow (1974), and Baldwin (1979) document a decrease in research orientation among older age cohorts. Faculty apparently turn their attentions away from research and more toward teaching and service to their institution and profession. No explanation of this apparent shift in orientation is offered. Is it a function of waning ambition? A reorganization of personal priorities? Do faculty simply begin to lose their intellectual curiosity? Nor is it clear to what extent this shift in orientation is responsible for fluctuation in actual publication activity. It may be that, at least to some extent, the drop in volume of publication activity is attributable to a change in the nature or focus of faculty research interests. Parsons and Platt (1968) present evidence suggesting that the research priorities of faculty tend to shift with age away from highly specific, empirical, and analytic inquiries toward broader, theoretical, synthetic and interdisciplinary endeavors. The nature of this new research focus would presumably require a period of prolonged incubation and would appear considerably less likely to result in "quick" publications than would more highly circumscribed, empirical inquiry. It may be that the incubation period is represented by the "low" in the saddle-shaped curve; and the final integration or synthesis, following the period of incubation, might result in the final peak just before retirement. Cole (1979) has sought to explain this pattern by reference to the operation of the academic reward system. By encouraging the able and discouraging the less able, the reward system reduces the number of scientists actively publishing, although the "best" continue to publish. A thoroughly satisfactory explanation, however, has yet to be put forward.

One final qualification must be highlighted. Hall (1975) and Blackburn et al. (1978) reported variation in the relative import of productivity determinants between college and university faculty. While interest in research and early publication remain powerful predictors of productivity for both groups, level of interaction with disciplinary colleagues and number of journal subscriptions prove much more powerful predictors for university than for college faculty. It would appear that faculty at four-year colleges are less likely to be at the heart of the disciplinary communication structure, but, apparently, their interest in research is powerful enough to fuel their productivity in the absence of intense collegial interaction. How the functions of disciplinary colleagueship are adequately substituted for remains unclear.

The Social Process of Research

Uncertainty with respect to the function of colleagueship in research performance is a specific symptom of our more general lack of understanding of the social process of research, that is, the sequence of events that constitute the "real life" referents of the research-oriented individual by colleague climate interaction we have posited. The role of social interaction processes have been treated at the most general level by several studies over the past decade. Both Biglan (1973) and Lodahl and Gordon (1972) examine the role of colleagueship in the conduct of inquiry as a function of academic discipline. They found that faculty in the "hard" sciences were more socially connected to their colleagues in the conduct of their research than faculty in the humanities and the "softer" social sciences. "Hard" scientists reported experiencing a lower level of disagreement with colleagues, were more likely to be influenced by them and to enjoy working with them, and evidenced a greater tendency toward coauthoring publications with them.[11] Moreover, Biglan (1971) and Glueck and Jauch (1975) reported that for hard scientists, the extent of social connectiveness with colleagues was positively related to publication productivity.

More recently, Finkelstein (1982) has suggested that it is the pattern or structure of collegial interactions rather than their overall level that is most supportive of faculty research and publication activity. Q-factor analysis of collegial interaction profiles identified four ideal types or patterns of faculty colleagueship: department-anchored cosmopolitanism (high interaction with off-campus disciplinary colleagues combined with high interaction with department colleagues on research and teaching issues), pure localism (interaction by and large confined to department and campus colleagues), and two varieties of "unanchored" cosmopolitanism (high interaction with off-campus colleagues combined with minimal department and on-campus connections). These patterns were relatively independent of a faculty member's overall level of collegial interaction. The most active publishers were those faculty showing a pattern of department-anchored rather than pure cosmopolitanism.

One particular aspect of collegial interaction that has received attention, especially recently, is the mentoring relationship that may develop between a senior professor and either a graduate student or a junior faculty member. Cameron and Blackburn (1981) identified the functional dimensions of that relationship from the perspective of the student, including collaboration on research and publication, the use of the research assistantship, and help in securing job placement. And, later, together with Chapman (Blackburn et al., 1981), they extended their purview to include the perspective of the mentors themselves. Their study does provide some insight into how mentors select prospective students (the principle of homophyly, that is, like selects like, does not appear to operate as uniformly as we may have supposed, especially with respect to student and mentor gender), but it tends to focus primarily on the attitudes and satisfactions of mentoring rather than its dynamics (how the relationship develops).

Crane (1964) does, however, provide some preliminary insight into the dynamics of the mentoring relationship, although somewhat obliquely, in her examination of the various modes by which young natural scientists and social scientists establish a research program at the beginning of their careers. Three modes proved dominant: continuing an interest developed as a graduate student; developing a new research interest, usually via association with an older colleague; or, for those who encountered difficulty in establishing a research program, becoming involved in research as expedience permitted (that is, according to the available on-going department research activities). All of these modes may, and frequently do, involve a mentoring process. The departmental and institutional conditions under which they operate, however, are only touched upon by Crane herself, and remain to be fully explored.

THE TEACHING ROLE

Since the pioneering observational studies of Mann et al. (1970) of the naturally occurring processes in the college classroom, there has been something of a general retreat from basic description and explanation of classroom dynamics. To be sure, there has been some recent work—primarily doctoral dissertations out of a single graduate institution—on levels of cognitive complexity of classroom discourse (based on Bloom's taxonomy), generally, and on faculty "questioning" behavior, in particular (Givens, 1976; Barnes, 1976, 1983; Fischer and Grant, 1983), as well as on lecturing behavior (Batchelder and Keane, 1977).[12] But the exploration of college teaching has become the province of the paper and pencil survey.

On what do these surveys focus? For the most part, not on classroom behavior. Gaff and Wilson (1975) constitute something of an exception here. They surveyed the incidence of a series of teaching practices and attitudes that define two broad teaching approaches: subject-matter centered (lecturing and using detailed notes) and student centered (favoring individual assignments; encouraging students to pursue their own interests; judging student performance in relation to their capacities) with the latter relying more on high degrees of instructor control of the classroom and extrinsic as opposed to intrinsic student incentives. For the most part, however, they eschew the use of these teaching practices as an outcome variable. Rather, these surveys tend to focus on three aspects of the teaching role:

1. The goals that faculty pursue in their teaching of undergraduates and, in a limited sense, how these goals relate to classroom teaching practices
2. Student ratings of classroom teaching performance and the personal and professional correlates of "effective" teaching as judged by students

3. Extension of the teaching role to faculty-student interaction outside the classroom.

Faculty Teaching Goals and Teaching Practices

What goals do faculty pursue in their undergraduate teaching? The available evidence suggests a rather startling consensus on the most important ones. Student mastery of knowledge in a discipline and development of the ability to think clearly consistently emerged as the most important goals for nine out of ten faculty *at all types of institutions* (Parsons and Platt, 1968, 1976; Bayer, 1973). Indeed, among the remaining top five educational goals emerging from the 1972–73 American Council on Education Faculty Survey—preparation for employment, increasing self-directed learning, developing creativity, developing a responsible citizenry—only the last showed as much as a 10 percent variation in the proportion of faculty endorsing it across institutional types. Where larger interinstitutional differences emerged (in the 15–20 percent range), they tend to be related to relatively secondary goals, such as character building and developing student research skills (endorsed by only about a third of the faculty respondents to the American Council on Education survey), and to be in the expected direction (university faculty are less oriented toward character building and more oriented toward research preparation).

Within this portrait of relative consensus, however, there is evidence to suggest some intra-institutional diversity, a diversity that seems to increase with institutional size and complexity (Blank, 1976). Table 5.2 below documents that diversity by juxtaposing faculty ratings of the top ten institutional goals and the top ten goals they pursue in their own undergraduate teaching. While there is a near perfect overlap between the two lists overall, five out of eleven goal statements do show differences greater than 10 percent in their endorsement as institutional versus personal teaching goals—suggesting some departure of individual faculty goals from perceived institutional goals. There appear to be two bases for this intra-institutional diversity. First, Gaff and Wilson (1975), Morstain and Smart (1976), and Stark and Morstain (1978) all uncovered significant differences in patterns of educational goals among disciplinary groups across several types of institutions, ranging from an eastern public university to a small midwestern liberal arts college.[13] Natural scientists were most likely to support the goal of career preparation and humanities faculty least likely; social scientists were the strongest proponents of general education and the pursuit of ideas

TABLE 5.2
FACULTY RATINGS OF THE TOP 10 GOALS OF UNDERGRADUATE EDUCATION

Goal	Rating as Institutional Educational Goal		Rating as Individual Teaching Goal	
	Percent[a]	Rank	Percent[a]	Rank
To master knowledge in a discipline	83.1	(1)	91.6	(2)
To develop ability to think clearly	79.3	(2)	96.9	(1)
To prepare students for employment after college	74.3	(3)	62.4	(5)
To increase capacity for self-directed learning	66.0	(4)	88.8	(3)
To develop responsible citizens	64.7	(5)	60.4	(6)
To provide community with skilled human resources	63.1	(6)	49.5	
To convey basic appreciation of the liberal arts	61.7	(7)	55.3	(9)
To develop creative capacities	56.0	(8)	76.6	(4)
To prepare students for graduate education	54.2	(9)	52.9	(10)
To provide tools for critical evaluation of society	50.7	(10)	56.9	(7)
To achieve deeper levels of student self-understanding	46.1		56.6	(8)

SOURCE: Based on data from Bayer (1973).
[a]Percent of raters indicating goal is "essential" or "very important."

and natural scientists the weakest. Second, on the basis of the professional life histories of faculty at a variety of institutional types, Ralph (1973) concluded that a faculty member's progression on the intellectual development continuum from "absolutism" to "relativism" (see Perry, 1970 and 1981) was accompanied by a change in his or her orientations to the goals of education and to knowledge. Faculty at the most rudimentary stage of intellectual development tended to define educational goals in accord with their professional group, to see knowledge as absolute and given, and to conceive of education as the filling of "empty vessels" with "the truth." In the course of development, the individual came to view knowledge as more problematic and context related, and thus, tended to become more open to diversity.

What do these findings mean in terms of actual faculty classroom teaching practices? Gaff and Wilson (1975) examined the relationship of faculty educational goals and institutional type to fourteen dimensions of faculty teaching practices. Their findings show that on eight of the fourteen dimensions, institutional type seems to account for more variation in teaching practices than individual faculty educational goals (Table 5.3). They conclude that teaching practices are more sensitive to institutional context (on-the-job socialization) than to individual faculty teaching goals (internal values and standards). Their conclusion, however, needs to be qualified in at least two respects. First, in choosing to juxtapose the two most extreme institutional types, community colleges and research universities, Gaff and Wilson are probably overestimating the institutional type effect. Certainly, Gaff and Wilson's own data show that community college and university faculty vary more extremely in terms both of teaching practices and teaching goals (see also Bayer, 1973) than do university and state college faculty. It is safe to as-

TABLE 5.3
TEACHING PRACTICES RELATED TO EDUCATIONAL GOALS (percents[a])

Teaching Practices and Attitudes	Skills and Mastery Groups		Self-Knowledge Groups	
	Community College (N = 41)	University (N = 136)	Community College (N = 54)	University (N = 55)
Subject-matter approach				
Lecture to class	2	37	7	27
Use detailed notes	39	52	21	33
Student-centered approach				
Favor individualized assignments	46	33	63	44
Encourage students to pursue own interests	27	25	54	40
Favor judging student performance in relation to capacities	49	23	62	51
Control and structure				
Feel class attendance should be optional	10	46	28	51
Give unannounced tests	29	19	15	7
Take precautions to prevent cheating	56	23	42	15
Describe objectives	56	36	46	36
Follow textbook closely	73	45	60	31
Intrinsic (student) motivation				
Basic interest in subject	63	63	39	51
Are challenged intellectually	29	44	28	42
Extrinsic (teacher) motivation				
Communicate own enthusiasm	83	53	70	56
Make courses relevant	46	20	56	36

SOURCE: Wilson and Gaff (1975).

[a]Percent of faculty members in each institution who scored in the upper third of the distribution for each item, except for the four motivation variables, where percent is the percent of faculty members indicating each of those variables.

sume that had they chosen to make the latter comparison, institutional context would have certainly emerged as a less powerful arbiter of teaching practices. Second, a close examination of the fourteen teaching practices reveals at least three conceptually distinct dimensions: subject versus student centered (5 of 14 items), degree of classroom control/structuring (5 of 14 items), assumptions concerning student motivation (4 of 14 items). When one disaggregates their analysis along these three dimensions, one finds that on three of the five items concerned with subject versus student centered approaches, faculty educational goals appear to account for greater variation than institutional type—even when the two extreme types, community colleges and universities, are compared; on the majority of items reflecting classroom control and student incentive practices, institutional type rather than educational goals appears to account for the greater share of variation. It would appear, then, that the relative impact of institutional context versus individual faculty educational goals varies by the nature of teaching practices examined as well as by the types of institutions selected for comparison. While a faculty member's teaching practices are conditioned by institutional context—especially those practices related to classroom control and student incentives and especially at the extremes of the institutional type universe—they are also conditioned by individual faculty educational goals—especially with respect to student versus subject matter centered approaches. Thus, although universities may breed a subject-centered approach to teaching in their faculty, there are pockets of student-centered faculty, following their own drummer, to be found even there.

Classroom Practices and Faculty Teaching Effectiveness

To what extent, and in what ways, are teaching practices associated with faculty effectiveness in the classroom as judged by their students? To what extent indeed is effectiveness in the teaching role linked to concrete, definable, and ultimately trainable behaviors or to more amorphous, fortuitous characteristics of the teaching situation, more enduring traits of faculty personality or status characteristics, such as rank, age, teaching experience?

Questions such as these have spawned an enormous corpus of research that has examined faculty teaching effectiveness as rated by students in relation to (1) enduring faculty status characteristics, both professional (discipline, rank, career age, teaching versus research orientation) and nonprofessional (sex, age, political orientation), (2) global personality characteristics (for example, self concept), (3) situational factors (course characteristics, such as level and class size; characteristics of the teacher-student relationship, for example, congruence/divergence in student-faculty orientations and expectations; extent of student-faculty interaction outside the classroom; the provision and timing of student feedback to the instructor); and (4) concrete in-class behaviors (presentation style, nonverbal cues; classroom management and faculty respect for, and sensitivity to, students). These studies have resulted in an enormously complex body of findings which, although sometimes mutually contradictory, seem to yield a series of defensible generalizations.

The most unequivocal and powerful of those generalizations is that the teaching practices that a faculty member adopts in the classroom are clearly and strongly related to perceived teaching effectiveness. Feldman (1976) attempted a comprehensive reanalysis of hundreds of studies of the correlates of student ratings of effective teaching via standardizing the ranks of correlates across studies. He uncovered three clusters or groups of critical correlates: those related to presentation of course material (for example, instructor's enthusiasm, clarity, knowledge of subject matter and ability to stimulate student interest), those related to the professor's interpersonal role as facilitator of the classroom process (respect for students, encouragement of discussion, availability), and those related to the professor's managerial role in course organization and administration (preparation and organization, clarity of objectives and requirements, fairness in evaluation, classroom management). Table 5.4 presents Feldman's rankings of the top ten correlates of effectiveness from studies of student ratings of their *ideal* or *best* teacher or of the characteristics *important* to good teaching (both for studies where student responses were prestructured and for those where student responses were unstructured) and from correlational studies of student ratings of their actual teachers.

In the first place, the table suggests a remarkable overlap in the qualities associated in student's minds with good teaching. A faculty member's knowledge and ability to stimulate student interests (both critical aspects of presentation skills) emerge among the top three in two of the three categories of studies examined. Indeed, quality of presentation skills dominate the top five in all categories with the exception of studies involving nonstructured student responses. Similarly, a faculty member's course organization skills emerge in the bottom five in both the structured and nonstructured response studies of student perceptions of the ideal teacher. Only

TABLE 5.4
RANKINGS OF THE TOP TEN CORRELATES OF EFFECTIVE TEACHING

Correlate	Nonstructured response studies Ideal (1)	Important (2)	Best (3)		Structured Response Studies Ideal (4)	Important (5)	Best (6)	Correlational Studies (overall evaluation × specific evaluations) (7)	
Respect students	6.5 (.28)	1 (.23)	2 (.27)	Knowledge	2.5 (.18)	3 (.26)	1 (.11)	Interesting	1 (.20)
Knowledge	5 (.23)	2 (.24)	3.5 (.33)	Interesting	1 (.14)	4 (.28)	2.5 (.26)	Clarity	2 (.25)
Interesting	6.5 (.28)	3 (.36)	3.5 (.33)	Class progress	4 (.19)	1 (.20)	5 (.40)	Challenge	3 (.39)
Availability	—	7 (.47)	1 (.20)	Clarity	5 (.21)	2 (.22)	6.5 (.42)	Class progress	4 (.40)
Discussion	[2 (.19)]	4 (.44)	7 (.45)	Enthusiasm	2.5 (.18)	6.5 (.35)	6.5 (.42)	Organization	5 (.41)
Clarity	1 (.17)	10.5 (.60)	5 (.39)	Organization	6 (.29)	5 (.29)	11 (.48)	Clear objectives	6 (.45)
Enthusiasm	[3.5 (.22)]	9 (.53)	11 (.50)	Challenge	7 (.39)	8 (.40)	[8.5 (.44)]	Enthusiasm	7 (.46)
Fairness	[9.5 (.40)]	6 (.46)	9.5 (.49)	Availability	10 (.45)	10 (.44)	[2.5 (.26)]	Knowledge	8 (.45)
Organization	11 (.56)	12 (.63)	6 (.44)	Discussion	8 (.40)	12 (.53)	14 (.64)	Elocution	9 (.49)
Elocution	[12.5 (.74)]	5 (.45)	12 (.52)	Respect students	11 (.48)	13 (.60)	10 (.46)	Expansiveness	10 (.54)

SOURCE: Feldman (1976).

NOTE: Figures in parenthesis are the average standardized ranks of a particular characteristic across studies, obtained by (1) dividing its rank in each study by the number of characteristics examined in that study and then (2) averaging this standardized rank across studies. The smaller the fraction, the greater the rank ordered importance of the characteristic. If the overall standardized rank is based on only one study, it and its rank placement in the table are given in brackets.

one aspect of the professor's facilitator role emerges in the top five—their sensitivity to class progress—while at the same time, the quality of the instructors facilitation (in terms of respect for, and availability to, students, and encouragement of discussion) appears to dominate students' nonstructured descriptions of the "good" or "ideal" teacher.[14]

The portrait that emerges of the effective teacher is of one whose strong presentation skills (knowledge, clarity, enthusiasm, and capability of stimulating interest) are bolstered by a sensitivity and openness to students, individually and as a group ("sensitivity to class progress"), and, to a lesser extent, by some course organization and class management skills. This portrait is corroborated again and again in individual studies of classroom practices. Thus, Wilson and Gaff (1975) found that a faculty member's scores on indices of "interesting presentation" and "discussion of contemporary issues" (bringing into the classroom issues and concerns directly related to students) as well as frequency of out-of-class faculty-student interaction were the most powerful predictors of the likelihood of their nomination as "outstanding" teachers by their student samples. Thus, too, Ware and Williams (1975, 1977), Elmore and LaPointe (1975), and Elmore and Pohlman (1978) all found faculty "expressiveness" and "warmth" (an important dimension of presentation as well as facilitation) quite independent of course content to be strongly associated with student perceptions of effectiveness.

What are the sources and determinants of this set of "effective" classroom practices? The available evidence permits us to locate them to varying degrees in faculty characteristics—personality, motivational patterns, and career statuses—as well as in the vagaries of the teaching-learning situation.

Personality. Beyond Maslow and Zimmerman's (1956) findings of a high zero-order correlation between their global assessments of faculty psychological health/maladjustment and teaching effectiveness, studies of the personality-teaching interface unmask no strong relationships—with three notable exceptions.[15] Both Usher (1966) and Choy (1969) reported a significantly positive association between overall perceptual orientation scores[16] and global student ratings of teaching effectiveness. Choy reported significant positive associations for all three perceptual dimensions (self, others, teaching task), and Usher reported that it was primarily the "positiveness" with which a faculty member perceived others (that is, students—Feldman's "facilitator" dimension) that was responsible for the fairly strong positive association with teaching effectiveness ratings (zero-order correlations ranging from about 0.40 to 0.55). Nearly a decade later, Sherman and Blackburn (1975) explored the relationship between student ratings of faculty personality on thirty semantic differential scales and their differentiated ratings of teaching effectiveness on two distinctive instruments (one, clearly oriented toward the assessment of the socioemotional climate of the classroom, the other concerned with issues in the organization and management of the course). A factor analysis of the semantic differential ratings yielded the following four personality factors in descending order of importance: intellectual competency, potency (active, energetic, extroverted), pragmatism (predictability, practicality), and amicability (sensitive, accepting, open minded). They collectively accounted for 77 percent of the variance in student ratings. Their two strongest factors, intellectual competency and potency, closely parallel Feldman's (1976) two primary aspects of presentation, interest stimulation and instructor's knowledge; the latter two closely parallel Feldman's facilitation and management factors. Together these exceptions suggest that to the extent faculty personality intrudes into the teaching process, it does so primarily by directly bolstering or undermining desirable classroom practices and behaviors bearing on presentation, facilitation, and to a lesser extent, classroom management.

Motivational Patterns. Wilson and Gaff (1975) reported that a faculty member's nomination by students and colleagues alike as an "outstanding" teacher was closely linked to the personal importance he or she attached to the teaching role: nominees were much more likely to display higher normative commitments to teaching than to research. Moreover, Linsky and Straus (1975) and Delaney (1977) reported a clear curvilinear relationship between years of teaching experience and rated teaching effectiveness. Initially low, ratings increased over the first four years, leveled out and then began to decline after about twelve years. This effectiveness pattern over time precisely parallels the temporal trajectory of faculty interest in teaching uncovered by Baldwin (1979). This near perfect correspondence of interest in teaching with effectiveness over time together with the direct evidence of the determining influence of individual teaching goals on teaching practices suggest that such classroom practices are rooted as well in fundamental values and motivational patterns of individual faculty—as these change over time.

Career Statuses. McDaniel and Feldhusen (1970), King (1971), Gaff and Wilson (1975), Linsky and Straus (1975) and Montenegro (1978) all reported that student ratings significantly increased with faculty rank. Employing differentiated ratings, Linsky and Straus found that the rank effect was primarily a function of the relatively high positive association of rank with instructor's knowledge ($r_o = 0.25$) slightly offset by a small, but statistically significant, negative association with instructor's personalization. This suggests that a faculty member's career stage, insofar as that is associated with subject matter knowledge and, up to a point, with teaching experience, may also influence classroom skills and practices.

Situational Factors: Course Characteristics, Faculty Training, and Student Feedback. Linsky and Straus (1975) reported that upper-division and more advanced courses tended to command slightly higher student ratings, primarily as a result of their positive correlations with instructor's knowledge and course content (r_o ranging from 0.09 to 0.17). Together with McDaniel and Feldhusen (1970), Elmore and Pohlman (1978), and Delaney (1977), they also reported a small negative relationship with class size, primarily insofar as size negatively affects instructor's personalization ($r_o = -0.22$; Linsky and Straus, 1975). Thus, quite beyond the characteristics of individual faculty members, the kind of course taught and the relative size of the course may affect classroom practices.

Delaney (1977) reported that among his sample of beginning assistant professors, in-service instructional development activities bore a small, positive, statistically significant relationship to student ratings (explaining approximately 2.5 percent of the variance in those ratings), whereas preservice training bore none. These results, together with the available evidence on faculty participation in instructional development activities (for example, the work of Francis, Finkelstein, and Stratton [1978] and Young [1976], which suggests that faculty who seek out such improvement opportunities tend to be drawn disproportionately from among those who are already "good") suggest the limited formative influence of instructional development on classroom practices and skills.

The evidence with respect to the effects of providing faculty with student feedback is more mixed. In some studies (Overall and Marsh, 1977), faculty "improved" in some respects at least according to subsequent student ratings; in others (Miller, 1971), they did not. In the majority of studies, whatever discernible improvement may occur is clearly "qualified" (Schultz, 1978). Ratings improve with feedback for female faculty (Pambookian, 1977), or those faculty whose own evaluations of their performance were higher than their students' (Centra, 1973), for moderately, but not for highly, rated faculty (Pambookian, 1974), and for faculty who confer with a measurement and evaluation expert (Aleamoni, 1978).

All of this suggests that the development of those teaching skills and practices that are most effective in the classroom is the result of a complex interaction of institutional norms, individual faculty goals, values, interests, and intellectual competencies as these evolve over the course of an academic career as well as the characteristics of the courses taught. These practices and skills are amenable only at the margin to the influence of student feedback and in-service training.

This complex picture is, however, muddied by evidence that the efficacy of these teaching practices and skills may vary substantially for different groups of students. Feldman (1976), although reporting fairly high consensus among student subgroups in the characteristics they preferred in faculty, uncovered some clear, consistent differences primarily by college class and by academic field. Underclassmen (either freshmen alone or freshmen and sophomores combined) tended to place somewhat more emphasis than upperclassmen on the importance of the instructor's fairness or impartiality as well as on his or her ability to get along with students. Moreover, upperclassmen tended to place somewhat greater value on the organization of the subject matter of the course than on the instructor's enthusiasm for teaching. Students in the natural sciences put relatively more stress on the importance of teachers being able to explain clearly. Together with students majoring in the social sciences, they also placed greater emphasis on the instructor's preparation and organization of the course material. Finally, emphasis on a faculty member's ability to stimulate thought and to be intellectually challenging is more evident in the social sciences, humanities, and fine arts than in other fields.

The picture is further muddied by evidence to suggest that the teaching practices and behaviors we have identified as "effective" or "desirable" may be more related to student ratings than to actual student learning as reflected in student achievement in the courses rated. Schultz (1978), in reviewing validity studies of student rating instruments, found that the relationship between student ratings and student course achievement remained inconclusive and subject to a host of qualifications. If, however, the proximate learning impact of these teaching practices remains unclear, Wilson and Gaff (1975) present data that suggest a clearer ultimate impact on general student intellectual development. In an analysis of faculty identified by students as "influential" on their intellectual development, they found considerable overlap between these nominees and those faculty who had been nominated as "effective" classroom teachers. These faculty differed from their colleagues in the normative importance they attached to teaching undergraduates, the frequency of their extra-classroom student contacts and in one, and only one, aspect of their classroom teaching practices—scores on the "interesting presentation" scale. All of this suggests that while those faculty identified by student rating instruments as effective in the classroom may not necessarily raise student achievement in the specific subject matter content of the course, they may achieve some ultimate, long-term impact on student intellectual development—and do so primarily via their capacity to stimulate student interest in the classroom.[17]

Faculty-Student Interaction outside the Classroom

A faculty member's teaching role typically extends beyond the boundaries of the classroom to include less formal, course- and career-related discussions with students in faculty offices, in the corridor, and perhaps even in the student union; and there is some evidence to suggest that these extra-classroom excursions are at least as powerful as classroom dynamics in their impact on students (Wilson and Gaff, 1975; Pascarella et al. 1978). How does such interaction come to take place? What determines its extent and its nature?

To begin with, it appears that the amount of such contact is shaped by institutional norms. Gaff and Wilson (1975) compared the University of California at Berkeley, on the one hand, with four-year colleges and smaller, less research oriented universities, on the other, and found that the former supported something less than half the rate of student-faculty contact as the latter institutions. Kenen (1974) reported that the proportion of institutional faculty holding the doctorate was negatively associated with the frequency of undergraduate contact. To what can we attribute these interinstitutional differences? To some extent, at least, they would likely appear attributable to variation in faculty characteristics across institutional types. What faculty characteristics? The available evidence suggests that they are not the ones that would be most readily expected. Thus, the incidence of faculty-student contact is not related to faculty orientations toward, and level of involvement in, the life of their discipline. Indeed, those faculty members who saw teaching as a major life satisfaction were no more likely to be high interactors than those who did not (Gaff and Wilson, 1975). Neither is incidence of interaction related to a faculty member's age or rank, their level of tolerance of student activism and permissiveness toward student personal behavior, or general political orientation (Gaff and Wilson, 1975). Thus, it is clearly not the case that younger, more permissive and liberal faculty, who can presumably identify more closely with student concerns, are the high interactors just as they are not the "effective" classroom teachers.

Gaff and Wilson (1975) uncovered three closely interrelated variables that appear to contribute most to variation in frequency of contact with students.

1. Scores on a scale designed to assess faculty beliefs in the intrinsic importance of interaction to the educative process—the incidence of interaction was significantly higher among those faculty who believed strongly in the intrinsic importance of faculty-student interaction to the learning process.
2. Faculty instructional practices, including (a) *classroom participation practices* (the extent to which students are encouraged to play a role in formulating classroom policy and to participate in discussions), (b) *discursive practices* (the extent of faculty openness to diverse points of view and the extent to which discussion of issues beyond course readings are encouraged), and (c) *evaluation practices* (the extent to which faculty prefer grading without a curve and using essay examinations and term papers)—faculty scoring low in these three areas were significantly more likely to be low than high interactors although no significant differences in interaction frequency emerged among high scorers.
3. Sheer physical availability—student contact was significantly higher among those faculty members who consistently kept their office hours and, generally, made themselves available to students.

The predictive power of even this triumverate, however, appeared to depend on the sort of faculty-student contact under consideration. No predictive power whatever was discernible for the two most frequently reported categories of faculty-student interaction by far: course-related matters and advice on academic programs. Indeed, the triumverate's strong predictive power was limited only to the four least frequently reported categories of interaction: career advice, personal counseling, discussion of campus issues, and personal friendship.

What do these findings suggest? First, it would appear that interaction with students related to course work and academic program constitutes something akin to a *requirement* of the academic role, and is, ipso facto, not subject to much fluctuation as a function of faculty personal characteristics. The source of this requirement would appear to reside in a kind of collective professorial unconscious of shared normative conceptions of the academic role. Second, along those dimensions of interaction that can be assumed to be "discretionary" (such as personal counseling and social friendship), frequency of contact appears to be determined largely by a faculty member's own conception of the proper role of interaction in the learning process—an internal standard.[18] It would appear, then, that a faculty member's interaction with students, although broadly sensitive to institutional context, is a function of internal standards of performance no less than are his or her general activity patterns, productivity in research, and teaching practices. The frequency of interaction in those arenas that are normally considered part of the academic role is relatively impervious to the influence of individual faculty characteristics; in those arenas that may be considered more "discretionary," it is the individual's own beliefs about the values of such interaction and the behaviors associated with these beliefs that are crucial.

This "intrinsic" explanation of faculty-student interaction is bolstered by Gamson's (1966, 1967) study of natural and social scientists at a small, general education college within a large state university. Gamson found that the two disciplinary groupings were differentiated by their distinctive normative orientations to education, including differing conceptions of students, educational objectives, and norms for student-faculty relations. And indeed, each of these normative orientations was directly translated into a distinctive pattern of interaction. Natural scientists tended to be more task-oriented and less selective in their contacts, focusing on the "average" student; social scientists tended to be more socioemotionally oriented and personalistic in their contacts, focusing on the more "interesting" students.

Additional supportive evidence is provided by Lodahl and Gordon (1972). They compared patterns of interaction with graduate students of faculty from disciplines differing in their level of paradigm development.[19] Faculty in fields characterized by a relatively high level of paradigm development (chemistry and physics) showed significantly lower conflict over time spent with graduate students and exhibited significantly higher willingness to help graduate students in their research than those faculty in fields characterized by a lower level of paradigm development (sociology and political science). Indeed, at elite research institutions, where faculty are most autonomous, the differences proved to be most pronounced. In explaining these findings, Lodahl and Gordon suggested that the higher degree of consensus with respect to research priorities and procedures among faculty in more highly "developed" fields facilitates task-related interaction and the conception of graduate students as colleagues. Thus, patterns of faculty-student interaction emerge as an intrinsic consequence of the nature of disciplinary tasks; and, where faculty are freest to do as they please—at elite universities— these intrinsic consequences assert themselves even more powerfully.

While the "intrinsic" explanation of faculty-student interaction may by itself account for the largest part of available findings, it is clearly only a partial explanation. Gaff and Wilson (1975) reported that although frequency of interaction was closely tied to a belief in its value for the sample as a whole, nearly a quarter of the "true believers" showed a low proclivity for student contact, while just over a quarter of the "nonbelievers" showed a high level of interaction. Moreover, while classroom teaching practices were strongly associated with frequency of interaction, it is only among *low* scorers on the three teaching practice scales that large significant differences emerge; high scorers on the three scales were just as likely to be low interactors as high interactors. This suggests that the interrelationships may not be strictly linear ones and that other determining influences may be at work.

What are some of these other determining influences? Bloom and Freedman (1973) suggested that a professor's stage of intellectual development along the continuum from absolutism to relativism, conceptualized by Perry (1970), affects his or her openness to new ideas and responsiveness to student diversity. Gaff and Wilson (1975) themselves suggested, on the basis of a separate analysis of student samples, that student characteristics, and more particularly their relative congruence with faculty characteristics, may powerfully influence the pattern and frequency of interaction. They found that students who reported frequent interaction with faculty tended to take greater initiative in the pursuit of their education, and tended to resemble more closely their teachers in interests, attitudes, and behavior patterns (they enjoyed writing papers and reading books for pleasure, had strong cultural interests, and indeed often expressed a desire to ultimately enter the professoriate).

In sum, the teaching role is shaped at least to some extent by institutional context; different kinds of institutions have different norms for classroom practices and faculty-student contact outside the classroom. University faculty tend to be more subject matter centered in their approach and interact less with students than faculty at four-year institutions. Within those broadly conceived norms, individual faculty personality and motivation—a function of interest and values as these evolve over the course of the academic career—permit considerable variation in actual classroom and extra-classroom practices and behaviors. The most critical teaching-related practices seem to involve a faculty member's ability to stimulate student interest and, to a lesser extent, to serve as a facilitator and classroom manager. The relative efficacy of such behaviors would, however, appear to depend on a number of situational factors, such as course characteristics, as well as on their degree of congruence with student characteristics and expectations. While such behaviors may not necessarily result directly in increased student academic achievement in a particular course, they may, nonetheless, be ultimately critical as a stimulus to general student intellectual development.

THE INTERRELATIONSHIP OF RESEARCH AND TEACHING PERFORMANCE

The inherent compatibility/incompatibility of the research and teaching roles we have just examined has been hotly debated ever since the advent of academic professionalization in the latter half of the nineteenth century. Can a single individual perform both well? To what extent, and in what ways, are the two mutually supportive or mutually exclusive? While the question tends to be raised most frequently in those settings that have historically emphasized both functions in the faculty role—the research universities—it is no less germane to the work of contemporary teaching-oriented institutions. Insofar as these latter have come to emphasize increasingly faculty research activity and publication (Blackburn et al., 1980; Michalak and Friedrich, 1981; Minter and Bowen, 1982), it has become critical to determine how this emphasis may enhance or detract from their historic mission.

While the debate has been pursued for the most part at the hortatory level, a discernible line of empirical inquiry has emerged that is founded on at least five conceptually distinct, if latent, hypotheses (Harry and Goldner, 1972). Two of these latent hypotheses assume an intrinsically positive relationship between research productivity and teaching effectiveness:

1. Faculty who are productive researchers keep abreast of the latest developments in their field and therefore are likely to display a higher degree of interest and expertise in their subject—this makes them better teachers.
2. Both research productivity and teaching effectiveness reflect a general ability factor—therefore, good researchers tend to be good teachers and vice versa.

Two of these latent hypotheses assume an intrinsically negative interrelationship, although they represent very different lines of reasoning:

3. Faculty who are productive in research tend to spend more time in research and concomitantly less time in teaching—this lesser amount of time and effort expended presumably results in poorer quality teaching.
4. Researchers and teachers are different sorts of people—teaching effectiveness may depend on personality attributes that are inversely correlated with those associated with high research productivity.

The final latent hypothesis assumes no interrelationship whatever:

5. Research productivity and teaching effectiveness are totally independent traits and are randomly distributed throughout the population.

Insofar as these hypotheses have latently structured both the debate and subsequent empirical inquiry, it will be instructive to assess the available evidence in terms of the relative support/nonsupport provided for each.

Table 5.5 presents the outcomes of 147 tests of the relationship of research and teaching performance across eight discrete studies (Wilson, 1943; Maslow and Zimmerman, 1956; Voeks, 1962; Bresler, 1968; McDaniel and Feldhusen, 1970; Hayes, 1971; Harry and Goldner, 1972; Linsky and Straus, 1975).[20] Examining the totals, we find that fully 70 percent of the tests proved statistically nonsignificant; only 30 percent of the tests achieved statistical significance, with positive outcomes outpacing negative outcomes by a 2 to 1 ratio. And even among the 30 percent of the tests achieving statistical significance, the relationship is generally small and of limited

TABLE 5.5
PATTERNS OF ASSOCIATION BETWEEN RESEARCH ACTIVITY AND
TEACHING EFFECTIVENESS

Measure(s) of Research Activity	Number of Tests	Nonsignificant (percent)	Significantly Positive (percent)	Significantly Negative (percent)
		Global Colleague Ratings		
Quantity of publication	1	100.0		
Colleague ratings	2	50.0	50.0	
Chairperson rating	1		100.0	
All	4	50.0	50.0	
		Global Student Ratings		
Quantity of publication	49	77.6	16.3	6.1
Quality of publication[a]	2	100.0		
Quantity and quality of publication	1	100.0		
Colleague ratings	1		100.0	
Chairperson rating	1	100.0		
Receipt of research support	2	100.0		
Time spent in research	1	100.0		
All	57	78.9	15.8	5.3
		Differentiated Student Ratings		
Quantity of publication	76	67.1	22.4	10.5
Quality of publication[a]	10	50.0	10.0	40.0
All	86	65.1	20.9	14.0

[a] Assessed by index of citations to published work.

practical significance (over one-half of the statistically significant tests emerging from a single, large sample study wherein zero order correlations below 0.10 could attain statistical significance).

On the basis of these "total" votes cast, it would appear that research productivity and teaching effectiveness are, for the most part, rather independent traits. In those cases where some relationship is uncovered, it is uniformly small.[21] But a closer look at Table 5.5 discloses two interesting patterns meriting further examination: the distribution of test outcomes varies both by measure of teaching effectiveness and by measure of research productivity employed.

An examination of test outcomes by measure of teaching effectiveness reveals the following:

1. Among those studies employing global student ratings, nearly four-fifths of all tests of the relationship proved nonsignificant.
2. Among those studies employing differentiated student ratings, not quite two-thirds of the tests proved nonsignificant.
3. Among those studies employing global colleague ratings, tests

are evenly split between significant and nonsignificant outcomes.

How can these differences be accounted for? In the case of global colleague ratings, at least two possible explanations suggest themselves: (1) In judging their colleagues' classroom performance, faculty may simply take "research-related" criteria into consideration (see Wilson and Gaff, 1975, for supporting data); teaching effectiveness may, thus, be in the eye of the beholder. (2) Since three of the four tests conducted with global colleague ratings of teaching effectiveness also employ global colleague ratings in the assessment of research productivity, some kind of "halo effect" may be operating, wherein both judgments reflect a single general ability factor.

That differentiated student ratings were more likely than global ones to yield statistically significant outcomes suggests that some dimensions of teaching effectiveness explicitly tapped in differentiated instruments may be related to research productivity, but that their impact is masked in global ratings; and an item analysis lends some credibility to this hypothesis. Across the differentiated rating instruments employed in three studies, at least two types of items can be discerned: (1) those items directly related to the instructor's subject matter knowledge and intellectual competence (for example, ratings of course content and instructor's knowledge) and (2) those directly related to socioemotional aspects of the learning situation (for example, ratings of the instructor's "personalization," accessibility, ability to motivate students).[22] If we then separately examine the distribution of test outcomes for each of the two dimensions of teaching effectiveness reflected in the item clusters identified above, a suggestive pattern emerges. In two of three studies, the vast majority of tests of the relationship of research productivity to the socioemotional dimension of teaching effectiveness prove nonsignificant, whereas the vast majority of tests of the relationship of research productivity to the intellectual competence dimension of teaching effectiveness are significantly positive, if low (with zero-order correlations ranging from 0.20 to 0.30). In one of three studies, the majority of tests on the rapport-socioemotional dimension are significantly negative, whereas the majority on the intellectual competence dimension are nonsignificant (McDaniel and Feldhusen, 1970).

Of the three studies, Linsky and Straus (1975) is the only multi-institutional study—they sampled student ratings of thousands of faculty members at sixteen colleges and universities. And it is the results of their study, displayed in Table 5.6, that reveal the starkest differences in the distribution of test outcomes by dimension of teaching effectiveness. Harry and Goldner (1972) lend added support to Linsky and Straus. Their factor analysis of the Wayne State student rating instrument showed that while the number of hours faculty spent in research weekly loaded nearly zero on the socioemotional/rapport factor, it loaded very highly on the intellectual competence/rigor factor.[23] It seems reasonable to adduce, then, that while research productivity is relatively unrelated to the socioemotional/rapport component of teaching effectiveness, it bears a small, consistently positive relationship to the intellectual competence/rigor dimension of teaching effectiveness.

If we now return to Table 5.5 and examine the separate distribution of test outcomes for each measure of research productivity employed, we find again a suggestive, if less clear, pattern. In the first place, research activity per se as reflected in time spent in research and receipt of research support appears to bear no relationship to teaching effectiveness, however measured. It is rather publication activity per se that bears whatever relationship to teaching effectiveness there may be, and the findings presented in Tables 5.7 and 5.8 specifically suggest that it is the form or quality of publication that makes the difference. Linsky and Straus (1975) found that the number of total publications was considerably more likely to bear a statistically significant relationship to teaching effectiveness (a modest, positive one) than the number of edited or coauthored books, or the number of articles published. Moreover, the quality of one's publications (as assessed by their frequency of citation) was considerably more likely than any other publication measure to

TABLE 5.6

RELATIONSHIP OF RESEARCH PRODUCTIVITY TO TWO DIMENSIONS OF
TEACHING EFFECTIVENESS

Dimension(s) of Teaching Effectiveness	Number of Tests	Nonsignificant (percent)	Significantly Positive (percent)	Significantly Negative (percent)
Rapport/empathy[a]	12	75.0	8.3	16.7
Intellectual competence[b]	12	25.0	75.0	0
All[c]	72	65.3	27.8	6.9

SOURCE: Based on data from Linsky and Straus (1975).

[a]Includes two items: "instructor's personalization" and "motivates students."

[b]Includes two items: "course content" and "instructor's knowledge."

[c]Includes all twelve items.

TABLE 5.7
ASSOCIATION OF TYPE(S) OF PUBLICATION ACTIVITY
AND TEACHING EFFECTIVENESS

Publication Measure(s)	Number of Tests	Nonsignificant (percent)	Significantly Positive (percent)	Significantly Negative (percent)
Total publications	12	58.3	41.6	0
Articles	12	75.0	25.0	0
Edited books	12	75.0	25.0	0
Joint books	12	83.3	8.3	8.3
Solo books	12	41.6	58.3	0
Citations (quality)	12	58.3	8.3	33.3
All	72	65.3	27.8	6.9

SOURCE: Based on data from Linsky and Straus (1975).

yield a significantly negative relationship to teaching effectiveness. If McDaniel and Feldhusen's (1970) findings are not precisely comparable to Linsky and Straus's, they do report considerably stronger relationships. Individual authorship of books and first authorship of articles, papers, or reports bore a strong negative association with global ratings of teaching effectiveness, whereas second authorship of articles, papers, or reports proved a fairly strong and positive predictor of global teaching effectiveness ratings.

What characteristics are associated with producing frequently cit-

TABLE 5.8
ASSOCIATION OF TYPE(S) OF RESEARCH/PUBLICATION ACTIVITY
AND TEACHING EFFECTIVENESS

Research/ Publication Measure	Number of Tests	Nonsignificant (percent)	Significantly Positive (percent)	Significantly Negative (percent)
Books	20	80.0	0	20.0
Articles, first author	2	50.0	0	50.0
Articles, second author	2	100.0	0	0
Reports, first author	2	50.0	0	50.0
Reports, second author	2	0	100.0	0
Receipt of research grant(s)	18	100.0	0	0
All	46	60.9	4.3	13.0

SOURCE: Based on data from McDaniel and Feldhusen (1970).

ed works that have a negative bearing upon teaching effectiveness ratings? What differences are associated with first versus second authorship that would explain diametrically opposed teaching effectiveness outcomes? Neither investigator offers any explanation, nor do any emerge from patterns in the findings themselves. If the "why" remains indeterminant, the findings nonetheless forcefully suggest that research productivity cannot be considered a unidimensional construct. Research activity is distinguishable from publication activity in its implications for teaching effectiveness; and, indeed, the very form that publication activity takes (presumably, some unknown faculty characteristics associated with the predilection for one form over another) may have a not inconsiderable impact on ratings of teaching effectiveness.

With the presentation of evidence now complete, what can we say about the mutual supportiveness/incompatibility of research and teaching activities? What status does the evidence accord the five latent hypotheses that have undergirded the debate? In the first place, the proposition of the total independence of research productivity and teaching effectiveness appears not quite on the mark. To the extent that judgments of teaching effectiveness are based largely on its intellectual competence dimension (and this appears to be the preferred criterion of faculty), then research productivity and the expertise that it engenders or the general ability that it signals does bear a fairly small, but consistently positive, relationship to good teaching. To the extent that judgments of teaching are based on socioemotional aspects of the learning situation (and students appear more disposed to this criterion), then the expertise developed via research activity appears a largely irrelevant factor. That good research is both a necessary and sufficient condition for good teaching, then, is not resoundingly supported by the evidence. Resoundingly disconfirmed, however, is the notion that research involvement detracts from good teaching by channeling professorial time and effort away from the classroom. Harry and Goldner (1972) found that the extra time faculty devote to research activity tends to be taken from their leisure and family activities and not from their teaching. Indeed, they report that the time a faculty member devotes to research is positively associated with the intellectual competence dimension of teaching effectiveness and not associated with the socioemotional component one way or the other. Similar findings are reported by McDaniel and Feldhusen (1970).

No direct evidence is provided by these studies bearing on the proposition that researchers and teachers are different sorts of people, that quality performance in each area hinges upon a distinctive set of personality attributes. The available evidence on the role of certain faculty personality characteristics in bolstering effective classroom behaviors as well as the limited data available on the personalities of eminent scientists (Roe, 1951a, 1951b, 1953) would tend to lend, if indirectly, some credence to this proposition.

ADMINISTRATION AND EXTRA-INSTITUTIONAL SERVICE

Beyond their research and teaching roles, we know very little about faculty performance in their administrative or extra-institutional professional service (to the discipline and the community at large) capacities. The near complete inattention to faculty as administrators comes despite evidence that nearly one-third of American academics as of 1973 had served as department chairpersons (Bayer, 1973) and that faculty tend to a somewhat distinctive "interpersonal" as opposed to "organizational" orientation to academic management—at least in their own departments (Gardner, 1971). And the near complete inattention to faculty as participants in the life of their disciplines comes despite evidence of the increasing "democratization" of professional and scholarly associations (the opening of participation to women, minorities, and younger scholars) and the increasing emphasis being placed by even the historically teaching-oriented institutions on participation in disciplinary life (Blackburn et al., 1980; Minter and Bowen, 1982).[24]

One dimension of such extra-institutional service, has, however, of late received a modicum of sustained empirical attention—the consulting role, and this is primarily in the wake of recent public outcries over the highly publicized abuses of some very active and absent consultants at public universities. What have we learned about the consulting role? In the first place, we have learned that three out of five American academics engage in some form of conslting (paid or unpaid) during a typical work year (Marver and Patton, 1976; Patton and Marver, 1979). Second, consulting constitutes the primary or secondary (to extra teaching) source of supplementary income for not quite one out of three American academics; about two out of three faculty consultants are paid (Marver and Patton, 1976). Third, although a significant segment of the professoriate engages in consulting and derives significant supplementary income therefrom, only about one out of five faculty devotes more than a half day and only about one out of twenty faculty devotes more than one full day per week to consultation activities. Thus, while consulting activity may be pervasive, it is a preemptive activity for only a minuscule segment of faculty.[25]

Who are the consultants? The available evidence suggests, not surprisingly, that the more productive, politically conservative (Lanning and Blackburn, 1979), higher ranking faculty in professional fields, such as medicine, law, and business (Marver and Patton, 1976; Lanning and Blackburn, 1979), tend to be most involved. Moreover, it appears that who is involved varies by the nature of the assignment. Paid consultants tend to come disproportionately from the universities, and nonpaid consultants tend to come disproportionately from the four-year and two-year college sector (Bayer, 1973; Patton and Marver, 1979). The most prestigious consulting assignments—those offered by the federal government, national corporations, and foundations—tend to draw on faculty at the prestigious research universities, and faculty in the four-year and two-year sector are more likely to serve local business and government (Parsons and Platt, 1968; Patton and Marver, 1979).

How is consulting reconciled with teaching, research, and other institutional obligations? The available evidence suggests that, overall, quite well. When compared with their noninvolved peers, faculty engaged in consulting teach as much (Marver and Patton, 1976; Patton and Marver, 1979), are as involved (Patton and Marver, 1979) or more involved and influential (Marver and Patton, 1976; Lanning and Blackburn, 1979) in departmental and institutional governance, publish more (Marver and Patton, 1976; Lanning and Blackburn, 1979; Patton and Marver, 1979), and are more involved in disciplinary networks (Lanning and Blackburn, 1979). Moreover, institutional activity level appears to differ little between paid and nonpaid consultants (Patton and Marver, 1979). It does, however, appear to differ to some degree by extent of consulting activity. Lanning and Blackburn (1979) found that their most active consultants (about 5 percent of the population) were significantly less active and involved in the affairs of their institutions. They provide no data on teaching activity, but their findings do raise the possibility that beyond a certain threshold, a high level of consulting activity may be associated with lower levels of institutional activity.[26] Within that threshold, however, the evidence clearly suggests that like the productive researcher, the faculty member who engages in consulting does so *not* at the expense of other parts of their role, but tends rather to do more of everything than nonconsultant colleagues. For the moderately active consultant, at least, consulting appears to be an integral part of academic role obligations

(Parsons and Platt, 1968) as well as a source of supplementary income.[27]

FACULTY ADAPTABILITY IN THE WORK ROLE

An institution's capacity to adapt to changing conditions has come to be recognized as perhaps the key element in institutional survival and even prosperity amid the fiscal and enrollment uncertainties of the 1970s and 1980s (Stadtman, 1980). While a large number of factors shape such adaptive capacity, perhaps none is more critical than the adaptive capacity of the faculty—as individuals and as a collectivity (Freedman et al., 1979). How do faculty respond to changing students, changing instructional demands, and new kinds of programs? What shapes their attitudinal support for, and actual decision to participate in, new and different institutional initiatives?

Attitudinal Support

Faculty who are attitudinally receptive to curricular change appear to be distinguishable from their more resistent colleagues on a rather general "change orientation" factor. This factor is reflected most broadly at the level of personality in a higher degree of open mindedness (Kazlow, 1977) and flexibility (Evans and Leepman, 1968) and a lower degree of dogmatism (Kazlow, 1977). More concretely, it is reflected at the level of daily work activities in a general orientation to students and teaching. Both Wilson and Gaff's (1975) supporters of curricular change and Evans and Leepman's (1968) supporters of instructional television appeared to share a common concern for pedagogy, the quality of the students' learning experience, and a disinclination toward traditional lecture approaches.

While such a general factor may be operative to varying degrees, its practical significance is circumscribed by the available evidence that faculty receptivity/resistance tends to be innovation-specific. Kazlow (1977) found no significant intercorrelation among levels of faculty receptivity to four distinctive innovations being proposed at a private urban university; and indeed, she uncovered significant differences in the strongest predictors of receptivity across the various proposed innovations. And the importance of this specificity factor would appear to explain why, beyond their similar student-centered approach, Gaff and Wilson's supporters of general curricular change differed so strikingly on a number of other dimensions from Evans and Leepman's proponents of instructional television.[28]

It would appear, then, that quite beyond any general receptivity factor, faculty tend to evaluate an individual change or innovation, curricular or otherwise, on multiple dimensions—its feasibility and desirability in their own field (Johnson, 1978), their familiarity with it (Johnson, 1978), and how it is likely to affect their organizational status (Kazlow, 1977)—and to reserve their support for those changes that pass their own idiosyncratic muster.

Actual Participation in Innovation

If attitudinal receptivity appears to hinge on innovation-specific professional considerations, two related questions yet remain: Does the formative power of such innovation-specific considerations extend to actual faculty participation (as opposed to mere attitudinal support) and how does it compare to the formative influence of institutional incentives or pressures for a particular change?

Four recent studies examine the impact of institutional pressure and support versus individual factors (that is, how faculty feel about participation in change) on actual faculty participation in particular innovations, ranging from adoption of instructional television (Kintsfather, 1977; Ittelson, 1978) to implementation of a new university calendar (Dykes, 1978) and general participation in faculty development activities (Young, 1976; Dykes, 1978). Across all four studies, individual factors—specifically, how faculty felt about participation in the change—emerge as the single best predictor of participation. And indeed, with the exception of Dykes (1978), organizational factors proved relatively impotent.[29] Thus, Young (1976) reported that the "perceived need to improve" explained 15 percent of the variance in the decision of Michigan State University faculty to participate in instructional development compared to the 1 percent explained by "institutional support and rewards." Ittelson (1978) found that faculty "confidence" in the instructional media office (their perception of availability, reliability, and convenience) was significantly more important than institutional encouragement in their deployment decisions. And Dykes (1978) found that, overall, individual incentives accounted for nearly one-third of the variance in faculty participation in the implementation of a new university calendar. And the preeminence of this internal standard is further corroborated by Kozma's study of the adoption and diffusion of innovations among faculty fellows and instructional-grant recepients at the University of Michigan. While the faculty fellows themselves increased their use of innovative instructional techniques at the end of their fellowship year, they were not very successful at diffusion.

Despite their discussions of innovative instructional techniques with many department and campus colleagues, few who were not already interested in such developments adopted them (Kozma, 1978).

There is some evidence to suggest, however, that the relative influence of both organizational and individual incentives are subject to situational pressures. Specifically, Dykes (1978) found the influence of organizational incentives on participation significantly greater for those faculty whose departments were "under the gun," that is, experiencing losses in students and increased student credit hour costs. Thus, while individual professional incentives remain paramount, faculty whose departments were most vulnerable proved most susceptible to organizational pressures.

It would appear, then, that like other performance parameters, faculty participation in innovation is a function of an internal standard—how such participation squares with personal and professional needs—rather than organizational pressures and incentives. Organizational factors may, however, increase their potency to the extent that faculty find themselves "organizationally vulnerable."

FACULTY AS ACADEMIC CITIZENS

Beyond their teaching, research, and consulting, faculty typically are called upon to play some sort of service role in the governance of their academic unit (departments, divisions, or schools/colleges) and of their institution as a whole. Such citizenship duties typically take the form of service on committees or other more inclusive decision-making bodies. While everyone serves at one time or another, both the extent and nature of faculty involvement vary considerably as a function of institutional norms, faculty characteristics (such as institutional and disciplinary status) as well as situational factors. And it is here that the dynamics of "academic politics" most clearly intrude into the work life of the professor.

The Faculty Role in the Governance of Academic Units

The academic department typically represents the most immediate point of contact between the individual professor and the organization that employs him or her. Moreover, it represents the nexus where the organizational and disciplinary professional lives of the typical faculty member meet. Academic citizenship begins here, and academic politics take shape most fundamentally in the give and take among professors and between professors and the head of their academic unit. What sort of dynamics characterize departmental governance processes?

In their efforts to examine the nature of influence exchange between departmental faculty and their chairperson, both Parsons and Platt (1968) and Cope (1972) asked faculty to rank five sources of power as most ("1") to least ("5") descriptive of the bases for their influence on their department chairperson and for the chairperson's influence on them. The aggregate rankings of the five bases of influence that emerged in each study are presented in Table 5.9.

What do the aggregate rankings suggest? In the first place, both faculty and chairpersons appear disinclined to wield their influence by the threat of sanctions (coercive power) or by holding out the proverbial "carrot" (reward power). Rather, influence tends to be exercised and accepted by both faculty and chairpersons on the basis of the perceived expertise and legitimacy of, as well as respect for, the influencer. Faculty, however, appear to differentiate between the primary basis for their influence on the department chairperson and the primary basis for the chairperson's influence on them. Above all else, faculty influence their chairperson by virtue of their *right* to do so and only secondarily by virtue of their expertise, or the

TABLE 5.9

RANKING OF BASES OF INFLUENCE EXCHANGE BETWEEN FACULTY AND DEPARTMENT CHAIRPERSONS

Case	Sample Composition	Sample Size	Referent	Expert	Reward	Coercive	Legitimate
			Chairman→Faculty				
Parsons and Platt (1968)	Arts and sciences faculty at 8 colleges and universities	420	3	1	4/5	4/5	2
Cope (1972)	Social scientists at a state university	71	1	2	4	5	3
			Faculty→Chairman				
Parsons and Platt (1968)	Arts and sciences faculty at 8 colleges and universities	420	3	2	4	5	1
Cope (1972)	Social scientists at a state university	71	2/3	2/3	4	5	1

esteem in which they are held by the chairperson. The chairperson, on the other hand, is perceived to exercise influence over faculty primarily by virtue of his or her expertise or the respect he or she commands, and only secondarily by virtue of a "right" to influence faculty. It is to the faculty, then, that the right to influence belongs first, and this right is accorded to a lesser extent to the department chairperson.

These aggregate rankings, however, conceal systematic variation among some faculty subgroups. Parsons and Platt (1968) reported that as one ascends the institutional prestige hierarchy,[30] faculty show a higher tendency to characterize their influence over the chairperson as a matter of their right, and they more often attribute the chairperson's influence over them to the former's expertise (as opposed to his or her right). And Cope (1972) found that level of departmental stress (impressionistically assessed by the investigator) as well as faculty professional orientations (cosmopolitanism-localism) affected faculty perceptions of the nature of influence exchange. Faculty in stress-laden departments perceived a higher emphasis on reward and coercive bases of influence than their colleagues in nonstressful departments. "Cosmopolitan" faculty placed emphasis on the use of reward and expert power, whereas their institutionally oriented colleagues both perceived and preferred influence exchanges based on respect and legitimacy.

How are we to interpret this subgroup variation? Differences attributable to institutional prestige presumably reflect the higher degree of professional autonomy characteristic of faculty at prestigious institutions. Why stress and professional orientation affect perceptions of influence exchange cannot be accounted for as easily. No explanation is offered by the investigator. Although a number of conjectures seem plausible (for example, stress may function to dissolve collegial relations based on respect and a sense of individual rights and obligations, and thus effectively remove all bases for influence other than reward and coercive power), none can be supported by the data itself. It would seem most reasonable, if not most satisfactory, to conclude simply that the nature of influence exchanges between faculty and department chairpersons is subject to some extent to the influence of institutional and professional characteristics as well as situational factors (for example, departmental stress).

Quite beyond these highly specific issues of interpretation is the more global issue of the internal validity and generalizability that can be attributed to the findings of these studies. At least three problems are posed by studies in the "influence exchange" genre:

1. Owing to the use of respondent rankings, bases of power are not independent—the high ranking of one necessitates the lower ranking of another.
2. No evidence is presented to support the assumption that respondents can clearly differentiate among the five bases of power and, furthermore, that their distinctions correspond to those of the investigator—one individual's "legitimate" power may be another's "referent" power.
3. Faculty perceptions of the bases of influence are "context-free"; that is, they are not elicited with reference to any particular decision or class of decisions—to the extent that faculty influence varies by decision type, we are in no position to assess the generalizability of the findings to various decision areas.

To what extent, then, do the findings as presented and interpreted actually reflect the real departmental situation? To what situations can the findings be generalized? Are they applicable to some decision areas and not to others? Or, are they applicable to no specific decision areas at all, but representative of some sort of "composite"?

The latter issue of generalizability muddies as well the interpretation of Parsons and Platt's (1968) case study of the decision-making process at the departmental level. In the course of their interview survey, the investigators asked faculty respondents to trace the decision-making process involved in the resolution of a particular, yet unnamed, departmental problem from its origin to final settlement. They uncovered systematic variation across institutional prestige strata:

1. *Origin of problem.* At more prestigious institutions, problems were more likely to originate with faculty rather than administrative dissatisfaction.
2. *Initiation of action.* At more prestigious institutions, action was more likely to be initiated by a faculty member than the departmental chairperson or an administrator.
3. *Handling of the problem.* At more prestigious institutions, the problem was more likely to be handled by the entire department or an ad hoc committee constituted therefrom than by the department chairperson or an administrator.
4. *The form of action taken.* At more prestigious institutions, the attempt at resolution was more likely to take the form of departmental committee meetings than administrative rulings.

5. *Uses of committees.* The higher the prestige of the institution, the greater the tendency to make use of departmental committees.
6. *Role of the administration.* The higher the level of institutional prestige, the lower the influence of administrators on problem resolution.
7. *Means of final settlement.* The higher the level of institutional prestige, the more likely that final settlement was achieved by a departmental vote rather than an administrative ruling.

To what types of department-related problems and decision areas can these findings be generalized? That Parsons and Platt request descriptions of problem resolution "from its origin to final settlement" sets a priori limits on the types of problem respondents might select, namely, those more "neatly packaged" problems that have both a clear point of origin and a clear point of solution. It would appear likely that an entire class of problems that might be characterized as either long-term or highly complex are excluded, although particular subproblems within these might be included. Do the solutions of such long-term, complex departmental problems show similar differences across institutional prestige strata?

Beyond Parsons and Platt, Blackburn and Lindquist (1971) provide the only context-specific study of faculty decision-making in action. They unobtrusively observed several faculty meetings over a one-year period at which professors in the school of education voted on a series of motions related to the establishment of a formal structure for student input into policy-making. The investigators were struck by the ebb and flow in the fortunes of the "student power" proposal—at the end of one meeting, approval seemed imminent; by the beginning of the next, victory had turned to defeat. How could these reversals in voting be explained? Neither rank nor department affiliation could account for them. Rather, voting patterns appeared to depend most heavily on political processes, such as:

1. Who stands on which side, and even the last speech before voting (some faculty who initially voted with their chairperson, later changed as everyone fell in line behind the dean)
2. Who attends in the first place
3. Who attends to observe the vote (for example, students)
4. Department unity
5. Whether a counterproposal or amendment is presented (even if defeated, it damages the chances of the original motion).

These findings suggest that when faculty confront a professional situation of general "political" significance, political ideologies and processes are more likely to determine their behavior than either rational argument or academic values, and this nascent hypothesis will gain added confirmation at the institution-wide level.

The Faculty Role in Institutional Governance

Curtis (1972), using data collected for the Stanford Governance Project, identified four modes by which faculty exercise influence at the institution-wide level and conceptualized them as points on a behavioral continuum: inactivity (doing nothing), formalized (regular participation in committees, writing letters, and otherwise seeking to influence administrators), strategic (active work in the American Association of University Professors [AAUP] or faculty unions to influence policy), and militant activity (strikes, picketing, withholding services, and other forms of protest). Although nearly half the faculty sample was inactive, Curtis was able to distinguish broadly between faculty adopters of formalized versus strategic and militant modes on the basis of how they felt about their institution, as reflected in their trust in the administration, their satisfaction with working conditions, and their sense of integration. Faculty who felt positively toward their institution (in terms of trust, satisfaction, and integration) were twice as likely to choose formalized modes of influence, while those faculty who felt negatively about their institution were three times as likely to resort to strategic or militant modes of influence.

Formalized Faculty Influence. Two conclusions can readily be drawn from the half dozen studies that examine formalized faculty influence on their institutions. Among institutional characteristics, type and prestige emerge as the most powerful determinants of variation in faculty influence (Parsons and Platt, 1968; Ecker, 1973; Kenen and Kenen, 1978); and among professional characteristics, rank and tenure status occupy a similar preeminent position (Parsons and Platt, 1968; Ecker, 1973; Gardner, 1971; Kenen and Kenen, 1978; Baldwin, 1979). That faculty at more prestigious institutions and at universities and those at higher ranks exert greater influence on governance seems readily explicable in terms both of organizational theory and of the academic career process. Both Ecker (1973) and Baldridge et al. (1978) have suggested that the greater "expertise" to which "high-powered" faculty lay claim is directly translated into greater professional autonomy, and Parsons and Platt (1968) have argued that the greater commitment of faculty at prestigious institutions to the values of cognitive rationality provides a fund against which influence may be "borrowed." Baldwin (1979) has demonstrated how over the course of career development, the professors' teaching and research interests wane and professional energies are increasingly channeled into institutional and disciplinary service. Moreover, it is virtually a commonplace of research on organizations that individuals with higher organizational status and those with greater levels of organizational commitment and loyalty—a function principally of longevity (Razak, 1969; Warriner and Murai, 1973)—tend to wield greater organizational influence. What is noteworthy is that the predictive power of institutional context varies considerably by decision area.[31] In the matter of faculty appointments and promotions, differences among institutional types are most marked; in matters of financial and educational policy, differences are barely discernible.

How can this be explained? It may be that the singular locus of faculty influence reflects the "nature" of their expertise. Since faculty expertise is primarily disciplinary, their claims for autonomy in matters of the evaluation of professional competence (appointments and promotions) may be considered legitimate and go unchallenged; however, insofar as their claims to expertise in fiscal and pedagogical matters is debatable, at the very least, faculty may have been less successful in legitimating their influence vis-à-vis administrators in these areas. The latter component of this hypothesis assumes, of course, that faculty have sought to assert their prerogatives in the fiscal and educational policy areas and have not been highly successful. It may, however, simply be a case of a lack of interest on the part of faculty in promoting those prerogatives. Indeed, Kerr (1963) has suggested that since 1945, American faculty members have tended to eschew serious debate on issues of educational policy, and have rather sought to channel their energies toward influencing faculty appointments. To the extent that faculty influence initiatives actually reflect their interests, then a change may be in the offing. As fiscal policy becomes more closely associated with retrenchment and as student clienteles become less academically oriented and seek closer articulation with the world of work, faculty interest may shift decidedly toward greater control of fiscal and educational matters.

Strategic and Militant Modes of Faculty Influence. The shift in faculty interests is most apparent in the rise of faculty collective bargaining as an alternative to traditional structures of institutional decision-making. By 1981, some 681 campuses, representing more than one-quarter of American academics, had unionized.

Nearly two-thirds of the unionized campuses are two-year institutions, but four-year campuses (predominantly public), owing to their larger size, account for two-thirds of all unionized faculty members (Baldridge et al., 1981). A variety of developments originating beyond the campus—passage by state legislatures of enabling legislation accompanied by recession and inflation in the general economy—have over the past decade furthered that general movement toward unionism, although the momentum may have slowed in the wake of the Supreme Court's 1980 *Yeshiva* decision, identifying faculty at that private campus as "managers" and ineligible to form a union under the National Labor Relations Act (Zirkel, 1981, cited by Baldridge et al., 1981). While these developments provide the *necessary* preconditions for the recent growth and imminent slowdown of unionism, they do not, however, provide a *sufficient* explanation for why any specific institution unionizes or why an individual joins a union. An answer to these questions would appear to lie in three clusters of variables, each of which investigators have advanced as potential explanations of individual and collective faculty behavior.

The first such potential explanation might be labeled the "general political culture/socialization" hypothesis of collective bargaining. It is founded principally on the findings of several multivariate analyses that report general political orientation to be the single most powerful predictor of attitudinal favorability to collective bargaining, after controlling for institutional context and a variety of faculty professional and nonprofessional characteristics (McInnis, 1972; Bryant, 1978; and, most notably, Ladd and Lipset, 1973). It is further supported by at least two additional types of evidence: (1) limited confirmation of the important role of prior political socialization and activity (such as, previous union activity and memberships) in faculty's current collective bargaining activities and (2) broadly based confirmation of the significant difference in support for collective bargaining among disciplinary groupings, with alignment of disciplines on the "favorability continuum" largely corresponding to their alignment on the "liberal-conservative" continuum, thus suggesting that disciplinary differences largely reflect group differences in political orientation.[32]

The second such cluster, consisting largely of demographic variables, has given rise to the not unrelated "class interest" hypothesis of collective bargaining (advanced most notably by Ladd and Lipset, 1973). This hypothesis is based on the relationships between certain demographic characteristics and collective bargaining attitudes.

1. *Age.* Support for collective bargaining was found to decrease significantly with age in six of thirteen studies (Ladd and Lipset, 1973 and 1976, found it to be the second most important predictor).
2. *Institutional type and prestige.* Support for collective bargaining was found by Ladd and Lipset (1973, 1976) to decrease significantly as one ascends the institutional prestige hierarchy and as one moves from community colleges to universities.
3. *Rank and tenure status.* Support for collective bargaining was found to be significantly higher among faculty at the lower ranks in four of eleven studies (Lane, 1967; Wainstock, 1971; Gress, 1976; Ladd and Lipset, 1976) and among untenured faculty in five of eleven studies (Wainstock, 1971; McInnis, 1972; Ladd and Lipset, 1973; Gress, 1976; Riley, 1976).
4. *Research productivity.* More productive faculty were found to be significantly less favorably disposed toward collective bargaining in four of five studies (Ladd and Lipset, 1973; Fox and Blackburn, 1975; Gress, 1976; Ladd and Lipset, 1976).
5. *Salary.* In eight of ten studies, lower salary levels were found to be significantly associated with higher support for collective bargaining (Lane, 1967; McInnis, 1972; Ladd and Lipset, 1973 and 1976; Feuille and Blandin, 1976; Gress, 1976; Plumley, 1978; Townsend, 1978); Ladd and Lipset (1973) and Nixon (1975), however, reported that variation in support seemed less a function of objective salary level than respondents' subjective estimate of salary adequacy.

Ladd and Lipset (1973) suggest that, collectively, these findings support a "class interest" explanation of attitudinal support for collective bargaining. Those faculty from less prestigious institutions with a lower degree of professional autonomy, those who are powerless (young and untenured) and least rewarded are most supportive of collective bargaining. Conversely, those faculty from the most prestigious institutions who boast a high degree of professional autonomy, those who are powerful (older and tenured) and most rewarded—the mandarins of the academic social structure—are least supportive.[33]

The third cluster of predictor variables includes situational factors, both campus specific and those specific to an individual faculty member's job. Among the campus factors examined, faculty-administration relations, and in particular overall faculty influence and involvement in institutional policy-making (Feuille and Blandin, 1976; Plumley, 1978; Kemmerer and Baldridge, 1975; Gress, 1976; Ladd and Lipset, 1976; Neumann, 1979) and trust in administration (Kemmerer and Baldridge, 1975; Curtis, 1972) as well as overall faculty satisfaction with their institution (Ladd and Lipset, 1976; Neumann, 1979; Curtis, 1972) emerged as uniformly highly significant predictors. Among individual job specific factors, salary, teaching/workload (Feuille and Blandin, 1976; Ladd and Lipset, 1976; Plumley, 1978; Townsend, 1978), and overall job satisfaction (Lane, 1967; Eckert and Williams, 1972; Ladd and Lipset, 1976; Plumley, 1978; Neumann, 1979; Kemmerer and Baldridge, 1975) proved nearly uniform predictors of collective bargaining activity.[34] Together, these findings suggest a "situational" theory of collective bargaining. Faculty who feel that they have a voice in their institution, who trust the administration, and who feel relatively satisfied with their own jobs and conditions of employment, are significantly less likely to turn to unionization than those who feel less represented, trusting, and satisfied. Bargaining sentiment on any given campus may, then, change with any concomitant change in administration and faculty sentiment *over time.*

What is the relative power of each of these explanations? In adjudicating their competing claims, one must look to those studies that simultaneously test the predictive power of more than one explanatory hypothesis on faculty unionization attitudes and involvement. In so doing, we find that the "class interest" hypothesis (and the cluster of demographic variables subsumed therein) proved second in importance to general political culture and socialization in all three studies in which the two were simultaneously tested (McInnis, 1972; Ladd and Lipset, 1973; Bryant, 1978)[35] and to situational factors in five of the six studies in which the two were simultaneously tested (Lane, 1967; Feuille and Blandin, 1976; Gress, 1976; Plumley, 1978; Townsend, 1978).[36] Moreover, beyond Ladd and Lipset (1973 and 1976), there has been a spate of recent evidence of the progressively declining discriminating power of intrainstitutional class interests in academic unionization.[37] Virtually all the corroborating evidence on the impact of age, rank, and tenure has come from studies completed in 1975 or earlier (Lane, 1967; Wainstock, 1971; McInnis, 1972; Ladd and Lipset, 1973 and 1976), while virtually all post-1975 studies report no internal age and status cleavages in faculty support patterns for collective bargaining (Galliano, 1977; Plumley, 1978; Bryant, 1978; Townsend, 1978). Kemmerer and Baldridge (1975) noting the same phenomenon in their studies of collective bargaining, suggest that as economic conditions worsen, older, tenured faculty are increasingly turning to collective bargaining to "preserve" their prerogatives and, in effect, joining with their junior colleagues in a common quest for job security. It would appear, then, that as class interests on campus realign themselves, that is, consolidate, faculty collective bargaining activity on any given campus will remain preeminently an expression of the faculty's general political ideology and culture as well as a reaction to the idiosyncratic character of faculty-administrative relations and faculty morale.

Faculty Responses to Student Activism. Very much the same formative influences are at work in shaping the attitudes of faculty toward student activism as in shaping their attitudes toward faculty militancy. In their sophisticated multivariate analysis of faculty response to student disturbances at Columbia, Cole and Adamsons (1969, 1970) found that general political orientation (on a liberal-conservative continuum) distinguished most strongly between supporters and opponents of student demonstrations. Beyond political ideology, considerable support was provided for a "class interest" explanation of attitudinal responses to student activism. Support was concentrated among the powerless (young and untenured), the least rewarded (in terms of salary), and the dissatisfied. Conversely, opposition was greatest among the mandarins of the university social structure (the powerful, older, and tenured), the productive, the most rewarded and satisfied. Moreover, the general prevalence of political over academic values was subject to much the same qualification in the case of "ideal-typical" academics. The most productive scholars who were generally most liberal in political matters placed academic standards above political ones in opposing student demonstrations as a disruption to free inquiry.

Cole and Adamsons, however, go one step further than investigators of collective bargaining attitudes. They sought to determine the extent to which attitudinal support or opposition was directly translated into behavior. They found that while nearly half of the faculty attitudinally opposed the student demonstrations, only one-third actually acted out their opposition by holding regular classes in the midst of the demonstrations. Why the discrepancy between faculty attitudes and behavior? Cole and Adamsons found their answer in the sociopolitical pressures brought to bear on individual faculty members by their departmental colleagues and their friends among the faculty. When social support for an individual's attitude was present in his or her department, 70 percent acted in accord with their attitude; when departmental social support was lacking, less than half did. Colleague friendship ties were even more influential. Radical faculty were more likely to hold regular classes than their most conservative colleagues if their friends on the faculty opposed the student strikes. Thus, not only are faculty attitudinal responses to student activism expressions of political as opposed to academic values, but the likelihood that such attitudes will be "acted out" is conditioned by the same social and political influence processes noted by Blackburn and Lindquist (1971) in their study of the political dynamics of faculty support for a student role in governance at the University of Michigan.

THE STRESSES AND SATISFACTIONS OF ACADEMIC WORK

Job Stress: Its Sources and Consequences

The stresses that faculty experience in their day to day work lives seem to be attributable to at least two analytically distinct sources. In the first place, there is the "structural" stress, that is, the institutionalized fluctuations of circumstance that attend the natural unfolding of the academic career as it has come to be organized. Baldwin (1979) has most fully documented the difficult "valleys" of professorial careers, including those first few years of a faculty member's initial apointment (years of intense on-the-job socialization), the period immediately preceding tenure and promotion decisions, as well as those later periods of new job responsibilities (such as administration) and career reassessment (occasions when failures, disappointments, conspicuous achievements, or new interests cause faculty to question the purpose or direction of their career pursuits). Klapper (1969), Fahrer (1978), and Rice (1980) have confirmed this picture, at least for the young, untenured faculty member. And, as the uncertainty surrounding the career prospects of younger faculty increases and as the mobility prospects for more senior faculty fade, one may expect the incidence of such career related stress to rise.[38]

Added to these career pressures are those that are organizational in character and stem from the number and nature of work demands placed on faculty at any one particular career stage. This organizational stress takes at least two forms:

1. *Placing excessive demands on faculty.* Fahrer (1978) found that the more complex, integrated faculty role at research universities tended to stimulate higher faculty stress levels. Similarly, the increase in faculty responsibilities at institutions in the

process of upgrading themselves (retaining high teaching loads but also insisting for the first time on faculty involvement in research and publication) may produce identical consequences. Thus, Parsons and Platt (1968) reported the highest incidence of role stress among faculty at institutions characterized by high teaching loads and increasing research demands. And Barnard (1971) found faculty bending under the weight of new demands for research and writing at a school of education whose new leadership was seeking to gain for it an international reputation.

2. *Placing incongruent demands on faculty.* Demands on faculty that are incongruent with their individual professional orientations and skills include the application of publication pressures to teaching-oriented faculty, the saddling of research-oriented faculty with a heavy teaching load, and subjecting faculty to increased bureaucratic "red tape" (Fahrer, 1978).

Thus, the sources of stress tend to center on the academic career process, and, at any one point in time, on faculty work load. For novice faculty or faculty at tenure time, the structure of the academic career itself is a major culprit. At any point in time, research demands are the chief culprit for teaching-oriented faculty at research institutions, or for faculty in institutions in the "up-grading" process; teaching demands are the chief culprit for research-oriented faculty at teaching institutions, or for faculty at elite, research universities.

What is it about research demands and teaching demands, respectively, that is stressful? In the case of research demands, it appears that the time squeeze is not the crux of the problem; rather stress ensues when faculty are called upon to display for the first time knowledge and skills that they may never have acquired. In the case of teaching demands, the time squeeze per se apparently emerges as the crucial factor. Morgan (1970) tested the relationship between the incidence of role stress and several different aspects of teaching demands, including the teaching load itself, the size of classes (as that affects the extent of prestructuring of the teaching experience), the amount of student contact involved, and the opportunities available for "naturally" integrating teaching and research via involvement of students in faculty research and teaching courses in one's area of research interests (or, more generally, integrating research topics in course content). He found that none of the "qualitative" aspects of the teaching situation affected the incidence of role stress; rather it was the teaching load itself that was largely responsible.

Indeed, Morgan reported that it was largely differences in teaching load that were reflected in variation among disciplines in the incidence of role stress; natural scientists reported the lowest incidence of role stress, and, by far, the lowest teaching loads (being the prime recepients of released time subsidized by extramural support), while humanists and social scientists reported a significantly higher incidence of role stress and significantly higher teaching loads.

To what can we attribute this ascendancy of teaching load over qualitative aspects of teaching demands? To some extent, it may be an artifact of the definition of the outcome variable. Given a focus on the *incidence* of *time* conflict, it is not surprising that that aspect of teaching that most directly affects the time commitment involved, that is, the teaching load, bears the greatest relationship to the incidence of stress. Although qualitative aspects of the teaching situation may not affect the incidence of time conflict, they may affect the level or intensity of the conflict and faculty attitudes toward the conflict (whether it is accepted as par for the course or is genuinely disruptive of performance). And it may be that these latter variables are more crucial in terms of the potential disruptive effects on academic work. Boyenga (1978) reported that the level of faculty job stress was negatively associated with job satisfaction ($r_o = 0.45$). DeVries (1975) reported that the incidence of role conflict per se affected neither faculty satisfaction nor research productivity. The "intensity" of conflict emerged as the crucial determinant, although it did not affect performance as expected: the highest level of productivity was reported for those faculty exposed to a moderate amount of stress. Clark (1973) and Clark and Blackburn (1973) reported that for a sample of liberal arts college faculty neither the incidence nor even the intensity of role conflict per se was associated with variation in performance. Rather, the impact of stress on performance was mediated by a particular set of personality variables. Those faculty characterized by a high level of anxiety, research orientation, self-esteem, and a low level of flexibility were likely to respond to stress with lower performance, while faculty with the opposite characteristics responded with higher performance. Thus, although the quantity of teaching required may affect the incidence of time stress, it may not directly, or in a linear fashion, affect the intensity of stress or its consequences for faculty performance.

How can stress, and its potentially negative consequences, be offset? Not much can be done about structural stress without changing the structure of the academic career. The incidence of time stress is, however, another story. Investigators provide a consensual response: align work load more closely with faculty orientations and capabilities. Senior faculty, to a larger extent than junior faculty, may have already achieved this; that a lower incidence of role stress is associated with higher rank is presumably a function of the greater control over individual work load by senior faculty as well as less uncertainty over the career process. What can be done for junior faculty? Klapper (1969) reported that institutional efforts to make work load assignment more flexible appeared to reduce the incidence of role stress among a sample of liberal arts college faculty. For research-oriented faculty, this involved granting released time, sabbaticals, and research support; for teaching-oriented faculty, a more flexible reward system. This approach is, of course, to modify the *source* of stress—be it workload, career progression, or institutional environment. Another complementary approach would involve increasing the capability of junior faculty for coping with stress via, for example, exercise or the use of spouse interaction.[39] This would involve "consciousness raising," a kind of personal faculty development.

Sources of Faculty Job Satisfaction

In several respects, job satisfaction may be conveniently viewed as obverse of job stress: more of one is usually associated with less of the other. Thus, Buerer (1967), Clark (1973), and Boyenga (1978) all reported a negative zero-order correlation between job stress level and job satisfaction level (Boyenga reported an r_o as high as -0.45). The sources of job satisfaction, like those of job stress, can be located in the structure of the academic career. Baldwin (1979), for example, found that job satisfaction, although generally increasing over the course of an academic career, did not follow a straight incremental pattern, but rather mirrored predictable career peaks and valleys. It was lowest among novice faculty; highest among imminent retirees; and dipped predictably during periods of rising stress (for example, before tenure).[40]

The organizational sources of faculty job satisfaction are not, however, as clear cut as are those of job stress. Investigators have for the most part sought to locate such satisfaction in administrative influence and leadership[41] and such organizational characteristics as complexity/differentiation (Parsons and Platt, 1968), goal structure (Kratkoski, 1969), and control structure (Oncken, 1971). What have they found?

While the amount of administrative influence is not significantly related to faculty satisfaction with their jobs (Wieland and Bachman, 1966; Bachman, 1968; McCord, 1970), there is some evidence to suggest that how that influence is exercised does matter. Washington (1975) reported higher levels of job satisfaction among faculty who perceived their chairperson's leadership style as above the median on "initiating structure" and "consideration" (the two major dimensions of leadership tapped by the Leader Behavior Description Questionnaire). Wieland and Bachman (1966), McCord (1970), and Cope (1972) all reported small positive associations between faculty job satisfaction and the administrator's use of "expert" and "referent" bases of power and a small negative association between job satisfaction and the administrator's use of the "carrot and stick" (reward and coercive) approach. It should be noted, however, that in those studies differentiating between faculty job satisfaction, on the one hand, and faculty satisfaction with the focal administrator, on the other, the administrative influence-satisfaction linkage proves statistically significant for satisfaction with the administrator but not for overall job satisfaction (Wieland and Bachman, 1966; Bachman, 1968; Coltrin and Glueck, 1977). It would appear, then, that while the amount of administrative influence does not make a difference, how that influence is exercised does; but that difference is a small one (Hill and French, 1967, reported the strongest relationship, with administrative influence accounting for approximately 17 percent of the variance in faculty job satisfaction) *and* is more closely related to satisfaction with the focal administrator himself or herself than to the overall level of job satisfaction.

If the character of administrative leadership contributes only modestly to faculty satisfaction, what about organizational structure? While there is virtually no overlap in the organizational characteristics investigators have examined, no single study presents evidence to suggest that any one or any combination of the organizational characteristics treated account for a substantial proportion of the variance in job satisfaction. Although no doubt of limited practical significance, one consistent and interesting relationship did emerge—that between level of organizational stress and faculty satisfaction. Parsons and Platt (1968) reported faculty job satisfaction to be lowest at emerging institutions in the process of upgrading; their new demands for scholarly productivity remain side by side with heavy teaching loads. Kratcoski (1969) found that among a sample of Catholic institutions, faculty job satisfaction was lowest at those in the process of transition from a more traditional to a more professional orientation. And finally, Cope (1972) found that a high level of stress at the departmental level was associated with lower levels of faculty job satisfaction.

Given the modest explanatory power of administrative leadership style and organizational structure, there remains, beyond the influence of career structure, a large amount of residual variation in faculty job satisfaction yet to be accounted for. Is there some key independent variable that can make an inroad into this unexplained variance? The available evidence suggests that factors intrinsic to academic work itself (that is, the tasks performed and the most direct conditions of work) can serve this function. Cares and Blackburn (1978) and Levine (1978) reported that faculty perceptions of their control over the work environment were highly related to satisfaction with their work and their career. The higher the sense of an internal locus of control (professional autonomy), the higher the satisfaction. Among that small group of studies that consider both intrinsic and extrinsic factors in relation to faculty job satisfaction, the former uniformly emerge as much more important (Stecklein and Eckert, 1958; Whitlock, 1965; Swierenga, 1970; Avakian, 1971; Eckert and Williams, 1972; Leon, 1973; Moxley, 1977; Willie and Stecklein, 1982). The absence of multivariate analysis precludes any precise specification of the magnitude of impact of intrinsic, job related factors, but it appears that their relative significance vis-à-vis extrinsic ones is most certainly higher.

Although a considerable body of evidence suggests that intrinsic, work related factors may be the most important determinants of job satisfaction, some further evidence suggests that the extrinsic factors examined earlier may be more important determinants of job *dis*satisfaction. Eckert and Williams (1972) and Willie and Stecklein (1982) reported that while tasks performed and the conditions of work contributed most heavily to job satisfaction, extrinsic factors such as salary and relations with administrators were among the most important determinants of job dissatisfaction. Theophilus (1967) reported the curious finding that while faculty did not find "material" incentives nearly as important as intrinsic, task related incentives to their job satisfaction, they expressed considerably more dissatisfaction with them. These findings, together with those reported by Swierenga (1970), Avakian (1971), and Leon (1973), suggest that satisfaction/dissatisfaction may not be a unidimensional construct, but may rather exist as two separate continua, subject to unique sets of determinants (roughly equivalent to Herzberg's (1959) "Hygiene"—job context—and "Motivator"—job content factors). And, indeed, Moxley's (1977) exploratory study of faculty in one professional area, higher education administration, largely confirms this distinction. If this were so, then it might explain the depressed zero-order correlation between such extrinsic factors as administrative leadership style and organizational structure and job satisfaction/dissatisfaction, measured as a unidimensional construct: the focal independent variables would strongly affect low scores on the satisfaction/dissatisfaction scale but have relatively little impact on high scores.

In sum, it would appear that faculty satisfaction with their work, while broadly shaped by the academic career process, is derived primarily from the nature of the work itself and the relative autonomy with which it is pursued, whereas dissatisfaction tends to center on extrinsic, organizational factors, such as administrative leadership and salary. The primary source of satisfaction, no less than of work motivation, is clearly internal.

Having located the sources of faculty job satisfaction, the question remains of the consequences of job satisfaction/dissatisfaction for faculty performance. While there appears to be no relationship between job satisfaction and productivity in industrial settings (Blackburn, personal communication), the available evidence suggests that in academic settings the relationship is problematic and unclear, at best. Only one study (Glueck and Thorp, 1974) reported an unequivocal, positive relationship between the two variables—and that, based on zero-order correlations with a very special sample of research-oriented faculty in a single state university. The evidence presented by other studies, most notably Ferguson (1960), Clark and Blackburn (1973), and Coltrin and Glueck (1977), suggests that the relationship is mediated by a whole host of situational factors. Thus, Clark (1973) reported that under conditions of high stress, high levels of satisfaction tended to be associated with high levels of performance; under low stress conditions, high levels of performance were associated with lower levels of satisfaction. Ferguson (1960) found that current productivity was associated with higher job satisfaction provided that past productivity had been rewarded (with promotion), but with lower satisfaction if past performance had not been rewarded. Insofar as contemporary concerns with faculty satisfaction and morale proceed from a concern with optimizing faculty productivity and indeed assume a positive satisfaction-productivity linkage, then the further exploration of the performance consequences of faculty job satisfaction demands the highest research priority.

FACULTY PERFORMANCE: SOME RETROSPECTIVE GENERALIZATIONS

What generalizations can be hazarded, in conclusion, about the determinants of faculty performance? In the conduct of their central academic functions, research and teaching, faculty appear to be most influenced by internal standards of professional performance. The translation of these internal standards into performance is not, however, direct, but rather mediated by work load assignment. To the extent that faculty are able to control their work assignment, they are satisfied and their performance appears to mirror their internal professional standards; to the extent that they cannot, stress appears likely to ensue. On the other hand, when in the course of their professional pursuits, faculty encounter situations of general "political" significance, their attitudinal responses are more likely to reflect their political ideology than their internalized academic values. Indeed, the probability of their "acting out" their attitudinal predispositions is conditioned by much the same social and political influence processes characteristic of less educated groups. Among the most productive scholars, however, academic values appear more likely to prevail over social or political ones, whatever the situation (whether it be a question related to the conduct of research or to a campus power struggle). In some quarters, the ideal-typical academic yet lives!

1. This consensus emerges from the two Carnegie Council surveys of faculty in 1969 and 1975 as well as the Ladd and Lipset faculty surveys of 1975 and 1977.

2. The term "research" is used here in its broadest sense to connote any scholarly activity—reading and/or writing—in one's field of specialization. The investigators generating these findings neither specify their own conception of research activity nor that of their respondents; and it would seem reasonable to assume considerable variation—from professional reading in one's field to the more strictly limited conception of research as the conduct and reporting of systematic, empirical inquiry.

3. In the Carnegie classification scheme, *research universities* include the one hundred leading institutions in federal funding for academic science who also awarded at least fifty doctoral degrees in 1973–74. *Doctorate granting universities* awarded at least twenty doctoral degrees in 1973–74. *Comprehensive colleges* and *universities* offer a liberal arts program as well as professional or occupational programs. Many offer the master's degree, but have no or very limited doctorate programs. *Liberal arts colleges* are four-year institutions offering a liberal arts program (Carnegie Council, 1976).

4. With the notable exception of elite liberal arts colleges.

5. Fulton and Trow distinguished among prestige strata on the basis of student selectivity, faculty qualifications, and institutional resources.

6. For faculty devoting less than half their time to administration.

7. This suggests that "self-perception theory" was not operating on Borland's fac-

ulty sample, and by implication, may not have been operating on Hinds's faculty sample.

8. It should be noted, however, that in nonuniversity settings, discipline appears to play something less of a role than career stage in differentiating among faculty activity patterns.

9. In all four studies that simultaneously examined both institutional type and prestige (Blau, 1973; Behymer, 1974; Kenen, 1974; Fulton and Trow, 1974) the latter clearly emerges as the more powerful predictor. Indeed, Fulton and Trow reported that faculty at the most prestigious colleges were at least as productive as faculty at mid-level universities.

10. This precisely reflects the pattern uncovered by Pelz and Andrews (1966) in their study of research scientists in a variety of organizational settings and by Cole (1979) in his study of natural scientists.

11. Lodahl and Gordon attribute this to the higher level of paradigm development in the natural sciences vis-à-vis the humanities and the softer social sciences—that is, their higher degree of consensus on the appropriate directions and methodologies for research—which creates a climate favorable to interaction.

12. The results of these behavioral observations suggests that things have not changed much. Lecturing was still, by far, the dominant mode of instruction at a state college—faculty lectured 83 percent of the time. Classroom teaching emerged as directive, teacher dominated, and heavily involved in low cognitive level thinking processes.

13. Although differing in instrumentation and analytical procedures, the three studies are roughly equivalent in their results. They do differ, however, in the explanation of those results. Wilson and Gaff speculate that disciplinary differences may reflect differences in the truth strategies employed by various fields of study, that is, the degree to which such strategies are highly codified/systematized. Morstain and Smart, on the other hand, see the results as reflecting Holland's theory of vocational choice—different types of personalities self-select themselves to fields consonant with those personality structures.

14. Feldman provides no persuasive explanation of the ascendance of facilitative practices in students' nonstructured descriptions, but one might speculate that insofar as students tend to rely heavily on socioemotional criteria in judging their teachers (see the interrelationship of research and teaching performance below) such predispositions tend to emerge most strongly in nonstructured response situations. This may also account for the relatively lesser import of professors' organizational skills in nonstructured ratings situations. The explanation of some of the few remaining large inconsistencies, such as the much lower ranking of instructor's knowledge in the structured ratings of actual teachers, remains unclear.

15. These studies have tested the association between student ratings and such variables as professor's self-esteem/self-acceptance (Sorey, 1967; King, 1971), degree of self-actualization (King, 1971; Stuntebeck, 1974) and scores on the Guilford-Zimmerman temperament survey, a factor analytic personality inventory (Bendig, 1955; Sorey, 1967).

16. Operationally, a faculty member's perceptual orientation can be defined as the degree of "positiveness" with which he or she perceives himself or herself, students, and the task of teaching.

17. Gaff and Wilson's findings need, however, to be interpreted with caution. The

same sample of students nominated "effective" and "intellectually formative" teachers, raising the possibility that similarities between the two groups may be as much a function of the operation of a "halo" effect (the tendency of students to generalize from classroom effectiveness to intellectual formativeness) as of a true congruence between the behaviors associated with pleasing classroom performance and long-term development impact.

18. Since a faculty member's "beliefs" are logically prior to teaching practices and physical availability, we are assuming that the latter, to a large extent, reflect the former.

19. Level of paradigm development is used in the Kuhnian sense to refer to the degree of consensus among disciplinary practitioners on the over-arching framework as well as the methodologies that guide research.

20. Owing to differences in the number of measures of research productivity employed and the number of dimensions of teaching effectiveness examined, studies vary substantially in the number of actual tests made of the relationship, ranging from one to seventy-two. The findings are thus presented for tests across studies rather than by individual study.

21. It should be noted that the validity of these results are open to question and qualification on at least two counts. First, all but one of the studies draw pure "convenience" samples from among faculty for whom student ratings are available, sometimes further excluding from this group faculty who boast no publications. Moreover, eight of these cases draw their convenience samples from among faculty at a single institution. Thus, the "generalizability" of the findings may be quite limited. Second, the majority of studies employ a single "global" rating of teaching effectiveness by students or colleagues; only three of eight studies employ "differentiated" ratings, all by students. This practice obscures the criteria respondents actually use in making their judgments; and evidence from several studies (Blackburn and Clark, 1975; Centra, 1974) suggests that there is some variation in those criteria. This documented variation in the meanings that can be ascribed to a single global rating of teaching effectiveness (1) renders problematic the interpretation of individual studies, (2) raises the issue of comparability across studies with respect to the dependent variable, teaching effectiveness, and (3) leads the integrator to rely unduly, in matters of interpretation, on the findings of those few studies that employ differentiated ratings, and ipso facto, clues to respondents' bases for judgment.

22. Bendig's (1955) factor analysis of the Purdue rating instrument yielded two factors that correspond precisely to our "eyeball" categorization of items: "competence" and "empathy." Harry and Goldner's (1972) factor analysis of a local teaching evaluation instrument developed at Wayne State University also yielded much the same factor configuration.

23. McDaniel and Feldhusen's (1970) study of seventy-six Purdue faculty members provides the only "discrepant" evidence. There is some question, however, concerning the stability of their findings since their sample size is actually smaller than the number of variables they examined (eight measures of research productivity × twelve measures of teaching effectiveness).

24. Bloland (1982) recently described the social dynamics of status striving and face-saving at convention meetings. Poole (1974) reported no relationship between the faculty member's reference group identification (institutional versus disciplinary) and either the incidence of convention attendance or the nature of faculty participation in convention activities.

25. Although these data are based on the 1969 Carnegie-American Council on Education Faculty Survey, Patton and Marver (1979) reported no significant changes by 1975. No comparable data subsequent to 1975 are available, but there is no basis for assuming any radical changes in these patterns.

26. There is no direct evidence, however, to suggest that these faculty would be more highly involved in institutional affairs if they were not engaged in consulting, or engaged in it to a lesser extent. Indeed, their significantly lower level of satisfaction (at least in matters of salary) vis-à-vis their less active colleagues may signal some broader disenchantment with their positions that is reflected in lower levels of institutional involvement (Lanning and Blackburn, 1979). Or they may simply represent Gouldner's prototypical "cosmopolitans."

27. Indeed, Parsons and Platt reported that among faculty at research-oriented institutions, consulting was highly likely to be "intrinsically" motivated, that is, engaged in as an academic role obligation.

28. Wilson and Gaff found support for broad-gaged change highest among humanists and social scientists, precisely those groups that Evans and Leepman found most opposed to the use of instructional television. Although Wilson and Gaff's supporters reported a significantly higher frequency of interaction with students, it was the *opponents* of instructional television who expressed the greatest concern with student contact. Finally, although the highest level of receptivity to broad-gaged curricular change seemed to reside among the lower professorial ranks, supporters of instructional television were found to have greater teaching experience at a wide variety of institutions.

29. It is not entirely clear why organizational factors emerged as significantly more important here. One possible explanation may lie in the nature of the innovation in question. The introduction of a new academic calendar represents a change that is clearly organizational in scope, although participation may still be a matter of individual discretion.

30. Parsons and Platt actually analyzed their data by "level of institutional differentiation," a composite scale built on three dimensions: institutional size (number of arts and sciences faculty), quality (income per student, percent of doctorate degree holders on faculty, student to faculty ratio), and research orientation (percent of students that are graduates, government dollars per faculty member, and number of library periodicals per faculty member). Since their SID is more highly correlated with Brown's (1967) prestige index ($r = 0.73$) than with quantitative indicators of internal institutional differentiation (that is, number of academic and administrative subunits), it is viewed within the context of our study as a proxy for institutional prestige.

31. The five decision areas examined across studies include general educational policy, financial policy, faculty appointments and promotions, course content, and overall influence.

32. See discussion of professorial politics in chapter 6.

33. That the most productive and well-placed faculty, who in political matters are generally more liberal than their less productive and well placed colleagues, are more resistant to collective bargaining cannot be explained by "class interest" alone. Indeed, Ladd and Lipset found that the opposition of the most productive faculty to collective bargaining was predicated most often upon the perceived threat posed by unionism to their "meritocratic" values. Thus, it would appear that among the "true

believers" (those who represent the ideal type of *homo academicus*), academic standards prevail over more general political values, even in professional contexts that are more political than strictly academic in nature.

34. There does not appear to be any clear pecking order of importance between or within these two subgroups of situational factors.

35. A major exception is, of course, provided by the case of the politically liberal "mandarins" at the prestigious universities (see above).

36. The major exception here is Ladd and Lipset (1976), who while conceding the importance of situational factors, such as teaching load, job satisfaction, and perceptions of influence over institutional policy, nonetheless assert the preeminent power of "class interest."

37. There is no such evidence of the declining salience of interinstitutional class interests, that is, cleavages among types and prestige strata of institutions, or class interests based on faculty disciplinary status, such as research productivity.

38. Beyond this shared structural or career-related stress, married women faculty are subject to the additional stresses of juggling career and family commitments—stresses that tend to be particularly acute early on before a successful modus vivendi has been developed. Thus, it is not surprising that married female faculty reported significantly higher stress levels than either married men or single women (Koester and Clark, 1980).

39. Boyenga (1978) reported that faculty who talked over work-related problems with their spouses showed significantly lower stress levels.

40. Baldwin's findings of a complex, nonlinear relationship between career age and job satisfaction appears to explain why previous studies (Hill and French, 1967; Theophilus, 1967) that assumed linear models report no statistically significant relationship between job satisfaction and such related variables as rank, career age, chronological age, and longevity in current position.

41. Those studies that have treated administrative leadership as an independent variable have sought, by and large, to determine the impact on faculty job satisfaction of (1) the amount of influence wielded by an administrator (be they department chairperson or dean) and (2) the means by which such influence was exercised. Following the conceptualization of French and Raven (1960) five bases of influence are examined: the *threat* of invoking sanctions, the capability of *rewarding* compliance, the perceived *legitimacy* of the influence agent, the *respect* accorded the influence agent, the recognized *expertise* of the influence agent.

6

Beyond the Work Role:
Faculty as People and Citizens

To what extent is the character of academic work reflected in the broader arena of personal life choices and conduct? How central is the academic role in the lives of faculty? Is it merely a job or rather an entire modus vivendi? In exploring these personal and social concomitants of the academic role, this chapter focuses on family life and leisure as well as on faculty participation in the religious, ethnic, and political life of the community in which they live.

FAMILY LIFE AND LEISURE

Most of the available data we have about faculty family life and leisure patterns are nearly two decades old and, strictly speaking, provide us with a portrait of the typical professor circa the early 1960s. What was it like then and in what ways is it likely to have changed or remained the same?

First, with an average work week variously estimated between fifty and sixty hours (Gerstl, 1959, 1971), the typical faculty member was likely to work irregular hours (Lee, 1968) and to spend significant amounts of time working at home, both during the week and on weekends (Gerstl, 1959, 1971; Kistler, 1967). The intrusion of work into home life appeared to vary substantially, however, for faculty in different academic fields. Kistler (1967) found that the extent of "carry-over of work roles into the home" was lowest among faculty in the scientific and technical disciplines, and highest among those in the social sciences and humanities. Lee (1968) confirmed that arts and sciences faculty were more likely than medical school faculty to work irregular hours and to place their work above their families. In thus "bringing their work home with them," the typical faculty member was likely to spend minimal time with their children and minimal time engaged in routine household chores (Gerstl, 1959, 1971; Anderson and Murray, 1967).

Perhaps in no other area was the typical faculty member as distinct from the general population as in patterns of leisure activities. Professors spent minimal time watching television and were quite selective in their viewing habits, largely confining their viewing to news and educational programing—with the exception of late movies and football (Anderson and Murray, 1967). They tended to spend much less time visiting relatives—if for no other reason than geographical distance (Gerstl, 1959, 1971)—and more time socializing with academic colleagues (Parsons and Platt, 1968). Indeed, Parsons and Platt reported that fully 43 percent of their national sample of faculty limited their social friendships to academic colleagues, though not necessarily members of their department.[1] They were likely to tie their vacations, directly or indirectly, to their work, typically by scheduling a vacation to coincide with attendance at a national conference or a sabbatical leave (Gerstl, 1971; Anderson and Murray, 1967). Perhaps most distinctively, they tended to be relatively voracious readers and consumers of high culture. About two-thirds of Anderson and Murray's (1971) faculty sample reported reading as their "favorite" leisure activity, and one-half had read "over twelve" books outside their specialty during the preceding year. Moreover, both Anderson and Murray (1967) and Gerstl (1971) reported that faculty were particularly high consumers of "highbrow" periodicals of criticism and general culture— the *New Yorker, Encounter, New Republic,* the *New York Times*— and tended to eschew the popular media, such as *Reader's Digest* and *Newsweek.*[2] Finally, the typical faculty member supported the arts on a regular basis. About two out of five had attended, in some combination, over twelve concerts, plays, ballets, and museum exhibits in the previous year (Gerstl, 1971).

How generalizable is this portrait of family life and leisure to contemporary faculty—particularly in light of the recent entry into academic ranks of the first generation raised on television, the advent of home computers, the women's movement, and the ascendance of dual-career couples as well as the cult of "personal growth"? Data generated over the past decade suggest that the portrait has, by and large, sustained itself over time. While estimates vary, contemporary faculty still appear to spend between fifty and sixty hours a week in work related activities (Doi, 1974; Shulman, 1980), and there is no evidence to suggest that faculty are any less likely to bring their work home with them. Indeed, Harry and Goldner (1972) reported that university faculty in pursuing their research and writing tended to cut into their evenings and weekends rather than slighting their teaching or other work responsibilities. An approximately equal plurality of professors (40 percent) still continue to limit their social friendships to academic colleagues (Bayer, 1973), and faculty continue to be voracious readers and relatively heavy consumers of high culture. Wilson (1979) cited a publisher's survey undertaken in the early 1970s that found faculty spending an average of twenty-six hours a week engaged in reading—fifteen hours on matters directly related to their specialty and eleven hours on nonprofessional materials. Ladd and Lipset (1976) reported a continued professorial proclivity for "highbrow" periodicals across all types of institutions and across faculty at all levels of scholarly attainment,[3] and approximately one out of every four faculty had attended at least one concert and one play a month during the preceding year; two out of five reported little or no attendance at athletic events (Ladd and Lipset, 1976).

There appears to be only one aspect of family life and leisure that has undergone some demonstrable change over the past two decades: the time faculty spend in household chores. Gappa and Uehling (1979) found that faculty in the late seventies were averaging several times as many hours per week, including weekends, in household chores and child care as faculty two decades earlier, as reported by Gerstl (1959, 1971); and academic women were spending nearly twice as much time as academic men (approximately twenty-eight hours a week on average). This suggests that although the family life of American academics has not changed much over the past two decades (at least as far as the available data tell us), it is significantly different for women, especially married women, than for men. Indeed, Herman and Gyllstrom (1977), Heckman et al. (1977), and Gappa et al. (1979) all found that academic women, even those in purportedly equality-oriented relationships, tend to revert to traditional sex roles in the family, assuming responsibilities for cooking and the household and retaining primary responsibility for parenting. The extra investment of time in household chores leaves them with 40 percent less time for professional work during the weekends (Herman and Gyllstrom, 1977). Thus the centrality of the academic role has tended to shape the nature of faculty family life and leisure activities, and it has done so most directly for academic men; for academic women, its shaping role has been limited in several important respects by the competing influence of sex role socialization.

FACULTY ORIENTATIONS TO RELIGION AND ETHNICITY

Religious and Ethnic Backgrounds

As noted earlier, nearly two out of three American professors are of Protestant origin, drawn disproportionately from those denominations that are more theologically liberal and of higher socioeconomic status, including Presbyterianism, Congregationalism, and Episcopalianism. Jews, constituting only about one-tenth of all faculty, are overrepresented compared to their proportion of the general population (3 percent), and Catholics (18 percent of the professoriate) are modestly underrepresented (27 percent of the general population).[4] Individuals of English origin are represented in the professoriate at nearly twice their concentration in the general population (37 percent versus 20 percent); blacks are underrepresented by a factor of three (3 percent versus 11 percent).

These patterns appear to be attributable to several factors: The impact of social class and discrimination (Ladd and Lipset, 1975e) as well as the impact of patterns of ethnic group migration and cultural values (Steinberg, 1974). Those religious and ethnic groups that have achieved relatively higher average socioeconomic status tend to be overrepresented (Presbyterians, Episcopalians and Congregationalists); those religious and ethnic groups that have historically been the victims of social discrimination (blacks and, until recently, Catholics) tend to be underrepresented. Jews belonged in this latter group until the post–World War II period. Their current overrepresentation seems to reflect the dismantling of discriminatory barriers after World War II and the group's movement upward in socioeconomic status.

These factors seem to account for not only the proportionate presence of religious and ethnic groups in the professoriate, but their level within the academic stratification system as well. Thus, Ladd and Lipset (1975e) found that professors reared in the high status Protestant denominations and those from Jewish families are relatively most numerous in the major research institutions, and their numbers declined sharply with movement down the ladder of institutional prestige. Lower status Protestants and Catholics showed exactly the opposite pattern: Catholics, for example, are twice as likely to be located at the lowest as at the highest prestige institutions.

Steinberg (1974) has reported that religious and ethnic groups are stratified by discipline as well as by institutional location. Protestants tend to be heavily concentrated in the practical sciences with roots in rural America (agriculture, home economics, industrial arts, education, business, earth science, geography); Jews are in fields that (1) are people oriented and concerned with ministering to physical or social ills (clinical psychology, medicine, law, social work) and (2) tend to be abstract and theoretical (physics, biochemistry, mathematics, especially at the major research universities). Catholics are in comparison much more evenly distributed across academic disciplines, although they tend to be overrepresented in the humanities (languages, philosophy, and religion) and in nursing. With few exceptions, these traditional patterns of concentration of religious groups within academic disciplines have not changed markedly over the past several decades nor do there appear to be significant departures in the offing among graduate students planning a career in college teaching.

Quite beyond the "facts" of professorial religious and ethnic affiliations, however, is the question of the meaning of those affiliations within the context of the academic role. Both religious and ethnic ties have at least a potential for conflict with academic obligations—conflict between the institution of religion, on the one hand, rooted as it is in faith and the institution of science, on the other, rooted as it is in skepticism or objectivity (Leuba, 1921); and conflict between the divisiveness of ethnic loyalties, on the one hand, and a shared, overriding interest in ideas and universal truth for its own sake (Gordon, 1964). How do faculty reconcile their background and their professional obligations? How do faculty manage potential conflicts? In addressing these questions, sociologists of religion have focused on three aspects of professors' enactment of their religious and ethnic allegiances in the professional context: (1) degree of religious involvement (religiosity), (2) modes of accommodation between religious and academic values (compartmentalization versus integration), and (3) degree of assimilation into the mainstream of intellectual culture. A consideration of these three aspects follows.

Religiosity[5]

Since the early work of Leuba (1921), sociologists have persistently confirmed that professors, other scientists, and artists are, as a group, significantly less religious than other professionals and the general public at large (Leuba, 1950; Thalheimer, 1965 and 1973; Anderson and Murray, 1971).[6] Most recently, Steinberg reported that one out of five American academics eschew even nominal religious ties (that is, reported no religious affiliation) as compared to only one out of twenty-five American adults; an additional one out of seven retains a nominal religious affiliation while remaining basically indifferent or opposed to religion.[7] These findings have raised a host of related questions. How, for example, can one account for the relative irreligiosity of academics vis-à-vis the general population? To what extent is it attributable to the "secularizing" influence of professional training and academic work or to early religious socialization? Is there substantial variation among academics in their religious involvement? If so, how can this internal diversity be explained?

The available evidence suggests that the relative irreligiosity of faculty is more likely attributable to a process of selection of irreligious individuals to the professoriate (via either self-selection or selective recruitment) rather than to the influence of professional training and academic work. Thalheimer (1963, 1965) examined the timing of changes in religious involvement by asking faculty about their religious affiliation, church attendance, private prayer, and beliefs about the Bible and God during five periods of their lives: childhood, high school, college, graduate school, and the present. He found that while faculty were, by and large, traditional in their early religious beliefs, they underwent a process of "secularization"; and the secularization process was completed for the vast majority during the precollege years, and to a lesser extent, during college. Indeed, change in the postcollege period was relatively infrequent. Following up on these results, Thalheimer specifically asked faculty whether their professional training and their subsequent teaching and research activities were, in any way, responsible for change in their religious involvement. The vast majority of respondents (about 70 percent) reported that academic influences had no effect whatever. Moreover, for that minority contingent who did report being influenced by their professional training and academic work, the *direction* of change was as likely to be toward increased religiosity as toward increased secularization. Thalheimer's findings for this group, presented in Table 6.1, would seem to indicate that insofar as the influence of academic training and work is at all salient, it operates to sustain or reinforce patterns of religious involvement established in earlier years. Current believers tend to be influenced in the direction of increased religiosity, and current nonbelievers tend to be influenced in the direction of decreased religiosity.

Thalheimer's findings, it should be noted, are open to question on two counts. Their internal validity rests on the assumption that respondents' conceptions of their past religiosity, the timing of changes, and the influence agents responsible constitute a fairly

TABLE 6.1
INFLUENCE OF PROFESSIONAL TRAINING AND WORK ON
RELIGIOSITY BY CURRENT RELIGIOUS ORIENTATION

Influence Agent	Percent Made More Religious	Percent Made Less Religious
	Current Believers	
Professional training	21.0	11.0
Professional work (teaching and research)	30.0	6.5
	Current Nonbelievers	
Professional training	4.0	22.0
Professional work (teaching and research)	7.0	14.0

SOURCE: Based on data from Thalheimer (1965).

accurate reconstruction of the actual course of events. Furthermore, their generalizability may be severely limited insofar as the sample of respondents is clearly not fully representative of faculty at the single state university from which it was drawn, let alone the professoriate at large. They do, however, gain added support from three other sources. Parsons and Platt (1968) found that, contrary to their expectations, faculty religious disaffiliation bore no relationship to age and hence to the length of time over which professors were exposed to academic values. Lehman and Shriver (1968) found that differences in early religious socialization accounted for some of the variation in religious involvement that they discovered among disciplinary groupings.

Most conclusively, Hoge and Keeter (1976) undertook a multiple regression analysis of the relative impact of early religious socialization (parent's church attendance, religious training, dogmatism), academic training (highest degree, doctorate prestige), discipline, and professional activities and standing (time spent in research, publication activity, and so forth) on current religiosity of a random sample of university faculty. They found that early religious socialization alone accounted for 28.6 percent of the variance in current religiosity; and, after controlling for such early socialization, all other factors combined (training, discipline, and professional activities) accounted for less than 8 percent of the variance in current religiosity. In light of this corroborating evidence, it seems most reasonable to conclude that (1) the process of secularization is, to a considerable extent, begun and completed in the preprofessional years; (2) change in the period immediately prior to, and after, entrance into the profession is more infrequent, and often in the direction of "reinforcing" already extant religious predispositions; and (3) the unexplained variation between academic and nonacademic groups in religious involvement is more likely attributable to processes of selection to the academic profession than to the influence of professional socialization.

Although professors, as a group, are more likely candidates for secularization than other segments of the population, there is, nonetheless, considerable variation in religious involvement within the academy. What factors contribute to this internal diversity? Steinberg's (1974) secondary analysis of data furnished by the Carnegie-ACE 1969 Faculty Survey suggests that the degree of faculty religious involvement varies across institutional prestige strata and religious groups. As one ascends the institutional prestige hierarchy, religiosity decreases significantly; and Jewish faculty, as a group, show lower religious involvement than their Catholic and Protestant colleagues. Both findings have been attributed to subcultural influences operating on faculty. It is assumed that at more prestigious, research-oriented universities, the canons of science are more fully institutionalized, thus providing more social support for skepticism than for faith. The lower religious involvement of Jews is attributed to the independent strength of Judaism's "cultural" as distinguished from its "religious" component; that is, one may reject the religious tenets and rituals of Judaism and still maintain links to its secularized, cultural heritage (Steinberg, 1974).

Beyond the effects of institutional prestige and religious affiliation, a veritable chorus corroborates the impact of disciplinary affiliation. Table 6.2 presents the distributions of disciplinary groupings across the religiosity continuum reported in five separate investigations. Two sets of observations are suggested by these data. First, there appear to be vast differences in religious involvement between faculty teaching in professional and applied fields and those housed in colleges of arts and sciences—the former, as a group, are significantly more likely to report extensive religious commitment. Second, differences among arts and science faculty are considerably less clear cut. Social scientists, as a group, generally emerge as least religious; the differences between humanists and natural scientists are small, and their position relative to each other varies from study to study. Moreover, in those cases where disciplines within the social sciences and humanities are disaggregated (Lehman and Shriver, 1968; Eaton, 1973), the data show considerable hetero-

TABLE 6.2
RANKING OF DISCIPLINARY GROUPS BY RELIGIOSITY

Rank by Religiosity	Thalheimer (1963)	Lehman and Shriver (1968)	Eaton (1973)	Steinberg (1974)	Wilson and Gaff (1975)
1 (lowest)	Social sciences	Sociology, psychology, English, history, religion	Sociology and psychology	Social sciences	Social sciences
2	Humanities	Education, economics, political science, modern languages, architecture	Biology	Humanities	Natural sciences
3	Natural sciences	Physics, chemistry engineering	History and Modern Languages	Natural sciences	Humanities
4 (highest)	Professional and applied			Applied	Professional and applied

geneity among social scientists and among humanists, suggesting that the sources of diversity are more discipline-specific.

How can this disciplinary diversity be explained? Both Thalheimer (1963) and Steinberg (1974) suggest that the distribution of religious involvement among disciplinary groups can be attributed to variation in the theoretical versus the applied orientation of academic fields—faculty in applied areas are more likely to be religious, and those in the most theoretical areas are less likely to be so.[8] This suggestion clarifies the differences between arts and sciences faculty, on the one hand, and professional school faculty, on the other; it sheds considerably less light, however, on diversity among arts and sciences faculty, in general, and among faculty within a given academic area (such as the social sciences or the humanities), in particular. Addressing themselves to this latter problem, Lehman and Shriver (1968), Eaton (1973), and Lehman (1974) sought an explanation in two characteristics along which academic fields vary: their scientism, that is, the extent to which they employ "scientific" procedures in formulating, presenting, and verifying knowledge, and their scholarly distance from religion, that is, the degree to which the discipline's normative structure involves the scholarly study of religion, and hence involves the individual academician in the application of the canons of scholarship to religious phenomena. They assumed that disciplines characterized as high in scientism and low in scholarly distance from religion (that is, devoted to the scholarly study of religion) would boast the least religious faculty, and those both low in scientism and high in scholarly distance from religion would boast the most religious faculty. The studies, however, yielded diametrically opposed findings: Lehman and Shriver (1968) and Lehman (1974) found that the extent of faculty religious commitment was almost solely attributable to their discipline's scholarly distance from religion rather than its degree of scientism, while Eaton recorded exactly the opposite pattern.

How can this discrepancy be explained? Differences in sampling certainly present one possibility: Lehman and Shriver sampled the entire faculty at a single state university in the South, whereas Eaton drew a much larger number of respondents from arts and sciences colleges at eight state universities in the West. Underlying these very different samples and very different findings may, however, be a common dynamic. Lehman and Shriver found that the effect of low scholarly distance from religion was a function of the relative lack of compartmentalization between religious and academic values among faculty in low-distance disciplines together with a colleague climate more supportive of skepticism. It may be that Eaton's scientists and Lehman and Shriver's scholarly students of religion share this tendency toward noncompartmentalization and that this latent dynamic explains both sets of findings. This hypothesis must, however, remain moot pending the accumulation of new evidence. To this point, attempts to explain the impact of discipline by reference to the characteristics of academic fields has produced no encompassing and powerful generalizations. This may mean that new ways of characterizing academic fields need to be conceptualized and applied or that the effect of disciplinary affiliation may be less a function of structural characteristics of the discipline per se than of prior selection of particular types of individuals to the various disciplinary groupings.

In sum, we may conclude that the academic role bears some relationship to individual religious expression and conviction. Faculty, as a group, tend to be less religious than the general population; and among the professoriate, religiosity varies by discipline, prestige of institutional affiliation, and religious affiliation. The best evidence available, principally Thalheimer (1965) and Hoge and Keeter

(1976), suggests that these observed differences are more likely attributable to selective recruitment or self-selection than to professional socialization.

Accommodation between Religious and Academic Values

Espy (1950, 1951) studied the willingness of faculty at Protestant four-year colleges to express their religious beliefs in their classroom teaching. He uncovered systematic variation in the willingness of his respondents to bring religion into the classroom by discipline, rank, and graduate training. Sociologists to a greater extent than either physicists or economists, senior faculty to a greater extent than junior faculty, and those who had taken graduate work in education or religion to a greater extent than those who had not, sought to integrate their religious ideas and educational practice by expressing their religious convictions to students and by making them an integral part of their teaching.

Thalheimer (1963), on the other hand, focused on the extent of faculty compartmentalization or integration of religion and scholarship at the attitudinal, rather than the behavioral, level of analysis. Thalheimer reported some variation among disciplinary groupings, but found that a compartmentalization or integration response was largely a function of religiosity, that is, more secularized faculty tended to compartmentalize religion and scholarship while "believers" tended to be more concerned about, and to actually achieve, a normative integration of the two spheres. To the extent that Thalheimer's sample disproportionately represents social scientists (as he himself clearly suggests), his findings would appear to contradict those of both Espy (1950 and 1951) and Lehman and Shriver (1968), who found the compartmentalization response to be characteristic of those professors who still held firmly to their religious convictions. Insofar as Thalheimer's sample is the most representative of the lot (albeit, by no means, representative of the professoriate at large), his findings would appear to veil in uncertainty the question of which kinds of professors respond how to the conflicting canons of religion and academic work.

Friedman (1971) took quite a different tack. Proceeding from symbolic interaction theory, he sought to explain the situational behavior of Jewish professors—the "priorization" between their ethnic and professional identities in a situation of hypothetical conflict (for example, being asked to present a paper on the high holy days). His sample displayed two major response patterns. About three-quarters opted to be true to *either* their professional *or* their religious obligations (the vast majority placing priority on the professional), displaying what Friedman termed "fixed or closed" priorization. Barely one-quarter showed "open or flexible" priorization, that is, anchored their responses in a variety of situational contingencies, or were simply uncertain. Friedman went on to speculate that "open or flexible" priorization might reflect personality tendencies, in particular, an individual's tolerance for ambiguity. If one were to view "fixed or closed" priorization as an index of the tendency to compartmentalize religious and professional considerations, then it would appear that Friedman's Jewish faculty tended to compartmentalize their professional and religious lives and to assign a higher priority to the former.

Ethnic Assimilation

Gordon, in his *Assimilation in American Life* (1964), posited that American intellectuals, among whom faculty are the most numerous group, form the outlines of an intellectual subsociety within which the divisiveness of ethnic background is largely eliminated by a shared overriding interest in ideas. His hypothesis, then, acutally has two components: the first concerned with ethnic assimilation, the second with the cognizance of participation in an "intellectual community." In putting it to the test, investigators (several of whom were Gordon's graduate students) have examined faculty self-perceptions (their ethnic identity, religious beliefs, cognizance of an intellectual community) as well as how those self-perceptions translate into behavior (friendship patterns, participation in ethnically oriented organizations, intermarriage, and child-rearing practices).

These tests of the "intellectual subsociety" hypothesis have, however, proceeded in the relative absence of controls. Only two studies actually compare faculty with the general population, and only one of these does so across all variables identified above. These two studies both appear to suggest that faculty are more likely than the general population to have broken their ethnic bonds. However, the single study that is large in scale and that simultaneously provides equivalent data on all variables for a control group from the "general population" presents evidence that would support an alternative interpretation—that observed differences between faculty and the general population may be attributable to differences in religious background. Anderson (1968) found that Protestant faculty were significantly more likely than their nonacademic coreligionists to be ethnically assimilated *but* were also significantly more likely to come from less religious families. Among Mormons, on the other hand, there were no significant differences between academics and their nonacademic coreligionists in either religious background or degree of current ethnic assimilation. To what extent, one may then ask, are "apparent" status effects (academic versus nonacademic) attributable to real differences in religious background between faculty and the general population? To what extent are individuals with weak ethnic ties actually "selected into" the academic profession? The large differences between humanists and social scientists, on the one hand, and natural scientists, on the other, *despite similar religious backgrounds* do suggest that while early religious socialization may account for some of the observed differences, it cannot by itself explain everything. The question as to whether we are witnessing here the effects of early religious socialization or those of an "intellectual subsociety" thus remains largely open.

The picture is further clouded by evidence of considerable variation in ethnic assimilation *among* academics. Anderson (1966, 1968), Mazur (1971), and Murray (1971a) together identified three factors directly related to professional activity which account for differences in ethnic orientation—the individual's institutional affiliation, disciplinary affiliation, and professional orientation. Faculty at more prestigious institutions and at secular institutions are more likely to report considerable ethnic assimilation as are those with a higher professional orientation and those in the social sciences and humanities. The effect of discipline, however, is apparently mediated by religious affiliation (Anderson, 1968). That the effects of a major professional determinant of ethnic assimilation are mediated by factors extrinsic to the academic role brings us to what is perhaps the most striking inference suggested by the findings—that variation among faculty in ethnic orientation is to a great extent attributable to characteristics that are, by and large, extraneous to academic status. Most prominent among these is the individual's intellectual orientation. Both Anderson (1966) and Murray (1971a) found that faculty characterized as "intellectuals" showed a higher degree of ethnic assimilation and were significantly more likely to identify themselves as part of the American intellectual community. Mazur (1971) reported that faculty teaching at institutions characterized by a less intensely intellectual climate were less likely to deviate markedly from the norms of the surrounding ethnic community. These findings must, however, be interpreted with reference to the criteria employed in differentiating faculty "intellectuals." Respondents were classified as intellectuals on the basis of median scores on a "media exposure index," tapping the kinds of books and periodicals read, the frequency of television watching, attendance at various performing arts, and so forth. Operationally, then, faculty intellectuals were those faculty participating in "high culture." If one assumes that an appreciation of "high culture" is as much an index of social class as it is of "an overriding interest in ideas" (and sociologists of leisure would likely support that assumption), then one might plausibly interpret the findings as indicating a higher tendency for ethnic assimilation among faculty with higher social class origins. Indeed, given the substantial evidence that faculty tend to be drawn disproportionately from the middle and upper-middle classes (Gustad, 1960; Crane, 1969; Eckert and Williams, 1972; Bayer, 1973; Lipset and Ladd, 1979), it may be that observed differences between faculty and the general population are attributable to social class differences, as well as differences in religious background, rather than academic status.

Beyond intellectual orientation, the operation of two other powerful, extra-academic determinants are in evidence—childhood and adult religious socialization. As noted earlier, Anderson (1968) found that differences in religious background accounted for a good deal of the variation between professors and their nonacademic coreligionists. In addition, both Anderson (1968) and Mazur (1971) reported that the individual professor's ethnicity appeared to be highly influenced by that of his or her spouse. Murray (1971b) reported that among Catholic college faculty, the religious composition of high school and college friendships proved influential in shaping later ethnic orientations. Although Anderson and Mazur disagree on the relative primacy of childhood (parents' religiosity) and later adult (spouse's religiosity) socialization influences, it seems fair to conclude that if earlier influences do not directly shape adult ethnicity, they would appear to play an important role in shaping the individual's choice of adult socialization influences (for example, the choice of spouse).

In sum, then, inquiry into faculty ethnicity has provided rather clear evidence that professors are more likely than other segments of the population to have broken ethnic ties, although some uncertainty remains as to what extent this can be attributed to their "overriding concern with ideas" or their differences vis-à-vis the general population in religious background and social class origin. The source of these intergroup differences is further clouded by the considerable variation in ethnic orientation within the academy. While professionally relevant factors such as prestige of institutional affiliation, professional orientation, and discipline account for some of the differences among faculty, the lion's share of variation appears to be attributable to factors extraneous to professional work, including intellectual orientation (cultural sophistication) and religious socialization during childhood and the later adult years. In this extra-academic aspect of their lives, then, the academic role per se appears to have little direct influence, but rather reinforces the proclivities and orientations developed in earlier years.

PROFESSORIAL POLITICS

Faculty Political Ideologies

If faculty are relatively less religious than the general public, they are also relatively more liberal, politically, and thus represent a classic negative case to the traditional equation of high socioeconomic status and political conservatism. Their relative liberalism is apparent from several different angles. Fifty-seven percent of college and university faculty in 1978, for example, were registered Democrats (Ladd and Lipset, 1978).[9] Since the end of World War II, college and university faculty have more consistently supported Democratic and left candidates for national office than any other occupational group, including manual workers (Ladd and Lipset, 1978).[10] When asked to describe their overall political inclinations on a seven-point scale ranging "far left" to "far right," 45 percent located themselves on the liberal side of the spectrum, 30 percent called themselves conservatives, while 20 percent chose the center option, "moderate."[11] These self-characterizations compare with those elicited from the general public by a survey of the National Opinion Research Center in the spring of 1977 which found 27 percent of the general population identifying themselves as liberal, 31 percent as conservative, and 37 percent as "moderate" (Ladd and Lipset, 1978).[12]

While faculty are relatively more liberal than the general population, there are enormous divisions in political ideology within the academy. A faculty member's disciplinary affiliation clearly emerges as the single most important line of cleavage. Social scientists (in particular, sociologists) emerge as most liberal and Democratic, followed by humanists and natural scientists, with faculty in the professional schools and in applied fields displaying the highest tendency toward conservatism and Republicanism (Eitzen and Maranell, 1968; Spaulding and Turner, 1968; Maranell and Eitzen, 1970; Ali, 1972; Berger, 1973; Faia, 1974; Ladd and Lipset, 1975f;

Wilson and Gaff, 1975; Ladd and Lipset, 1978). Within disciplinary groupings, faculty who have shown the highest levels of professional achievement, as evidenced in their research contributions, and who are more oriented to the research component of the academic role, display a higher tendency toward liberalism than their more teaching-oriented colleagues who have published less (Ali, 1972; Berger, 1973; Ladd and Lipset, 1975f). Indeed, the impact of academic achievement at the individual level appears to be duplicated at the institutional level; as one moves from smaller colleges to larger, graduate-oriented universities and as one ascends the institutional prestige hierarchy, one finds increasingly higher concentrations of liberal faculty. Thus, those segments of the professoriate that are most prominent and influential—the more prolific scholars at the more prestigious institutions—and whose scholarly concerns involve them most readily in public policy debates—social scientists— show the most marked leftward inclinations.

How can one account for this relative liberalism, on the one hand, and enormous ideological division, on the other? Political scientists have variously posited the operation of disciplinary, institutional, and even teaching versus research subcultures which exert socializing influences on faculty members within their boundaries. However, evidence of variation within the posited subcultures, as well as evidence of the impact of family background factors and social characteristics largely extraneous to the academic role (such as age, religious affiliation, and religiosity), suggest that influences quite beyond professional socialization are at work.[13] Most prominent among these is the influence of childhood political socialization as reflected in the politics of the family of origin. Spaulding and Turner (1968) reported large and consistent *intradisciplinary* differences in parental politics between Democrats and Republicans. Democratic, liberal parents were significantly more likely to produce Democratic and liberal progeny. Ladd and Lipset (1975f), on the basis of their secondary analysis of the 1969 Carnegie-ACE survey data, reported a zero-order correlation of 0.49 between respondents' politics as a college senior and that of their fathers' and a strong positive correlation between the former and their current political predispositions.[14] The evidence less clearly supports the influential role of childhood religious socialization, community of origin, and parental socioeconomic status. Spaulding and Turner (1968) reported that social scientists, their most liberal respondent group, were more likely than either natural scientists or faculty in applied areas, their most conservative respondent groups, to have had Jewish parents, and the latter were more likely to have had Protestant parents. Moreover, within academic areas, Republicans, as a group, were 20 percent more likely than Democrats to have been raised in the Protestant faith. They further report that within academic areas, Democrats were more likely to have grown up in large cities than Republicans, and the latter were more likely than Democrats to have been raised in the Northeast. Finally, Spaulding and Turner (1968) found a not quite consistent pattern of intradisciplinary differences in parental socioeconomic status between Democrats and Republicans. Although not in itself persuasive, this finding gains plausibility in light of the strong, if indirect, effect Ladd and Lipset (1975f) attributed to parental socioeconomic status: the higher the socioeconomic status of the family of origin, the more likely is the individual faculty member to be affiliated with a high-prestige institution and the less likely he or she is to be in a professional or applied field. Collectively, these findings together with a lack of relationship between career age (that is, postdoctorate years) and a leftward shift in political orientation (Faia, 1975)[15] provide the first chink in the armor of the professional socialization explanation. They suggest first that selection to disciplinary or institutional subcultures may be nearly as important a factor as socialization and second that the background one brings to these subcultures may determine individual susceptibility to their socializing pressures.

The ascendancy of the professional socialization explanation of faculty political orientation is further undermined by evidence of the significant influence of age, religious affiliation, and religiosity—all variables extraneous to the professional role. Turner et al. (1963), Berger (1973), and Ladd and Lipset (1975f) corroborate a neat progression from political liberalism to conservatism with movement from the youngest to the oldest faculty age groups. Moreover, the factors associated with age that make older faculty more conservative than younger faculty operate as strongly in "liberal" disciplines and institutional environments as in relatively conservative ones. What are these "factors" associated with age? At least two possibilities have been identified: First, it may be the effects of aging per se, that is, the development of a firm stake in the extant sociopolitical system; or it may be that age reflects generational differences in political socialization. Ladd and Lipset (1975f), however, investigated the claims of both these alternatives and concluded, on the basis of their own data and those of Lazarsfeld and Thielens (1958), that the aging process itself provided the more plausible explanation.

A similar consensus has developed around the role of faculty religious affiliation. Jews tend to be more liberal than their Catholic and Protestant colleagues and indeed show lower variation in political orientation by discipline and prestige of institutional affiliation (Turner et al., 1963; Spaulding and Turner, 1968; Steinberg, 1974; Ladd and Lipset, 1975f). Ladd and Lipset conclude that the relative liberalism of Jewish faculty represents the predominance of cultural factors over academic ones, but it may be attributable as well, to some extent, to their relatively low degree of religiosity. The available evidence strongly supports the proposition that liberalism increases with decreased religious involvement (Turner et al., 1963; Spaulding and Turner, 1968; Ladd and Lipset, 1975f), and Steinberg (1974) found that as religiosity decreased, so did differences in political orientation between Jews and non-Jews, to the point where no differences could be observed among apostates across religious groups.

Collectively, these findings suggest that faculty political orientation is the result of a complex array of interacting forces, including childhood political and religious socialization, later adult socialization (religious affiliation, religiosity), the aging process, and experiences related directly to professional practice. The prospective faculty member enters the professoriate with a set of political predispositions established, and we have no direct evidence of any change in those predispositions during the course of an academic career, except for the findings of several cross-sectional studies that *suggest* that observed differences among age cohorts may be a function of the aging process itself (which is, of course, independent of the academic career). Disciplinary and institutional affiliations undeniably explain considerable variance in political orientations within academe, but the distribution of individuals over disciplines and institutional types may hardly be considered "random." The relative liberalism of sociologists is, no doubt, due in part to the disproportionate representation of apostate Jews from urban, Democratic families, and this suggests the important role of selection. Moreover, to take our example one step further, the large minority of relatively conservative sociologists (about 30 percent of the population, extrapolating from the Carnegie-ACE 1969 survey data) who tend to share the background and social characteristics associated with conservatism suggests the limits of professional socialization. It may be most reasonable to speak rather of *selective* professional socialization—when subcultural norms fit individual political predispositions, they tend to reinforce them; when they do not, they tend to be rather ineffectual. In the absence of longitudinal data on the actual timing of changes in political orientations, our conclusions must, of course, remain tentative. Nonetheless, the single effort to elicit from faculty retrospective reports of their political orientation during childhood and as college seniors (Ladd and Lipset, 1975f) shows a marked durability and consistency in political attributes from the earliest age of political awareness.

Political Participation

Professors are more likely than the public at large to "act out" their ideological commitments in the arena of civic life. Ladd and Lipset (1975c) found that college and university faculty were twice as likely as other college-educated Americans to be active in political campaigns and in public policy groups (49 and 45 percent, respectively, were active in these) and 50 percent more likely to be involved in the affairs of a political party (29 percent were so involved). Generally speaking, it is the most liberal faculty who are most active, especially at the national level. Thus, the most liberal faculty Democrats were two and a half times as likely to be involved in politics and twice as likely to be involved at the national level as the most conservative Republicans (45 percent scored high on a political involvement scale, and 41 percent indicated involvement at the national level).[16] Social scientists, the most politically liberal segment of the professoriate, were twice as likely as faculty in applied fields to be so involved (41 percent versus 19 percent); and faculty with moderate publications records were more involved than nonpublishers.[17] It would appear, however, that party loyalty may be as important a determinant of civic participation as party membership or political ideology; the most active faculty proved to be those who always voted straight tickets, Democratic or Republican. Among those who always vote straight tickets, 45 percent scored high in political involvement compared to only 18 percent of those who regularly split their ballots (Ladd and Lipset, 1975c).

Perhaps nowhere are these patterns of political activism more dramatically apparent than in professorial reaction to the Vietnam War. During the late 1960s and early 1970s, close to one-third of American professors wrote to public officials, signed petitions, or attended meetings related to American involvement in Vietnam; approximately one out of five actually took part in war-related demonstrations (Ladd and Lipset, 1975d). As early as 1966, the majority of faculty opinion had turned against the war, and such anti-war sentiment tended to be concentrated, quite predictably, among the most politically liberal faculty, social scientists at the major. research universities (Schuman and Laumann, 1967; Armor et al., 1967; Ladd, 1969; Ladd and Lipset, 1975d). It was precisely these liberal, anti-war faculty who were most likely to act out their sentiments. In comparing the political activity levels of anti-and pro-war faculty,[18] Ladd and Lipset (1975d) found the former three times as likely as the latter to have written to government officials (45 percent versus 16 percent) and four and a half times as likely to have signed a published petition (67 percent versus 15 percent). Three out of four of the pro-war faculty never attended a single meeting concerned with the war, and two out of three never signed a statement or wrote to a public official. In sum, then, the relatively liberal professoriate led all other groups in opposition to the Vietnam War: anti-war forces were much more active than pro-war forces and were drawn disproportionately from the most prestigious and visible segments of the profession.

ACADEMIC WORK AS A WAY OF LIFE

This chapter began with the question of the "preemptiveness" of the academic role, that is, the extent to which it pervades the non-work-related aspects of faculty lives. A review of the findings of some three dozen research studies suggest three broad generalizations.

1. The academic role is associated with a distinctive lifestyle. Faculty, as a group, show consistent differences from the general population in the nature of work-family relationships, friendship patterns, religious involvement, the strength of ethnic ties, and political allegiances.
2. The preemptiveness of the academic role, however, varies substantially among different types of professors. The degree of distinctiveness from the general population varies by professional statuses, such as disciplinary affiliation, professional orientation and type and prestige of institutional affiliation, family background, and nonacademic ascriptive, social characteristics (age, religious affiliation).
3. The dimensions of faculty lifestyles examined are closely interrelated insofar as group differences on one dimension are, for the most part, systematically replicated on other dimensions. Thus, for example, social scientists, as a group, tend to bring their work home with them, tend to be least religious, and tend to be most liberal.

How are these findings to be explained? To what extent are differences between faculty and the general population and differences among faculty a function of the kind of people professors are and have always been, or, the kind of work they do and the colleagues with whom they share it? Three types of evidence bearing on this question were reviewed.

1. Retrospective reports on lifestyle before entry to the professoriate (Thalheimer on religious involvement; Ladd and Lipset on political orientation)
2. Data on the relative contribution of academic characteristics versus extraneous, background and social characteristics to variation in the "distinctiveness" of faculty lifestyles
3. Data on changes in lifestyle over the course of the academic career (cross-sectional analyses of faculty age groups).

This review leads to the following conclusions:

1. In the areas of faculty religious and ethnic ties and political orientation, current predispositions were largely formed before graduation from college.
2. Although academic characteristics such as discipline and level of professional achievement do differentiate faculty, background and extraneous social characteristics differentiate disciplinary and professional achievement groupings and account for variation within them.
3. What change does occur over the academic career is attributable to the developmental process of aging itself (Baldwin, 1979) rather than any specific or generalized professional influences.

Together, these findings suggest that in matters of lifestyle the academic role is "preemptive" chiefly by *selection* rather than by *socialization*. Professional socialization may selectively reinforce extant predispositions, but it is apparently resisted when it runs counter to them.

1. There was some modest variation in the professorial propensity to "academize" their friendships by discipline and prestige of institutional affiliation. Academization was highest among natural scientists and among faculty at more prestigious, research-oriented institutions (Parsons and Platt, 1968).

2. It should be noted, however, the consumption of such highbrow periodicals was most pervasive among Jewish faculty and among those faculty who identified themselves as intellectuals (Anderson and Murray, 1967).

3. Ladd and Lipset did, however, note modest variation in the nature of faculty reading habits by discipline, by level of political activism, and by geographic region.

4. Ladd and Lipset's (1975e) and Steinberg's (1974) cross-sectional comparison of

age cohorts suggest, however, that while the Protestant presence is modestly decreasing among newer entrants to the profession, that of Catholics has been increasing and that of Jews leveling out following a substantial increase in the post–World War II period.

5. With the exception of Wilson and Gaff (1975), who sought respondent self-reports of religiosity on a unidimensional scale, students of faculty religiosity have followed the lead of Glock and Stark (1965) in conceptualizing religious involvement as a multidimensional construct, including ideological components (beliefs which the followers of a given religion are supposed to share), experiential components (religious feelings or experiences), and ritualistic components (practices such as church attendance and prayer).

6. This is not to suggest that in *absolute* terms a majority of American academics have renounced religious ties. Indeed, data from the 1969 Carnegie survey show that a majority of American academics consider themselves either moderately (48 percent) or deeply (16 percent) religious (Steinberg, 1974).

7. This latter group of "indifferents" consists primarily of Jewish academicians who while eschewing any traditional religious beliefs appear to cling to their Jewishness as more of an ethnic/cultural identification (Steinberg, 1974).

8. The greater religiosity of faculty in applied fields and in some of the physical sciences may also reflect the overrepresentation of Catholics—who tend to have more orthodox religious beliefs and higher levels of church participation than Protestants or Jews—in those fields (Hoge and Keeter, 1976; Anderson and Murray, 1971).

9. There is some evidence to suggest that "academic" Democrats constitute something of a special breed. If on traditional New Deal issues, such as government spending for social welfare and support for organized labor, faculty Democrats line up with all Democrats, on newer sociocultural issues, such as women's rights, abortion, environmental protection, and legalization of marijuana, they stand considerably to the left of the rank and file party membership (Ladd and Lipset, 1975b).

10. In 1972, 57 percent of academics voted for George McGovern or "left" candidates compared to 31 percent of all those in professional and managerial occupations and to 37 percent of all voters who had attended college. In 1976, two out of three faculty members voted Democratic or left compared to two out of five college educated Americans. Indeed, since 1956 about 20–30 percent more faculty than "other professionals" have supported Democratic presidential candidates (Ladd and Lipset, 1978).

11. Additional evidence from the Carnegie–American Council on Education 1969 Faculty Survey suggests that faculty ideological self-identifications have remained nearly perfectly consistent over the entire decade of the 1970s.

12. As in the case of professorial apostasy, it must be emphasized that American academics are "liberal" relative to other occupational groups and not in absolute terms. Indeed, the data show that the majority of faculty (55 percent) characterize themselves as either "moderate" or "conservative" (Ladd and Lipset, 1975a). Moreover, even among faculty "liberals," radical views, such as the nationalization of private enterprise, are decidedly rare (Ladd and Lipset, 1978).

13. Since none of the studies treating background factors employ multivariate techniques, one cannot assess the precise "pecking order" of impact among them, let alone the precise relative importance of their contribution vis-à-vis discipline and institutional prestige to variation in political orientation.

14. In the absence of longitudinal data, however, they were unable to further specify the relationship.

15. Faia's findings were, however, based on a cross-sectional, rather than a longitudinal, analysis of faculty age groups.

16. While faculty liberals and conservatives differ markedly in their levels and patterns of voluntary political participation, they do not differ in terms of their actual experience in official positions, such as consultantships to government agencies or service on government boards, committees, or task forces. This Ladd and Lipset (1975c) attribute to two factors: (1) the attempt by public officials, especially in Republican administrations, to achieve partisan and ideological balance by seeking out more conservative and Republican faculty for such posts and (2) the fact that many consultants are drawn from the ranks of faculty in the applied professions—the most politically conservative segment of the professoriate.

17. Moderate publishers showed higher activity levels than either heavy publishers or nonpublishers. It would appear that heavy research and writing commitments limit political activity even as they shape political ideology.

18. Anti-war faculty were operationally defined as those faculty who reported being totally against any U.S. involvement at the start of the war (25 percent); pro-war faculty were operationally defined as those 10 percent of the professoriate who maintained a hard line in favor of military victory until the end.

7

Women and Minority Faculty

INTRODUCTION

The decade of the 1970s witnessed a heightened consciousness of the status of women and minorities in academe—a function of the heightened self-consciousness raised by the women's and civil rights movements. This self-consciousness has been translated into government policy and legal mandates, such as antidiscrimination legislation, executive orders, and affirmative action regulations, and new federal structures such as the Office of Women's Equity in the United States Office of Education. It has also intruded both directly and indirectly into academic and professional structures. On campus, we have seen the growth of women's studies and minority studies programs, black student unions, minority and women faculty caucuses, resource and research centers, as well as affirmative action offices; off campus, we have seen the emergence of women and minority caucuses in most major professional associations (and projects within higher education associations, such as the Association of American University's project on the status of women), new national resource and support organizations, such as HERS, as well as new professional journals, such as *Sex Roles* and *The Journal of Educational Equity,* and special issues of extant journals, such as the *Harvard Educational Review*'s special issues on women in 1979 and 1980 and the 1980 special issue of the *Educational Researcher.*

As the academic arm of the women's and civil rights movements, women's and minority study programs have sought to develop a knowledge base to form the intellectual foundations of the movements. In the case of the women's movement, in particular, there has been a massive effort to direct social scientific inquiry toward an understanding of biological and psychological sex differences, socialization and sex roles, the relationships among gender, race, and class, the historical roles of women and minorities, the history and function of the family in the United States, and, cross-culturally, women and minorities in the labor force and before the law (Howe, 1979). Most immediately, investigators have sought to develop a knowledge base on women and minority professionals in higher education—the "soldiers" in the intellectual arm of the movement. This latter knowledge base has at least three components.

1. "N of 1" autobiographical accounts of life as a woman or minority professional (for example, Nielson (1979) and Abramson (1975)) that draw on subjective experiences to illuminate in a very immediate way the trials and tribulations of being different in academe
2. Opinion and hortatory pieces that provide armchair analyses and descriptions of discrimination
3. More broad-based empirical studies of women and minority professionals in academe.

This chapter focuses on an examination of the third component of this evolving knowledge base on women and minority professionals in higher education. This component includes a diverse array of status reports initiated by individual institutions and professional associations, independent studies of women and minority professionals, as well as national level surveys of new doctorates and academic professionals that employ sex or race as independent or control variables (for example, the National Research Council's annual survey of doctoral recipients, the American Council of Education–Carnegie Commission's faculty surveys, and the Higher Education General Information Survey directed by the National Center for Education Statistics). All of these studies have focused primarily on the then current status of women and minorities (vis-à-vis a matched sample of majority males) on a variety of career-related variables in an effort to assess the existence and extent of discrimination. Salary has been the central career-related variable examined, followed by promotion and tenure, work assignments, and location within the institutional stratification system. The results of such studies suggest that in many respects women and minorities differ from majority males, but in others, they do not. The question of what sense to make of the patterns of differences and similarities that do exist is at once less often and less carefully addressed. Are differences a matter of choice, overt discrimination, or differences in level of performance/productivity? And it is to this sort of question that the present chapter addresses itself. Specifically, this chapter seeks to (1) provide a relatively brief overview of the current status of women and minority faculty (much of that overview is available in greater detail elsewhere, for example, for women faculty, Kane, 1976; Gappa and Uehling, 1979; for minority faculty, Rafky, 1972, and Moore and Wagstaff, 1974) and (2) to identify alternative explanations for patterns of differences that do exist and to weigh the extant empirical evidence related to each of these alternative explanations. It is assumed that an understanding of the sources of status differences and their relative weight will provide a surer guide to approaching any inequities that exist.

CURRENT STATUS OF WOMEN FACULTY

What is the current status of women in the academic profession (their proportionate presence, their distribution by institutional type and discipline)? What is the academic woman's status at her own institution (in terms of rank, promotion, compensation, and participation in administration and governance)?

In 1980–81, women constituted 26.3 percent of all full-time faculty. This figure evidences a 1.7 percent decline in proportionate representation over the past half century (women constituted about 28 percent of all faculty in 1929–30), but it also represents a 7 percent increase in their ranks during the decade of the 1970s. Women are disproportionately located at community colleges (35.5 percent of all community college faculty) and at less prestigious four-year colleges (26 percent). They are underrepresented at universities, generally (18.2 percent), but particularly at major research institutions (National Center for Education Statistics, 1982). There is some evidence, however, of a shift in institutional location among "new hires" in the early and mid-1970s. Bayer (1973) reported a 2 percent gain in proportionate representation for women in universities (15 percent to 17 percent) between 1969 and 1973, balanced by slight losses in proportionate representation at the four-year and community colleges. Both Centra (1974) and Cartter (1976) found that between 1967 and 1973 the proportion of women among new hires was two to five times greater than their proportionate representation in faculty ranks at the most prestigious research universities. Cartter's (1976) data (Table 7.1) documents a progressive convergence in the first job placement pattern of male and female doctoral degree holders during the early 1970s. That convergence resulted from a steady decrease in job opportunities for males while females held their own in a declining job market.

The distribution of academic women across disciplinary fields ap-

TABLE 7.1

PERCENT OF NEW DOCTORATES TEACHING AT INSTITUTIONS EQUAL OR SUPERIOR
TO DEGREE-GRANTING INSTITUTIONS BY SEX, 1967–73

Degree-granting Institutions	1967	1968	1971	1972	1973
			Men		
Group I	20.1	18.8	13.4	13.8	10.3
Group II	23.0	21.2	18.8	17.3	14.5
Group III	25.8	25.6	19.1	19.5	16.0
Group IV	41.1	36.4	32.3	30.8	26.4
Group V	60.8	56.1	50.7	48.7	44.3
All universities	29.2	27.6	24.4	23.9	20.6
			Women		
Group I	8.9	15.3	10.0	11.4	12.8
Group II	19.8	19.6	17.6	15.7	17.9
Group III	23.8	25.9	22.4	27.4	21.7
Group IV	27.0	35.6	33.0	31.5	30.5
Group V	51.6	55.8	46.9	45.6	44.8
All universities	22.8	26.7	24.4	24.9	23.8

SOURCE: Cartter (1976).

pears to display a similar pattern. In 1970, 55 percent of all female faculty were to be found in just four fields: the performing arts (art, drama, music), foreign languages, health-related professions, and English. They were scarcest in fields such as economics (8 percent of all full-time faculty), law (7 percent), engineering (6 percent), physics (5 percent), and agriculture (4 percent). These patterns of concentration and scarcity in faculty ranks clearly reflected patterns of distribution by field among doctoral degree recipients. By 1979–80, however, disciplinary patterns by sex among new doctorate recipients and current graduate students had begun to change. Academic women were being increasingly drawn to law, economics, engineering sciences, the physical sciences,[1] and agriculture and natural resources[2] (Tables 7.2 and 7.3). Precisely when these changing foci of graduate study will be reflected in a swelling of female faculty ranks in more traditionally masculine fields, and even whether this will occur, remains to be seen.

The winds of change are less evident in the woman scholar's status at her own institution. Women have historically been concentrated in the lower ranks, and in 1980–81, 70.7 percent of all women faculty were at or below the assistant professor rank or were unranked (National Center for Education Statistics, 1982). The influx

TABLE 7.2

PROPORTION OF FEMALES AMONG DOCTORAL RECIPIENTS IN
SELECTED FIELDS, 1979–80

Field	Percent Female
Engineering	3.8
Physical sciences	12.3
Chemistry	16.7
Physics	7.6
Agriculture and natural resources	11.3
Food sciences	26.6
Law (J.D. or LL.B.)	30.2
Economics	15.1

SOURCE: Based on NCES data (National Center for Education Statistics, 1982).

of female new hires during the 1970s was absorbed at the lower
ranks, as evidenced by the rank distribution of female faculty between 1973–81 presented in Table 7.4. The table shows no change in
the proportion of full professors who are female over the past decade
and only a 4 percent increase in female representation at the associate professor level, in contrast to a notable swelling of academic
women in the assistant professor and instructor ranks. Moreover,
the concentration of the woman scholar at the lower untenured
ranks seems to be intensified as one ascends the academic prestige
hierarchy. Table 7.5 suggests that among tenured faculty, female
representation is lower at universities than at other four-year colleges, and lower again at four-year institutions than at the community colleges. These inequities in rank beyond the initial appointment suggest that women are promoted at a slower rate than their
male colleagues. Indeed, Kane (1976) found that to be the case,
although promotion rate appeared to vary by discipline. The relatively small group of women scholars in the natural sciences were

TABLE 7.3

PROPORTION OF FEMALES AMONG ENROLLED GRADUATE AND PROFESSIONAL
STUDENTS IN SELECTED FIELDS, FALL 1980

Field	Percent Female
Agriculture and natural resources	24.2
Engineering	8.9
Law	34.0
Physical sciences	19.6

SOURCE: Based on NCES data (National Center for Education Statistics, 1982).

TABLE 7.4
PERCENT OF WOMEN AMONG ALL FULL-TIME INSTRUCTIONAL
FACULTY BY RANK, 1973–81

Rank	1973– 74	1974– 75	1975– 76	1976– 77	1977– 78	1978– 79	1979– 80	1980– 81
Professor	9.8	10.1	9.8	9.6	9.7	9.6	9.9	10.1
Associate professor	16.3	17.0	17.0	17.7	18.0	18.9	19.7	20.3
Assistant professor	23.8	27.3	28.9	30.4	31.7	32.9	33.8	34.8
Instructor	39.9	41.0	40.7	50.6	50.0	51.5	51.9	51.9
Lecturer		38.9	40.4	40.8	42.8	43.6	45.2	43.6
Total	22.3	24.1	24.3	25.2	25.5	25.8	25.9	26.3

SOURCE: Based on data from Gappa and Uehling (1979) and National Center for Education Statistics (1982).

promoted on a par with men, and the larger group of females in the humanities and social sciences were promoted less rapidly than their male colleagues (Kane, 1976).

In the matter of compensation, over fifty major studies completed during the past decade point incontestably to a single conclusion: women are paid less than men, even after controlling for rank, institutional type, and discipline. Although the male-female disparity in compensation actually began increasing midway through the 1970s after remaining fairly constant since World War II, the most recent evidence suggests that it is narrowing slightly during the early 1980s. In 1981–82, academic women were earning approximately 85 percent as much as academic men compared to a figure of 80 percent in the mid 1970s. Moreover, in that year, academic women received salary increases on a par with their male colleagues (8.9 percent) after receiving a 0.8 percent differential over men in the previous year (*Chronicle of Higher Education,* 1981).

During the 1970s, there had been a tendency for these disparities in compensation to widen over the course of an academic career.

TABLE 7.5
PROPORTION OF MALES AND FEMALES AMONG TENURED FACULTY
BY INSTITUTIONAL TYPE, 1979

Institutional Type	Males among Tenured Faculty	Females among Tenured Faculty
Universities	88.9	11.1
Four-year colleges	80.6	19.4
Community colleges	69.2	30.8

SOURCE: National Center for Education Statistics (1980).

Bayer and Astin (1975) reported near equity in entry-level salaries at the junior ranks but aggravated disparities at the higher ranks. Simon, Clark, and Galway (1967), LaSorte (1971), Robinson (1973), Centra (1974), Johnson and Stafford (1974), Fulton (1975), Kane (1976), and Tuckman (1976) all attested to a compensation pattern of near equity during the first five career years, followed by an increasing gap, which narrowed only during the final years of the academic career. By the early 1980s, however, this widening gap was becoming perceptibly attenuated. Female associate professors earned 95 percent as much as their male counterparts in 1980–81— a figure corresponding precisely to that for assistant professors and instructors. Although the gap was wider for full professors (females earned 90 percent as much as their male counterparts), it had closed in absolute size since the mid-1970s (National Center for Education Statistics, 1982).

Beyond career age, disparities in compensation continued to vary by institutional type and discipline. Disparities are highest at the doctoral degree granting universities where males earned nearly a quarter more than their female colleagues in 1981–82, lower at other universities and comprehensive colleges (a male differential on the order of 20 percent), and lowest at colleges granting the baccalaureate degree only (12.7 percent male differential over females) and at community colleges where males earned only 4.6 percent more than their female colleagues. Among disciplinary groupings, the male differential varies enormously from just over one-third in the arts and just over one-quarter in the sciences to 6.6 percent in physical education and 8.9 percent in business. Overall, academic women fare worse in the traditional arts and sciences than in the professions (*Chronicle of Higher Education,* 1981). A number of investigators have suggested a relationship between the size of these disparities and the proportionate representation of women in a given discipline (Gordon et al., 1974; Johnson and Stafford, 1974; Kane, 1976), that is, the disparity increases as the proportion of females in a discipline increases, but there appear to be a sufficient number of exceptions to this rule (for example, business, the arts) to make it tenuous (Fox, 1981). The source of these wide variations may indeed be specific to certain internal conditions of the various disciplines.

Women scholars' relatively low institutional status in comparison to their male colleagues is reflected as well in institutional administration and governance. Oltman (1970) found that among a sample of 454 colleges and universities, fully one-third had no female department chairpersons, and those females holding such positions were in traditionally female fields. In the American Council on Education's 1972–73 faculty survey, females were 10 percent less likely than their male colleagues to have served as department chairpersons, especially at universities, and were half as likely as their male colleagues to have held major faculty-wide offices, such as deanships. Baldridge et al. (1978) reported that females in his representative sample of 200 colleges and universities were significantly less likely to serve on university committees than their male colleagues, and those females who did serve were less likely to be in leadership positions or to view their committee activities as significant. At the departmental level half as many women as men reported significant influence on policy. These disparities tended to be exacerbated at the larger institutions, primarily universities. Although much of the disparity seemed attributable to rank rather than sex per se, the concentration of female scholars in the lower ranks, especially at universities, has effectively neutralized the role of academic women in governance.

By way of summary, the following conclusions can be drawn about the current status of women scholars:

1. Female faculty have gained in their proportionate representation during the 1970s but still lag behind their strength of a half century ago.
2. Female scholars tend to be segregated by discipline (although there has been a noticeable opening up in some traditionally male fields, particularly over the latter part of the 1970s) and by institutional type (although there have been gains in the 1970s at the university level, especially among new hires).
3. Females are disproportionately represented at the lower ranks, reflecting the recent infusion of new hires during the 1970s.
4. Females have generally been promoted at a slower rate than their male colleagues, especially in those fields in which they are most fully represented.
5. Female scholars have been compensated at a rate averaging 85 percent of their male colleagues; although the gap appears to be narrowing somewhat, there are still wide variations across institutional types and disciplines.
6. Female scholars have a lesser role in administration and governance (the latter largely as a result of their concentration in the lower ranks).

CURRENT STATUS OF MINORITY FACULTY

Before proceeding to an examination of the current status of minority faculty, two initial observations are in order. First, the vast majority of studies have focused on black faculty.[3] Second, while the majority of black faculty are located at black colleges, investigators have focused their attention on black faculty at predominately white colleges and universities. Therefore we know very little about black faculty at black colleges with the exception of Thompson's (1956) dated analysis of black college faculty and the work of Mommsen (1974) on black Ph.D.s and Hayden's (1978) study of the purposes of black higher education as perceived by black college faculty.

With these observations in mind, what can we say about the current status of blacks in the academic profession at large?[4] In 1960, before the civil rights movement, Rose (1966) counted some 5,900 black faculty across the country—about 3 percent of the academic profession. By 1975, blacks still constituted about 3 percent of a professoriate that had grown from just under 200,000 to nearly one-half million (National Center for Education Statistics, 1979). While the proportionate representation of blacks in the professoriate has remained stable, the past fifteen years have seen a considerable shift in their distribution within academe. Black faculty have been historically concentrated in predominately black colleges in the south. As late as 1969, fully 75–85 percent were so located, depending upon whose estimates one chooses to take (Bryant, 1970; Mommsen, 1974; R. Freeman, 1978). During the first half of the 1970s the proportion of black faculty in black colleges decreased to about half, while the proportion in predominately white universities increased by 8 percent overall and by 12 percent at the most prestigious research universities. Moreover, the shifts have been most pronounced among the youngest cohorts of black faculty (R. Freeman, 1978). Therefore, while two-thirds of black professors in the mid-1970s were still clustered at the lowest prestige strata institutions (especially in black colleges) and significantly underrepresented in universities and predominantly white, private liberal arts colleges, there has been some movement toward a greater similarity in distribution with majority faculty, especially among the younger age cohorts.

Like academic women, black faculty in predominantly white institutions tend to be concentrated in a few select fields: Fully one-half are concentrated in education and selected fields of the social sciences (especially black or ethnic studies departments), while another one-quarter are evenly distributed between the humanities and the natural sciences. The older age cohorts tend to be more completely concentrated in education, while younger black faculty are more heavily concentrated in the social sciences and humanities (Rafky, 1972). Unlike academic women, however, there seem to be no major shifts in disciplinary distribution in the offing. The latest available data on the disciplinary distribution of black recipients of doctorates (National Center for Education Statistics, 1982) shows a continued high concentration of blacks in education and the social sciences and reveals no striking increases in proportionate representation in other fields.

What of the status of the black professor at his or her own institution? Like academic women, black faculty tend to be clustered in the lower ranks, although the extent of that clustering appears to vary by institutional type and sex. Among the studies of black faculty in predominantly white institutions only, the concentration in lower ranks is marked (Rafky, 1972; Moore and Wagstaff, 1974); the proportion in part-time and nontenure track positions is considerably higher vis-à-vis their white colleagues by a ratio of about twenty to one; and the likelihood of black faculty holding tenure is about one-half that for their white colleagues (Rafky, 1972; Moore and Wagstaff, 1974). Among those studies of black faculty at *all* institutions, the black/white rank discrepancy appears considerably smaller. Among males, there was no significant discrepancy except at the full professor level, whereas among females whites were more likely to be represented at the higher ranks (R. Freeman, 1978).

As a group, black faculty fare significantly better than academic women in matters of compensation. On the basis of American Council on Education 1972–73 faculty survey data, Tuckman (1976) found no significant black/white salary discrepancy for males, but black female faculty earned significantly more than their white colleagues (on the order of four thousand dollars per academic year on average). Supplementing the 1972–73 survey with the results of the earlier (1969) American Council on Education–Carnegie Council survey, Freeman (1978) largely corroborated Tuckman's findings. In a more detailed analysis, Freeman develops separate regression equations to determine the predictors of salary for black and white faculty. The predictors were largely similar for males, except for the differential impact of publication rate. Black male faculty who published extensively obtained a premium in the two to three thousand dollar range over equally productive white faculty, reversing the comparative disadvantage of the most productive black scholars that emerged from the 1969 data. This reversal would appear to suggest a shift in demand in the early 1970s for more productive black male faculty. The comparative advantage of black female faculty over their white colleagues emerged largely as a function of the differential impact of age, experience, publication rate, and institutional type. Black women gained on a par with majority males with increased experience while their white female colleagues lost; they also received a premium for publication similar to majority males and did particularly well at community colleges and less prestigious universities.[5]

While no systematic studies specifically examine the participation of black faculty in institutional or departmental governance, two impressionistic studies look more broadly at black faculty participation in various aspects of institutional life.[6] Anderson et al. (1979), in their survey of forty-two black faculty and staff at the University of North Carolina, Chapel Hill, uncovered a sense of relative isolation: a majority of respondents were the only black members of their department, did not feel close to their white department colleagues, and felt that they were not regarded as part of the team. This portrait of isolation is largely confirmed in Middleton's (1978) multi-institutional interview study of black faculty. Although black faculty may play an important role in committees concerned with affirmative action and other black-related issues, they appear to participate less actively in the central policy channels of their institutions.

By way of summary, the following conclusions can be drawn about the current status of black faculty:

1. Blacks as a group have made considerably less progress than women in entering the academic profession, although they began in the 1970s to hold positions in predominately white institutions in greater numbers than heretofore.
2. Black faculty are concentrated chiefly in education and several areas of the social sciences, and even though there is some broadening in disciplinary distribution among the younger age cohorts, this trend appears likely to continue.
3. In terms of their institutional status, black faculty, like academic women, have tended to be concentrated in the lower ranks and at least the impressionistic evidence suggests that they may also be relatively isolated from a major role in institutional administration and governance.

4. In the area of compensation, black faculty, especially females and the most prolific publishers, began to do quite well by the early 1970s.

How can we account for the differential status of women and black professors vis-à-vis majority males? Investigators have by and large explored two potential explanations. Differential treatment may be a function of overt discrimination based on sex and/or race or may simply attend on differential performance, that is, women and minorities as a group are not as productive as majority males and therefore are not as rewarded as a group.

Those who sought to explain differential treatment by differential performance do, however, make important distinctions in the bases or sources of the differential performance. Some would argue that women and blacks perform differently because they *choose* to, that is, as a group, they bring different values, orientations, and activity preferences (the results of differential early socialization) to their academic careers than majority males (for example, for women, an orientation to cooperation rather than to competition, to human relationships rather than to academic tasks; for blacks, an orientation to action rather than to abstraction); *and* those activitity preferences happen to be less rewarded by the academic system.

Others would attribute performance differentials to differentials in educational background and training, suggesting that current performance patterns result from more subtle patterns of discrimination to which women and minorities have been subjected in their academic training as a result of their race or sex or their socioeconomic background.

Still others would attribute differential performance to the differential context within which the academic career is pursued by women and minorities vis-à-vis majority males. This differential context includes (a) the added social/cultural constraints on women and minorities pursuing professional careers—the stress of reconciling the academic role with extra-work roles (for example, for women, the stresses of combining work and traditional family roles; for blacks, the challenge of relating to both the academic and the black communities) and (b) the "token" status of women and minorities, that is, the pressures generated by being different in a majority, male-dominated culture (see Kanter, 1977).

The following sections identify and weigh the evidence that has been generated in testing these competing explanations.

THE THESIS OF OVERT DISCRIMINATION

Three principle sources of evidence are available to test the thesis of overt discrimination.

1. Studies of actual hiring decisions, focusing on interview and hire rates for women and minorities vis-à-vis majority males and on the criteria employed in hiring decisions
2. Studies of discriminatory attitudes on the part of majority males, including attitudes manifested in letters of reference and reactions to scholarly work as well as attitudes toward affirmative action
3. Studies of inequity in the distribution of salary, promotion, and other rewards, including empirical analysis of the determinants of rewards for males and females, blacks and whites, as well as studies of self-perceptions of discrimination among women and minority groups.

Hiring Decisions

Investigators have taken basically two sorts of approaches to the study of hiring decisions. The earlier studies (Simpson, 1969; Levin and Duchin, 1971; Fidell, 1970) sought to detect inequities via experimental simulations, for example, requesting subjects who were usually department chairpersons, deans, or members of faculty search committees to react to curriculum vitae, varying in the sex or race of the applicant. Two-thirds of these studies (Simpson, 1969; Fidell, 1970) did indeed detect discrimination. Males were generally preferred over females, although this preference was significantly lower among female employers and among the youngest and oldest employers; and when hypothetically offered a position, female applicants were less likely to be placed on the tenure track and more likely to be offered a lower rank. The negative case (Levin and Duchin, 1971) uncovered no evidence of discrimination among department chairmen in the physical sciences only. This suggests some variation in discriminatory attitudes by discipline—discrimination appears to surface more readily in the humanities and social sciences (those fields with relatively high proportions of women) and less readily in fields such as the physical sciences, which have the very lowest proportionate representation of women.

The later studies (Amsden and Moser, 1975; Shoemaker and McKeen, 1975; Steele and Green, 1976; Thornberry, 1979) focus explicitly on affirmative action and its impact on interview and hire rates of women and minorities. Together, these studies permit a number of generalizations about the impact of affirmative action. In the first place, affirmative action increases the likelihood that institutions will carefully look at women and minority candidates although it does not significantly increase the likelihood that they will actually hire them. Shoemaker and McKeen (1975), for example, in a study of hiring at 191 colleges and universities advertising positions in the *Chronicle of Higher Education* reported that qualified blacks and nonblack minorities were significantly more likely than qualified white candidates[7] to be *interviewed* (20 percent of qualified black applicants versus 6 percent of qualified white applicants over all positions sampled) but were significantly less likely than white applicants to be hired as a result of the interview. About 6 percent of minority interviewees were hired as opposed to nearly 24 percent of white interviewees, although, overall, qualified minorities and whites were about equally likely to be hired (about 2 percent of the qualified applicant pool of both minorities and whites were ultimately hired).

Institutional pressure for affirmative action, by itself, then, does not significantly affect *hiring* rates of minorities; rather, the findings suggest that the effect of affirmative action on hiring is mediated by individual department circumstances, that is, the department's current utilization index[8] and its level of attrition among women and minority group faculty. Thornberry (1979), in a survey of ninety department chairs in two large state universities, found no significant difference in hiring rates by extent of institutional affirmative action pressures. Steele and Green (1976), however, in a case study of new hires at a public research university over a two-year period, found that general affirmative action pressures are transformed at the department level by situational factors. When department utilization is negative, the pursuit of women and minority candidates is stimulated (departments with a negative utilization index for women made 35 percent of all offers to women during the two-year period under study although they constituted only about 12 percent of the availability pool); when utilization is positive, the extent to which a department pursues affirmative action depends upon attrition among extant women and minority faculty, that is, those departments with little or no minority attrition made but a single offer to minority candidates in the course of sixty-six searches and made less use of those informal recruitment procedures that are most effective in finding minority candidates, whereas those departments with high minority attrition made over one-quarter of all offers to minority candidates and persisted in informal avenues of recruitment. It would appear that once compliance has been achieved (that is, operationally defined as a utilization index greater than or equal to zero), women and minority candidates were pursued only when a vacancy was created by the loss of another woman or minority faculty member. Departments, then, tended to single out a small proportion of positions for allotment to women and minorities and once these were filled, to abandon the pursuit of women and minority candidates, *regardless* of the number of positions that subsequently became available.[9]

If differential treatment of women and minority candidates is manifest in the *results* of the hiring process, Steele and Green (1976) provide additional evidence about the operation of differential treatment in the process of evaluating candidates itself. Following up on their study of hiring decisions, they examined the hiring criteria that department chairpersons applied to unselected minority and white candidates. Specifically, they examined the importance assigned by department chairs to each of twenty-five hiring criteria as well as the ratings on each criterion of unselected candidates. For unselected minority candidates, the majority of correlations between the rated importance of each criterion and the rating of each candidate on that criterion were negative, that is, on those dimensions rated most important, minority candidates were rated lowest, and on those dimensions viewed as less important, minority candidates were rated higher. This was emphatically not the case with unselected white candidates. It would appear that the standing of unselected minority candidates on these hiring criteria changed the importance assigned to these criteria so as to emphasize candidates liabilities and underplay their assets.[10]

Less directly, the differential evaluation of faculty candidates based on sex and/or race is reflected in several content analyses of letters of reference written on behalf of job candidates. Hoffman (1972), in a study of letters of reference prepared by members of the Modern Language Association, detected blatant sexism in the references to physical appearance, marital/parental status, sexual preference, participation in the women's movement or womens studies that found their way into letters written in behalf of women candidates but not those written in behalf of men. Guillemin, Holstrom, and Garvin (1979) in a content analysis of letters of reference written on behalf of candidates for a junior position in sociology at a northeastern university, uncovered sex differences in the appraisal of career performance and potential. Female candidates were less often described as "capable of serious work," and were more frequently referred to as "students" rather than "faculty"; the letters written on behalf of females made fewer references to "intellect" and contained fewer superlatives. While these letters, to be sure, directly reflect the values and orientations of the writers rather than the employers, we can assume that referees are attending to those characteristics they believe are of interest to employers, that is, they are writing for an audience as they perceive it.

Not only do academics attend to different characteristics in evaluating women and minority group candidates for academic employment, there is even some evidence that the ascriptive characteristics of sex and/or race affect the evaluation of scholarly work itself. Goldberg (1968) asked college students to rate pairs of scholarly articles, differing in the sex of the author. Fully 80 percent of the comparisons favored male authors. And that favorable bias tended to be exacerbated in judging scholarly work in the traditionally masculine fields, such as law, linguistics, and city planning.

Salary Discrimination

Differential treatment accorded in the hiring process appears to extend into the actual work situation as well—most notably in the area of salary. We have already noted that academic women as a group earn about 15 percent less than male academics. In an effort to determine whether salary disparities are attributable to sex discrimination or other factors, investigators have sought to control predictor variables other than sex that might explain salary differences. Specifically, they have developed separate regression equations to predict male and female salaries. Collectively, the findings of these studies suggest that

1. Controlling for academic rank, research productivity, and experience, academic women still earn considerably less than men (Bayer and Astin, 1975)
2. The salaries of male academics are more predictable than those of female academics. Tuckman (1976) was able to account for 55 percent of the variance in male faculty salaries but only 32 percent of the variance in the salaries of academic women. Similarly, Bayer and Astin (1975) were able to account for nearly half the variance in male faculty salaries as compared with barely 10 percent of the variance for academic women. It would appear that more intangible factors are operating in the salary determination process for women
3. While in 1969 there was a high degree of similarity in the predictors for male and female faculty, by 1973 considerable

male-female differences in salary determinants were emerging (Bayer and Astin, 1975). These findings suggest that the criteria for salary determination may be in the process of change or realignment or that they are not being uniformly applied to men and women. Table 7.6, based largely on Tuckman's (1976) analysis, highlights the major salary determinants that show differential impacts on academic men and women.

What do these differences mean? An examination of Table 7.6 suggests that females are most rewarded in the areas of their relative aggregate weakness. Although female academics as a group are half as likely as their male colleagues to hold the Ph.D., publish less, and are notably scarce in the natural sciences, they are rewarded for possession of a doctorate, publication, and choosing the natural sciences as a career. Males, on the other hand, are rewarded most heavily in precisely those areas of their greatest comparative strength vis-à-vis academic women. They are more likely to publish, discharge administrative responsibilities, engage in public service, and they receive a premium over academic women for so doing. Similarly, they are more likely to be married and affiliated with more prestigious institutions and receive a premium over academic women for so doing. It would seem fair to conclude, then, that current academic compensation practices tend to recognize historically

TABLE 7.6
DIFFERENTIALS IN THE SALARY DETERMINANTS FOR MALE AND FEMALE FACULTY

Research productivity	1969: Males receive a higher return for publication (Bayer and Astin, 1975) 1973: Females receive a higher return for article publication (Tuckman, 1976)
Career age/experience	Females receive a lower return for experience (Tuckman, 1976)
Public service/administration	Males receive a 100 percent higher return for public service activities and a 50 percent higher return for administrative activities
Prestige of institutional affiliation	Males receive a higher return for affiliation with prestigious institutions (Tuckman, 1976)
Field	Male-female disparity highest in the professions and lowest in the natural sciences and engineering
Highest degree	Females receive a significantly higher return for the doctorate (Bayer and Astin, 1975; Tuckman, 1976)
Doctorate prestige	Prestige of doctorate is a significantly more important predictor for males (Bayer and Astin, 1975)

male strengths and female weaknesses, that is, they are defined in terms of male strengths.

Discrimination in the Allocation of Other Rewards

Academic Women. In terms of the likelihood of gaining an appointment at a prestigious university, six out of seven investigators (Rossi, 1970; Morlock, 1973; Cole and Cole, 1973; M. Patterson, 1971; Baldridge, et al. 1978; Cole, 1979) reported that academic women were significantly less likely than academic men to be at "top" departments (however "top" might be measured), even after controlling for highest degree, Ph.D. prestige (Morlock, 1973), and research productivity (Cole and Cole, 1973; Cole, 1979). Patterns of disciplinary differences did, however, emerge. Females tended to do better in some fields, such as sociology and biology, than in others, such as chemistry and psychology (Cole and Cole, 1973; Cole, 1979; Rossi, 1970). Moreover, the evidence presented by Cartter (1976) suggests that by the mid-1970s academic women had begun to do better at the entry level. The findings of Menninger and Rose (1978), based on 1976 data, that women scientists were concentrated in the high prestige departments may indeed be attributable to this shift at the entry level. They may also, however, be a function of their failure to distinguish between women in faculty positions and those in research or other professional positions. Their findings may thus reflect a concentration of females in the least prestigious jobs (postdoctoral and research associate positions) at the more prestigious institutions.

In the matter of rank, receipt of professional honors, and reputational standing (visibility and perceived quality of work), sex appears to be significantly less of a disadvantage. Bayer and Astin (1975) reported a small significant sex effect on the attainment of higher rank (partial correlation in the neighborhood of 0.15). Cole and Cole (1973) and Cole (1979) found that females were only slightly less likely to receive professional honors, although the magnitude of the disadvantage varied considerably by discipline (from none in biology to a partial correlation of 0.19 in chemistry). They further reported only the most minor independent effect on reputational standing (beta = -0.05). In both the receipt of honors and reputational standing, the lion's share of any sex effects proved attributable to male-female differences in research productivity. The clear and large disadvantage of sex in matters of compensation, then, remains, albeit less strongly, in matters of promotion and virtually disappears in the allocation of professional honors and the recognition of one's peers.

Black Faculty. No multivariate analyses of the impact of race on promotion and the distribution of professional honors and recognition are available. The analysis of the impact of race on compensation suggests that in matters of salary, racial or ethnic minority status is considerably less of a disadvantage than sex.

Self-Perceptions of Discrimination

Beyond the data on actual discriminatory behavior, there is the evidence provided by women and minorities themselves on their self-perceived status. In the case of academic women, Berwald (1962) and Crim (1978) reported a pervasive sense of limited opportunity. Ladd and Lipset (1976) uncovered significant sex differences in views concerning discrimination as opposed to perceptions of the current status of academic women. While 90 percent of both male and female faculty agreed that women scholars are proportionately underrepresented in colleges and universities, fully two-thirds of the women agreed, and nearly 60 percent of the men disagreed, with a statement suggesting that appeals to the concept of merit merely constituted a smokescreen for discrimination. While apparently conceding the obvious, academic men are reluctant to attribute it to their own discriminatory behavior.

In the case of black faculty, the findings of Moore and Wagstaff (1974) and Rafky (1972) suggest that a large proportion of black academics in predominately white colleges and universities feel that blacks are sometimes excluded and discriminated against, even if they are well qualified. The perceptions of discrimination, however, appear to be mediated by institutional type, age, and faculty qualifications. Rafky (1972) found perceptions of discrimination to be highest among the least-qualified faculty and among faculty at lower-prestige-strata institutions and correspondingly lowest among the best-qualified faculty and faculty at higher-tier institutions (among which younger faculty are disproportionately represented). And indeed, Elmore and Blackburn (1983) found an overall perception of equity among their sample of well-qualified and well-located black faculty at the big ten universities—further evidence of the relatively advantageous position in which highly productive black faculty began to find themselves in the early and mid-1970s.

By way of summary, what can be said of the case for overt discrimination? In the first place, the evidence clearly suggests overt discrimination in the hiring process insofar as tokenism (the designation of a few token slots reserved for women and minorities) operates and differential evaluation criteria are applied to women and minority candidates. Although affirmative action pressures appear to be moving women and minority group hiring ratios in line with availability pools, newly entering females appear to have the edge over racial and ethnic minorities—if for no other reason than the latter's uncertain availability pools. Academic women are being subjected to clear and large inequities in compensation and, to a lesser extent, in promotion, while they have achieved near equity in the allocation of professional honors and peer recognition. Black faculty, on the other hand, while not subject to the same inequities in compensation, have not been increasing in proportionate representation in the academic profession during the 1970s. While the objective evidence and the self-reports indicate a relatively advantageous position for the most productive black faculty, the "average" black faculty member at predominantly white institutions appears to be a relatively scarce commodity, concentrated in the lower ranks, and decidedly isolated.

THE THESIS OF PERFORMANCE DIFFERENTIALS

Although, then, a considerable portion of the current status of academic women and minorities is clearly attributable to overt discrimination, there is considerable evidence as well that their current status may be attributable to differences in the type of work performed and to differential levels of performance and productivity.

Differences in Type of Work Performed

Academic women spend more time teaching (Astin and Bayer, 1972; P. Patterson, 1974; Simon and Rosenthal, 1967; Centra, 1974; B. Freeman, 1977; Baldridge et al., 1978) and, specifically, more time teaching undergraduates (Bayer and Astin, 1972; Baldridge et al., 1978) and less time teaching graduate students (Bayer and Astin, 1972; B. Freeman, 1977; Baldridge et al., 1978).[11] Their teaching is more concentrated in small classes, whereas male professors are more likely to teach large lecture sections (Bayer and Astin, 1972). Academic women spend concomitantly less time in research—they spend about half as much time (Baldridge et al., 1978) and are twice as likely as males to spend no time whatever (Eckert, 1971)—and less time in administration—male faculty are nearly twice as likely to hold administrative positions (Centra, 1974).

There is some evidence of variation in the extent of this work activity disparity by institutional type. Bayer and Astin (1972) reported that the differences held firm across all work settings; B. Freeman (1977) found that male-female differences were somewhat attenuated at the most prestigious institutions, that is, the research universities (less than a 10 percent disparity). This suggests that the overall male-female work activity disparity may be a function of the higher concentration of females in the less-research-oriented universities and comprehensive colleges.

In the case of black faculty, Moore and Wagstaff (1974) report that (1) nearly two-thirds are limited in their teaching to undergraduates only, (2) nearly four-fifths spend 15 percent or less of their time in research, and (3) black females tend to have higher teaching loads than black males and spend very little time on research. When black and white professors are compared directly, however, racial differences in the distribution of work effort disappear. Rafky's (1972) sample of black faculty in predominantly white universities was as likely as a comparison group of white faculty to report research and administration as their major activities; and Elmore and Blackburn (1983) reported their samples of black and white faculty at big ten universities to be about equal in time devoted to teaching, research, and university service. There are conflicting findings on the role of black faculty as student counselors. Rafky (1972) found black faculty to be significantly more involved in student academic and personal counseling than their white colleagues, but Elmore and Blackburn (1983) did not. This may be a function of a more limited counseling role played by black faculty at major research universities (Elmore and Blackburn, 1983) or a function of a shift in the role of the black professor over time—as educational opportunity centers and other structures that provide services to minority students have developed over the past decade, they may have relieved black faculty of some of their student counseling burden.

Beyond teaching, research, and administration, women and minority faculty appear to be less involved in off-campus professional activities. Cameron (1978) reported that academic women were significantly less likely than their male colleagues to have developed strong professional network ties; and Bayer (1973) found academic women less likely to spend time off campus in professional activities. Morlock (1973), examining over thirty studies of faculty in fourteen disciplines, reported that academic women were less likely to participate in national meetings and to hold professional association offices or journal editorships. Rafky (1972) reported similar findings for black faculty at predominantly white institutions.

This lowered off-campus professional participation is reflected in patterns of colleagueship and collaboration. Kaufman (1978) found that academic women were significantly less likely than men to separate friendship from colleagueship and tended to include in their colleague networks friends with whom they shared no professional interests. And this distinctively social concept of colleagueship is reflected in patterns of collaboration in research and publication. Cameron (1978) found that while academic women were as likely as males to collaborate on research, they tended to limit their collaboration to a very few colleagues with whom they worked more intensively. Males, on the other hand, tended to work with a much larger network of different collaborators, interacting on a more task-specific basis. Thus, although females are no more likely than males to be married to academics (Bayer, 1973), females are more likely to collaborate with their spouses—a "primary" tie. And when academic women do collaborate with their male colleagues, they tend to receive second authorship nearly two-thirds of the time (Wilkie and Allen, 1975).[12]

The picture that emerges of black faculty, based to be sure, on limited evidence, is one of relative isolation from their white colleagues and of searching for professional and social support from other blacks. While the collaboration rate of black faculty approaches the norm (over one-half had not coauthored publications with colleagues (Moore and Wagstaff, 1974)), Middleton's (1978) admittedly impressionistic findings suggest that the nature of that collaboration may be rather distinctive; many black faculty tend to look to a different set of colleagues beyond their department and with these other black faculty they effectively form a "black network." These findings are echoed by those of Anderson's (1979) case study of faculty at a major public research university.

In the area of paid consulting, academic women appear to be at a greater disadvantage than black faculty. Bayer (1973) found that women scholars were only two-thirds as likely as men to have engaged in paid consulting, with the disparities being greatest at the university level. Elmore and Blackburn (1983), on the other hand, found no significant differences in consulting among black and white faculty at the university level.

Differences in Research Productivity and Performance

Academic Women. Female academics are not only significantly different from their male colleagues in what they do, but in how productive they are in their work. The results of some two dozen studies in the last decade provide overwhelming evidence that males outpublish females across all types and prestige strata of institutions by as much as two or three to one (Fulton, 1975; Ladd and Lipset, 1976; Baldridge et al., 1978;). Whether focusing on cumulative production or publication rate, one dominant pattern emerges again and again (Astin and Bayer, 1972; Centra, 1974; Weidman and Weidman, 1975; Fulton, 1975; B. Freeman, 1977; Astin and Hirsch, 1978; Cameron, 1978 and 1981): men are significantly overrepresented among prolific publishers; females are disproportionately represented among nonpublishers; and academic women are either similar to (Astin, 1973; Centra, 1974; Weidman and Weidman, 1975; B. Freeman, 1977), or significantly higher than (Fulton, 1975; Astin and Hirsch, 1978; Cameron, 1978), males in their proportionate representation among moderate level publishers. Thus, although academic women are significantly more likely not to engage in publication, when they do, they are more likely to be moderate rather than prolific in their publications.

A sizeable portion of this publication disparity seems to be attributable to academic women's "weaker" position on a constellation of correlates of research productivity. They are less likely to be found at the more prestigious institutions and at research universities, less likely to be found in the higher ranks, and less likely to be found in the most productive disciplines (for example, the natural sciences). Although most studies control for one or more of these factors, and none controls for all of them, there nonetheless remains some kind of residual, independent sex effect—an effect that varies considerably from study to study (depending, in part, on the number of control variables examined). Controlling for only one or two of these yields partial correlations of a magnitude of 0.35 (see Cole and Cole, 1973 and Cole, 1979, controlling for institutional type and prestige). Simultaneously controlling for most in a multiple regression analysis yields beta weights of a magnitude of 0.10 (Blackburn et al., 1978).

While the male-female publication disparity, then, tends to withstand the scrutiny of multivariate analysis, it does show marked fluctuation—most notably, by discipline. The disparity is lowest in the natural sciences (Astin, Folger, and Bayer, 1970) and in some of the social science disciplines, especially sociology (Cole, 1979). Indeed, examining publication rate, Fulton (1975) found that the proportion of prolific publishers among women in the natural and social sciences was fully two times higher than that for the sample as a whole. And Centra (1974) reported almost no gender disparity in cumulative publication among physical and biological science doctorates.

Several studies have further documented fluctuation in the disparity over the course of the academic career. The initial disparity is small, but begins to widen measurably about five to ten years after receipt of the doctorate (Converse and Converse, 1971; Cole and Cole, 1973; Centra, 1974); and that pronounced mid-career disparity appears alternatively to narrow by about the twentieth year after receipt of the Ph.D. (Converse and Converse, 1971; Centra, 1974) or to stabilize (Cole and Cole, 1973; Centra, 1974) depending on the type of institution with which faculty members are affiliated (Centra detected a narrowing among college faculty and a stabilization among university faculty) or their disciplinary affiliation (Cole and Cole's sample of natural scientists displayed a stabilizing pattern). The pattern of a narrowing disparity over the course of the academic career is reflected (in combination with a "selection" factor), to some extent, in the finding of a significant rank effect. Fulton (1975) and Astin and Hirsch (1978), in their secondary analyses of the 1969 and 1972 Carnegie–American Council on Education Faculty Surveys, respectively, found the publication disparity declining as faculty ascended the hierarchy of academic ranks. With increasing rank, the proportion of female "inactives" declined, approaching parity with males at the full-professor level; and the proportion of moderate female publishers substantially increased (there was, however, no substantial reduction in the disparity at the highest levels of publication prolificness).

The disparity in publication productivity is replicated in women academics' performance in "grantsmanship" (grantspersonship). Simon and Rosenthal (1967), Bayer (1973), and Lipset and Ladd (1979) found academic women significantly less likely to receive research grants across all types of institutions. Moreover, when they did, they were less likely than their male colleagues to be *principal investigators*. Bayer (1973) found that while one-third of the female academics in his sample had received some grant, only about one-eighth of the sample were serving as principal investigators compared to nearly one-third of the men.[13]

Black Faculty. Three of the four available studies (Rafky, 1972;

Moore and Wagstaff, 1974; R. Freeman, 1978) found a pattern of black-white disparity in publication productivity similar to that between male and female faculty. Rafky (1972) found that black faculty in predominantly white colleges and universities were significantly more likely to be nonproducers and significantly less likely to be high producers—and about as likely as white faculty to be moderate publishers. And R. Freeman's (1978) secondary analysis of the 1969 and 1972–73 Carnegie–American Council on Education Faculty Survey data found that white faculty outpublished black faculty by a ratio of two to one when faculty at the black colleges were excluded. The sole discrepant findings are advanced by Elmore and Blackburn (1983), who found no significant productivity differences between black and white faculty at the Big Ten universities. The failure to find a significant difference may be an artifact of their relatively small sample size (eighty-one black and ninety-two white faculty), or, alternatively, it may reflect the increased demand for highly productive black faculty noted by R. Freeman (1978) in the early and mid-1970s, who were selected to the Big Ten universities.

The Teaching Effectiveness of Academic Women

If academic women are less involved and less productive in research, in the area in which they focus the lion's share of their effort—teaching—they appear to be no more effective overall than their male colleagues. Among a dozen studies that examine the relationship of instructor's sex to student ratings of teaching effectiveness, five reported no significant differences (Choy, 1969; Katz, 1973; Ferber and Loeb, 1973; Ferber and Huber, 1975; Barnett and Littlepage, 1979). Four additional studies yield nonsignificant findings overall; however, they report significant differences either on only a few teacher rating instrument items or for certain disciplines and not others. No clear pattern emerges from the items that do yield significant sex differences. And only one item yielded significant differences in more than one study—both Wilson and Doyle (1976) and Elmore and LaPointe (1974, 1975) found that male faculty were more highly rated in matters of clarity of presentation and speaking. A clear pattern does, however, emerge for disciplinary differences. Female faculty were rated higher in the traditionally female disciplines (such as home economics) and lower in the traditional masculine disciplines (such as engineering and agriculture) (Kajander, 1976; Ferber and Huber, 1975). It would be a mistake, however, to overstate these differences for, although they attain statistical significance, they are generally quite small and explain by themselves only very minute portions of the variance in teaching effectiveness ratings.

That academic women are not rated better teachers overall may nonetheless mask their particular efficacy with some groups of students. Tidball (1976) and others have suggested that female faculty are particularly effective as role models for female students. It may be, then, that they are more effective teachers for female students. This hypothesis has been tested in several recent studies of the interaction effect of instructor and student sex on teaching effectiveness ratings. While three out of five studies show no significant interaction (Elmore and LaPointe, 1974 and 1975; Wilson and Doyle, 1976), two of the five studies do. Ferber and Huber (1975), in a study of faculty of the University of Illinois, found that although male faculty were similarly rated by male and female students, female students tended to rate female faculty much higher than male students rated these same faculty, and significantly higher than they rated male faculty. These findings are corroborated by Mackie (1976) in a study of student ratings at the University of Calgary. They are, however, difficult to interpret. The negative evidence (Elmore and LaPointe, 1974 and 1975; Wilson and Doyle, 1976) is furnished by studies of faculty in the humanities and social sciences, and the positive evidence (Mackie and Ferber and Huber) is furnished by studies of faculty in home economics, agriculture, physical education, and sociology. Any special efficacy of female faculty in the instruction of female students may therefore vary considerably by discipline. Moreover the generalizability of the findings of all of these studies is clouded by the nonrandom sampling of faculty within sex groups (they simply use all available courses that have both male and female instructors). The male and female faculty evaluated can in no way be viewed as representative of male and female faculty, even at the single universities from which the course evaluations were drawn. And, finally, except for Wilson and Doyle, none of the studies control for course level, instructor rank, format, content area—all variables beyond sex that may be affecting student ratings in unpredictable ways. It would appear that, at least at this point in time, no robust inferences can be made.

How to interpret these performance differentials—whether they can be seen to justify the differential status of women and minorities—depends on what we choose to attribute them to. To the extent that they result from the free choice of participants according to their preferences (these preferences, to be sure, may be influenced by differential socialization), then performance differentials may indeed justify differential treatment (provided, of course, we are willing to accept the biases of the extant academic reward system). To the extent, however, that they are attributable to inequitable training opportunities or to externally imposed constraints on the academic career, then performance differentials may merely mirror inequities in the larger society. We therefore turn now to an examination of the evidence bearing on the sources of these performance differentials.

THE THESIS OF CHOICE

Jessie Bernard (1964) was among the first students of academic women to suggest that their status was to a considerable extent a matter of choice. Women, she claimed, by virtue of their prior socialization were more oriented to the teacher than to the man-of-knowledge role, to the socioemotional (nurturant) aspects of working with students than to the cerebral, competitive tasks of research. She argued that it was these differences in orientation that led female faculty to choose less-rewarded academic activities and self-select themselves to those types of academic institutions (teaching-oriented colleges) that permitted them to most freely pursue their preferences.[14]

To what extent does the evidence support this position of inherent male-female differences in orientation and activity preferences resulting from prior socialization? Perhaps the strongest evidence is provided by the sizeable sex differentials in the goals faculty ascribe to their undergraduate teaching. In the 1972–73 American Council on Education Faculty Survey, 20 percent more females than males endorsed student emotional development, helping students achieve deeper levels of self-understanding, and preparation of students for family living as goals of their undergraduate teaching; 10 percent more females than males endorsed development of moral character, development of responsible citizens, conveying a basic appreciation of the liberal arts, and provision of the local community with skilled human resources as goals of their undergraduate teaching. These sex differences are largely replicated in faculty ratings of the importance of the educational goals of their institution, although the size of the differentials is somewhat attenuated. Moreover, these sex differences, by and large, hold across institutional types at the same level of magnitude (although absolute percentages are slightly lower at the universities). It would appear, then, that these differences persist regardless of institutional context and cannot be ascribed to differences in the distribution of academic women over institutional types.

The particular orientation of women academics as a group is further reflected in their tendency to endorse teaching effectiveness, rather than publications, as the primary basis for promotion (Bayer, 1973; Tidball, 1976; Lipset and Ladd, 1979). Indeed, it is academic women in the universities who are nearly twice as likely as the sample as a whole to endorse teaching effectiveness over publications as a basis for promotion, suggesting that female faculty feel even more strongly about the importance of teaching effectiveness at those institutions where it is most challenged by the research ethic (Bayer, 1973). It is not surprising, then, that female faculty as a group proclaim themselves more oriented to teaching than research. Lipset and Ladd (1979) found that 11 percent fewer academic women than men indicated a primary interest in research. Even among the youngest age cohorts, while the absolute proportion preferring research rose slightly, fully 15 percent fewer women than men indicated a preference for research. These sex differences in research orientation held across institutional prestige strata and, with the exception of faculty in the social sciences, across academic fields.[15] Moreover, even among those female faculty who are more research oriented, we find significant sex differences in the character of the research they undertake. Academic women were significantly less likely to undertake pure or basic research and significantly more likely to pursue literary or expressive (Bayer, 1973) or "soft" or qualitative (Ladd and Lipset, 1976) approaches. And it is the pure or basic research orientation that is most significantly associated with high research productivity (Astin and Hirsch, 1978).

The evidence supporting racial or ethnic differences in teaching orientation is considerably sparser. While Hayden's (1978) study of the educational goals of minority faculty in black colleges and black studies programs draws no direct comparisons with white faculty, her findings do suggest racial and ethnic differences in the nature of faculty educational goals. These black faculty rated as least important the goal of "assimilating the student into the dominant culture," but they heartily endorsed goals such as "preparing the student to help promote an economic system that is cooperative rather than competitive," "developing a commitment to serve the black community," "fostering racial solidarity," and "enhancing the self-concept of the student." Although it is not clear to what extent black faculty at predominantly white institutions outside of black studies would support these latter goals, it does seem fair to conclude that a significant group of black faculty orient their teaching activity to goals that would not be of the highest priority to majority male faculty.

Another arena in which free choice influenced by early socialization may be operating is in the distribution of faculty by discipline. In our earlier discussion of the status of academic women, we noted a historic pattern of segregation by discipline: while scarcely represented among faculty in the natural sciences and in the more quantitative fields (such as engineering, economics, and business), fully half of all female faculty were teaching in a cluster of historically feminine fields—the performing arts, education, library science, health-related professions, and English and modern languages. Although the number of females pursuing advanced degrees increased fully 50 percent during the 1970s (National Center for Education Statistics, 1982), changes in patterns of segregation by discipline have been only slight in comparison. Women are increasingly drawn to law, economics, the physical sciences (chemistry rather than physics), and engineering, but they continue to constitute a majority of the graduate students in education, the health professions, English, foreign languages, and library science (Lipset and Ladd, 1979; National Center for Educational Statistics, 1982). These continued sex-related variations do not appear to result from admissions barriers. A study of graduate school admissions at the University of California, Berkeley, cited by Lipset and Ladd (1979), revealed that women tended to apply to departments with a high ratio of applicants to places—largely those that did not require mathematical preparation. As the authors of the study pointed out, "women are shunted by their socialization and education toward fields of graduate study that are generally more crowded, less productive of completed degrees, and less well funded, and that frequently offer poor professional employment prospects" (Bickel et al., 1975).

Black graduate student enrollments display a pattern similar to that of women, except that there has been no dramatic numerical swelling of black graduate school enrollments during the decade of the 1970s. By 1979, blacks constituted 4.6 percent of all doctoral degree recipients (up from about 3 percent a decade earlier) but continued to segregate themselves into a few fields: education, a few of the social sciences, and the humanities (National Center for Educational Statistics, 1982).

One final note on the issue of sex and race-related differences in faculty orientation to cooperation versus competition. While we have no direct evidence on the attitudes of women and black faculty toward competition, several studies offer suggestive findings. Bayer (1973) solicited faculty perceptions of their relative career success compared to male and female colleagues in their field with comparable training. He found that whereas male faculties' perception of their career success was largely independent of the sex of their comparison group, female faculties' perception were not, that is, female faculty tended to compare themselves favorably with their female colleagues, but much less favorably with their male colleagues. While these sex differences may merely reflect the reality that males are more likely than females to have received the tangible rewards (promotion, affiliation with a prestigious institution, and higher salaries) associated with career success, they may also reflect a disinclination on the part of women academics to compete with their male colleagues. Middleton (1978) reported that some young black faculty had "become discouraged by the pressures of working in white institutions and voluntarily have gone back to black colleges or left higher education altogether." To what extent such withdrawal represents a response to the harsh economic realities of the academic profession during the late 1970s or a more general disinclination toward the competition for promotion and tenure is not clear.

DIFFERENCES IN TRAINING AND EDUCATIONAL BACKGROUND

Female faculty defy the law of social class influence on academic careers—higher socioeconomic background tends to be associated with attendance at more prestigious baccalaureate and graduate institutions, which is, in turn, associated with more favorable placement in the academic stratification system (see Crane, 1969). Women have historically come to an academic career from higher socioeconomic backgrounds than male academics (Bernard, 1964; Astin, 1969) and continue to do so (Strober, 1975; B. Freeman, 1977; Lipset and Ladd, 1979)—indeed, younger female faculty come from the most privileged backgrounds in the entire profession; and yet, they have been unable to translate the advantages of their background into status within the academy.

What intervenes between socioeconomic origin and career entry to attentuate the effect of socioeconomic origin? Since academic women do not differ appreciably from their male colleagues in the prestige of their baccalaureate or graduate institutions, the most obvious factor appears to be sex-related differences in the attainment of the doctorate. Through the early 1970s, academic women have been about half as likely as their male colleagues to hold the Ph.D. (Eckert, 1971; Bayer, 1973; Morlock, 1973; Kane, 1976; Baldridge et al., 1978); and possession of the doctorate is importantly associated with teaching in universities rather than colleges, publication, and salary and promotion (Blau, 1973; Finkelstein, 1978). However, if male-female differences in attainment of the doctorate were the major determinant of male-female status disparities, one would expect non-Ph.D. males to be as bad off as non-Ph.D. females. This is decidedly not the case. The Modern Language Association Commission on the Status of Women (1971) found that more men without the doctorate reached the rank of full or associate professor than women. And data from the American Council on Education 1972–73 Faculty Survey corroborate this finding: male faculty without the Ph.D.—some 25 percent of the male faculty sample—were distributed nearly evenly over the ranks of assistant, associate, and full professor, whereas nondoctorate females—just over half the sample of academic women—were heavily clustered at the assistant professor level. These data, no doubt, overestimate the sex effect since they do not take career age (years of experience) into account—the proportion of academic women in the under-thirty age category is nearly twice that for academic men and one would expect this entry-level group to be clustered at the lower ranks. Overall, however, the age and experience distribution of male and female faculty is quite similar (Bayer, 1973) (only about 5 percent more females than males are just embarking on their service in the academic profession), so that the disadvantage of the academic women appears to persist, irrespective of the terminal degree issue.

What background factors beyond mere possession of the Ph.D., then, contribute to the relative disadvantage of academic women? There is evidence of sex-related inequities in several components of graduate training that investigators have found to be associated with later performance and career success (Cameron, 1978 and 1981). Graduate assistantships in teaching and research provide an opportunity to work closely with a faculty member outside the classroom; and, especially in the latter case, provide an opportunity for the development of research skills and for early publication (the major determinant of later career publication productivity; see Clemente, 1974; Blackburn et al., 1978). It is these very sorts of opportunities that are conducive to the development of a "mentoring" relationship with a faculty member who may then serve as sponsor in the early stages of an academic career—a critical factor in gaining access to the best academic positions (Cameron, 1978; Blackburn, Chapman, and Cameron, 1981). Yet, academic women at all types of institutions were only half as likely as men to have held research assistantships and two-thirds as likely as men to have held teaching assistantships (Bayer, 1973; Centra, 1974; Strober, 1975; B. Freeman, 1977).[16] Moreover, both Sell (1974) and B. Freeman (1977) found that academic women at research universities were significantly less likely to report having a faculty sponsor in graduate school. That likelihood, however, varied considerably by discipline—with the disparity approaching zero in the case of social science faculty, that very group which shows no sex-related disparity in research orientation and productivity (Lipset and Ladd, 1979).

There is at least one sign that the gap may be narrowing. Cameron (1978) in a 1977 study uncovered no sex-related differences in graduate school sponsorship. Her negative findings may be attributable to particulars of sample size and composition. The small sample size would require very large disparities to attain statistical significance and the preponderance of social science faculty would tend to narrow any sex-related disparities. They may also, however, be attributable to changing attitudes and practices in graduate education. Cameron collected her data fully five years after Sell and Freeman, following a period that saw both increasing pressures for affirmative action and a rise in female graduate school enrollments. Nonetheless, for most current female faculty, trained in the first half of the 1970s or earlier, the evidence suggests sex-related differentials in training opportunities precisely in those aspects of graduate education associated with initial job placement and later productivity. And, all of this quite beyond any sex differences in the likelihood of Ph.D. attainment.

If women faculty defy the law of socioeconomic status and academic careers, black faculty at predominantly white institutions conform to it—with a vengeance. Black faculty are twice as likely as their white colleagues to come from low socioeconomic origins, with younger black faculty even more likely to do so than their older colleagues (Rafky, 1972). At the baccalaureate level, the top ten producers of black faculty are all black colleges, with younger black faculty more likely to have attended the least prestigious predominantly white institutions, especially public comprehensive colleges and universities (Bryant, 1970; Mommsen, 1974). At the graduate level, black faculty, like academic women, are about half as likely to hold the Ph.D. as their white colleagues (Rafky, 1972; R. Freeman, 1978); and those who do attain the doctorate tend to take much longer to do so than their white colleagues.[17] Unlike academic women, however, black faculty were less likely than their majority male colleagues to pursue their doctoral studies at the most prestigious research universities—and this is especially true for the younger black faculty cohort (Rafky, 1972). In light of these conditions, the careers of black faculty, even more so than those of academic women, are likely to be adversely affected by their education and graduate training.

THE DIFFERENTIAL CONTEXT OF THE ACADEMIC CAREER

Female Faculty

While academic women are more likely than men to interrupt their graduate study for childbirth and other domestic responsibilities (P. Patterson, 1974; Strober, 1975), they tend to complete their degrees about as quickly (Strober, 1975) if at a slightly later age (Tuckman, 1976); and, upon degree completion, typically plunge right into an academic career (Gappa and Uehling, 1979). Once having embarked on their career, they are no more likely than men to interrupt it for personal and family reasons (Astin, Folger, and Bayer, 1970; Bayer, 1973).

While, then, academic women pursue their career trajectory as directly as, though a little later than, academic men, a number of constraints operate on that pursuit. Marriage and family responsibilities appear to be a primary one.[18] While it is true that academic women are only half as likely to be married as academic men (45 versus 90 percent—Fulton, 1975; B. Freeman, 1977) and the plurality is indeed single, the proportion of married academic women is increasing among each new age cohort entering the profession—to nearly 60 percent among the most recent female entrants. Marital constraints, therefore, are particularly significant for younger female faculty—those who are in the thick of the tenure race—and will be even more so in the future should present trends continue.

Several recent studies (Herman and Gyllstrom, 1977; Koester and Clark, 1980) report that married female faculty experience more conflict between work and family roles than unmarried female faculty or married male faculty. The primary source of that strain appears to be sheer lack of time to meet opposing demands. Koester and Clark (1980) and Mayfield and Nash (1976) reported time management to be the number one source of tension for married female faculty. Herman and Gyllstrom (1977), Heckman et al. (1977), and Gappa, St. John-Parsons, and O'Barr (1979) found that academic women, even those in purportedly equality-oriented relationships, tended to revert to traditional sex roles in the family—assuming responsibility for household maintenance, cooking, etc., and maintaining primary responsibility for parenting. Thus, female faculty were found to spend 50–100 percent more time in home mainte-

nance during the work week and during weekends than academic
men (about twenty-eight hours overall, Gappa and Uehling, 1979)
and 40 percent less time in professional work during the weekends
(Herman and Gyllstrom, 1977)—all of this despite the extensive use
of full-time childcare.

Beyond the day-to-day time constraints, marriage also constrains
the career mobility of academic women. While less likely to be married, they are two or three times as likely as academic men to have
spouses who are professionals—frequently also professors (Simon,
Clark, and Galway, 1967; Astin, 1969; B. Freeman, 1977; Blackburn, Chapman, and Cameron, 1981). This results in several sorts of
constraints.

1. *Enforced mobility when the spouse moves.* Berger et al. (1977),
   in a study of job-seeking strategies among dual-career couples,
   found that although most couples initially chose *egalitarian*
   strategies (optimization of opportunity for both), in response to
   market unfavorability they tended to revert to the traditional
   strategy of giving the husband's career precedence. Astin
   (1969) found married female doctorates more mobile than the
   unmarried, primarily as a result of spouse job moves. And Reagan (1975) found that even female economics faculty who were
   equal or major earners in their family, were significantly more
   likely than men to have given up a good job in the past because
   their spouse had to move (nearly one-third of the females compared to 4 percent of the males).

2. *Immobility owing to spouse's employment.* Baldridge et al.
   (1978) reported that although female faculty were more dissatisfied with their jobs than their male colleagues, they were
   significantly less likely to move as a result, among other
   things, of family considerations. Rose (1978) and Marwell et al.
   (1979) found that although male and female faculty made
   about the same number of job shifts, women tended significantly more often to remain in the same geographic location
   (33 percent as compared with 7 percent of the men). And Reagan (1975) found that although female economics faculty who
   were equal or major family earners were as willing as men to
   move, their past mobility patterns indicated that the spouse's
   career had taken precedence.

Recognition of this enforced immobility leads to exploitation. Heckman et al. (1977) found that among 200 couples holding joint membership in the American Psychological Association, nearly 20 per-

cent cited professional exploitation, that is, colleges and universities taking advantage of a female academic's geographical "stuckness" to pay her less and offer her a nonregular appointment.

It appears clear, then, that marriage and family have an especially negative impact on the job mobility of female faculty and ultimately on their careers insofar as mobility, or the threat of mobility, has traditionally been associated with moving up in the academic world—both in rank and in salary. Academic women simply do not have that ace in the hole working for them. When they do change jobs, it is more likely to be in the same geographical location, and they are less likely to advance in rank and salary than their more geographically mobile male colleagues (Marwell, 1979).

If marriage and family responsibilities constrain the career mobility of female faculty and increase the stress level under which they must operate on a daily basis, the evidence suggests that the preemptiveness of the family role may not directly account for sex-related differences in performance, especially in the area of research. Nine recent investigations have sought to examine the relationship between marital and parental status and the research productivity of female faculty (Simon, Clark, and Galway, 1967; Astin, 1969 and 1978; Astin, Folger, and Bayer, 1970; Cole and Cole, 1973; Centra, 1974; Weidman and Weidman, 1975; Ferber and Loeb, 1973; B. Freeman, 1977; Hamovitch and Morganstern, 1977). Two-thirds of these studies found no significant difference in research productivity between married and unmarried academic women.[19] Indeed, two out of three of the discrepant studies (B. Freeman, 1977; Astin, 1978) found that married women were actually more productive than their single colleagues. Initial differences at the assistant professor level were quite small, but swelled to the point that at the full-professor level, married females outpublished single females by two or three to one and also outpublished married males. The third discrepant study, Astin (1969), reports lower productivity among married women academics—but, the relationship is very small ($r_p = -0.06$) and of limited practical significance. Still further doubts are cast on the significance of the relationship by the peculiarities of Astin's sample. Astin extended her survey to female Ph.D. recipients, generally, rather than limiting it to those who were employed full-time in the labor force. By including nonworking doctoral recipients and those employed part-time, who are more likely to be married, to be parents, and to be nonproductive, Astin increased the likelihood of finding a negative relationship.

While it would appear, then, that marital and parental responsibilities cannot account for sex-related differences in research performance, this consensus needs to be interpreted with caution. While the studies focus on cumulative publication over the academic career, they seek to relate it to respondent marital status only at the time of the survey. This creates a high potential for the misclassification of individual respondents. A faculty member just married, yet single during most of their career would be classified as married; similarly, someone who has been married most of his or her career and is recently just widowed or divorced would be classified as single. How might such misclassification affect the findings? It may be that they effectively cancel each other out (about equal numbers of married and single respondents are misclassified); or, it may be that errors of classification hide any real relationship that might exist. We have no way of telling.

To the extent, however, that we lend credence to these findings, then we are led to conclude that while family role constraints make for added stress and reduce the advancement opportunities that attend mobility, they do not explain male-female differentials in research performance. And that explanation still seems to reside in activity preferences and orientations that seem attributable to earlier sex roles socialization or in differential training opportunities.

Black Faculty

While black female faculty experience the same conflict between professional and family responsibilities, they, together with black male faculty, seem to be subject to the additional tug-of-war between their professional and community responsibilities (the larger family, as it were).

Walker (1973) detected a double-consciousness among black university professors as they struggled to reconcile the frequently incompatible behaviors demanded of them by the academic and black communities—incompatibilities between the action research orientation demanded by the Afro-American community and the academic research orientation demanded by tenure and promotion committees; the incompatibility between the role of scholar and the role of community activist: incompatibilities between the communicative style characterizing the two communities; and, the sheer time demands imposed by service to both.

This double-consciousness is reflected in the goals black faculty pursue in their teaching—the preparation of students to compete in the economic system and the development of commitment to the black community (Hayden, 1978). More immediately, it is reflected in the tensions of daily work. Moore and Wagstaff (1974) and Middleton (1978) report on the individual psychological repercussions of at once pursuing promotion and tenure and serving as the resident black, that is, becoming involved in the counseling of black students, serving on a disproportionate share of committees, especially those concerned with affirmative action and minority affairs, attending black events on campus, as well as maintaining relationships with the black community. Moreover, the dilemma is confounded insofar as most black faculty are in education, the humanities, and the social sciences, and their research and teaching directly or indirectly touches on matters of race.

While no studies empirically test the effect of these tensions on black faculty performance and career advancement, impressionistic evidence suggests that for those black faculty caught on the wrong side of the dilemma, both performance and career advancement may suffer (Middleton, 1978).

The Peculiar Stresses of Being a "Token"

Quite beyond the conflicts generated by divided loyalties to the profession and to the family and community, women and minority faculty, single and married, are subject to the additional stress of frequently being the only one of their kind in a department—the deviant individual in an otherwise racially or sexually homogeneous group.

Kanter (1977) has examined the impact of low proportional representation of a particular social category on group functioning in business organizations. In skewed groups, that is, groups in which one social category predominates over another by a ratio of more than 85 to 15, she uncovered a set of dynamics that empirically defines tokenism. In such skewed groups, tokens (1) tend, as deviants, to have high visibility (which creates performance pressures of its own) and to function as symbols of their social category for the dominant group (creating the additional pressure of representing all women or all blacks to the dominant group); (2) provide the impetus for increased self-consciousness among the dominants of their common culture and ipso facto the token's deviance (and this is reflected in the tendency to isolate tokens on the periphery of colleague interaction—the token is not quite to be trusted); and (3) are stereotyped, that is, subsumed under preexisting generalizations about their category as a group and forced into playing limited and caricatured roles (for example, the female faculty member relegated to taking minutes at the committee meeting; the minority faculty member assigned responsibilities related to affirmative action).

Although there has been no full-scale empirical test of Kanter's concept as it operates in academe, a number of related pieces of evidence suggestively support the operation of group dynamics associated with tokenism.

1. Kaufman's (1978) studies of colleagueship and network involvement among female faculty reveal a pattern of greater relative scholarly isolation as do Middleton's (1978) and Anderson et al.'s (1979) studies of black faculty
2. The phenomenon of viewing individual female and minority faculty as representatives of their social categories is a familiar pattern in academe (for example, the black faculty member is the instant expert on black students)
3. Studies of job satisfaction show that women scholars (single as well as married) are significantly less satisfied with their jobs than male academics (Herman and Cyllstrom, 1977; Baldridge et al., 1978). Moreover, those at the most prestigious institutions (where women are scarcest) and those who are youngest (and have not yet developed successful coping strategies) are the least satisfied of all.

Just how token status per se affects performance (the comparison of token and nontoken women and minorities) remains to be examined. To the extent that tokenism is a major determinant of the work performance of women and minorities, then the most viable solution will be to increase the proportion of women and minority group members of academic departments (move toward more balanced groups)—a goal that appears to be mitigated by current responses to affirmative action pressures, such as the establishment of token slots in academic departments (Steele and Green, 1976).

A FINAL WORD

On the basis of the preceding analysis, what conclusions can be drawn about the status of women and minority faculty in academe?

Most importantly, it appears that the situation of women and minority faculty is the result of many forces. Beyond inequities in training opportunities and in hiring, promotion, and compensation practices that may be attributable to overt discrimination on the part of the professoriate, a number of less directly manipulable factors are at work. There is, first of all, the matter of early socialization and the orientations and activity preferences to which it gives rise. The evidence clearly suggests that a heightened orientation to teaching and student development, a disinclination to empirical research, and selection to more teaching-oriented institutions cannot be attributed solely, or even primarily, to discrimination against individuals on the sole basis of their sex or racial or ethnic origin. Similarly, the sex and race-related constraints on the pursuit of an academic career seem more attributable to culturally prescribed family and community roles than to purposeful discrimination against individuals. Colleges and universities, in and of themselves, are hardly in a position to attack differential early socialization and prescribed family and community role relationships directly.[20] They are, however, in a position to more directly attack inequities within the academy itself. They can recognize the peculiar impacts of early socialization and sociocultural constraints and attempt to adjust employment practices and the organizational reward system to accommodate group differences. It should be recognized, however, that current practices and the current reward system have evolved over time to meet the needs and orientations of the largest number of academics—majority males. It would be most reasonable to expect change to occur only to the extent to which the composition of the professoriate actually changes, that is, to the extent that numerically significant minorities emerge that can mobilize significant support for change. In the case of academic women, that numerical significance in graduate education and in the professoriate itself and that mobilization of support began to emerge in the late 1970s— at the very same time that the women's movement was mobilizing significant support for change in early socialization and family roles. Thus, institutions of higher education have begun to respond to the negative impact of antinepotism regulations, to needs for pregnancy leave and child care centers, etc. In the case of racial minorities, that numerical significance and mobilization of support has yet to emerge; and the data on graduate school enrollments are not encouraging.

If indeed numerical growth is the key to change, then the decade of the 1980s brings with it a bitter irony (at least for academic women). At the very time when social conditions support a significant infusion of women into the professoriate, the opportunities for an academic career are declining dramatically; and, if current enrollment projections are credible, will continue to do so for at least the next decade and a half. To what extent the significant contingent of academic women among "new hires" will fall prey to the tenure squeeze or retrenchment or will make their way into the senior ranks of the professoriate and further empower themselves and the cause of equity should determine the situation of women and minority faculty well into the twenty-first century.[21]

1. Much of the increase in the physical sciences is, however, attributable to increased representation in chemistry, whereas representation in physics remains around the 5–6 percent level.

2. It should be noted, however, that over two-thirds of the female doctoral recipients in this area specialized in "food sciences," that is, the more traditionally female area of home economics.

3. This is hardly surprising since the overall proportionate representation of blacks in the academic profession is twice that of Asian Americans and more than three times that of Hispanics and Native Americans.

4. Since the National Center for Educational Statistics does not annually provide breakdowns of its faculty data by race as it does by gender, the data for our assessment of the status of black faculty is older than for female faculty.

5. Nonblack minority faculty did not do as well. They are paid somewhat less than comparably productive white colleagues and showed no consistent improvement in compensation between 1969 and 1973.

6. Given the lack of systematic sampling, the results of both of these studies need to be interpreted with extreme caution.

7. An equal proportion—about two-thirds—of both black and white applicants were considered to be "qualified."

8. For affirmative action purposes, a department's utilization index is defined as the percentage of women and minorities hired divided by the availability pool times the number of full-time equivalent faculty in the department, and it provides a generally accepted indicator of the extent to which department hiring practices reflect the availability pools for women and minority group faculty.

9. In the case of minority faculty, in particular, there is the further problem of determining the availability pool upon which utilization indexes are calculated. Unlike academic women, no national organization maintains data on the disciplinary distribution of minority doctoral degree recipients. In current institutional practice, the availability pools of minority candidates tend to be calculated on the basis of annual doctoral degree conferrals by a handful of the most prestigious research universities, thus effectively excluding from their availability estimates doctorates conferred by Howard University and other major producers of black Ph.Ds. Current practices thus tend to underestimate the availability pool of minority candidates and thus indirectly contribute to inequities (Steele and Green, 1976).

10. It should be noted that these findings are based on the responses of only five department chairpersons and may, in fact, reflect defensiveness at the line of questioning rather than an actual bias operating during the hiring process.

11. The largest male-female differences occur at the high end of the spectrum. Thus, while male and female academics are about evenly distributed at the low and midrange of the teaching load continuum, academic women are much more likely than men to be teaching more than nine hours—nearly two-thirds of the women compared to less than half of the men (Astin and Bayer, 1972; B. Freeman, 1977).

12. Although one cannot clearly attribute the high incidence of second authorship to discrimination based on these descriptive data alone, the size of the male-female disparity certainly leads one to wonder whether or not treatment was equal.

13. Cameron (1978) found virtual parity between males and females in her sample in the proportion receiving one or more grants and in the average number of grants received over a three-year period. Her findings may reflect the effort of federal agen-

cies during the latter half of the 1970s to be more self-consciously evenhanded in their distribution of funds. Or, they may merely reflect the exclusion of faculty in the natural sciences from her sample—that group which is most likely to receive grants and which is simultaneously least likely to count academic women among its ranks.

14. She has since recanted and moved into the feminist camp (see Bernard, 1981).

15. The greater orientation toward research among female social scientists may be related to the fact that they also turn out to be much more committed to the ideology of the women's liberation movement than their colleagues in other fields. Perhaps as a result, they have also rejected other traditional feminine orientations, which have been reflected in the preference of female academics for the less competitive person-related teaching role (Lipset and Ladd, 1979).

16. The issue remains, of course, as to what extent these sex differences owe to the operation of preference—that is, women self-selecting themselves out of research assistantships and into teaching assistantships, in which they achieve near equity with men—or discrimination on the part of graduate faculty.

17. Rafky (1972) found that the median time for doctoral degree completion for black faculty was thirteen years subsequent to receipt of the baccalaureate at a median age of thirty-six compared to a median completion time of seven and a half years after the baccalaureate at a median age of thirty for white faculty. These differences probably, however, reflect differences in the disciplinary distribution of black and white faculty. Blacks tend to be disproportionately located in those disciplines, such as education, whose average time to degree completion has been historically high, and whites tend to be more evenly distributed over disciplines—including those, such as the natural sciences, with historically shorter average degree completion times.

18. Marriage has traditionally been more of an advantage to the professional male than to the professional female. For men, the spouse functions as a source of support, a household attendant—minimizing family distractions to work—and even as a research assistant; for women, marriage and a family become something they have to juggle with their professional responsibilities (Koester and Clark, 1980).

19. Among these studies, all three that examined the relationship for males found that married men were indeed more productive than unmarried men; and four out of five that examined the impact of parental status found it to be nonsignificant.

20. They can, to be sure, serve as a forum for highlighting these social inequities and even for mobilizing intellectual resources to respond to them.

21. Insofar as academic women tend to be significantly more sensitive to general issues of discrimination and equity than majority males (Ladd and Lipset, 1976), it seems reasonable to assume that, at least to some extent, their rise in significant numbers to senior ranks will bring with it an increased push toward equity. The possibility remains, however, of co-optation and for the new elite to overidentify with the "academic establishment" and turn against their own—a phenomenon Kanter (1977) observed among new women managers.

8

Summing Up

Looking back over some four decades of social scientific inquiry, one can identify at least three axes of generalization across the host of discrete facts and insights. Taken together, these three axes provide a convenient structure for summing up, and more importantly, they form the outlines of a substantive framework which may be brought to bear in understanding academics.

The Distinctive Character of Academic Workers:
Sources of Motivation and Satisfaction

In at least one fundamental respect, professors are a world apart from most other workers: their-on-the-job performance is determined to an extraordinary degree by their own professional values and standards. Studies of faculty performance lend strong support to the proposition that in acquitting themselves of their core academic obligations of teaching and research, faculty are most influenced by their own internalized standards for professional performance. At the same time, their activity patterns appear to be relatively impervious to the performance demands reflected in institutional incentive structures. Notwithstanding the likelihood of "payoff," research-oriented faculty tend to do research, and teaching-oriented faculty tend to devote themselves to teaching—whatever their institutions may want them to do. Notwithstanding obvious fiscal and enrollment pressures, and even the prospect of layoffs, faculty react to new instructional procedures and programs, and new kinds of students, in a highly differentiated fashion, based primarily on the test of "normative congruence" and not on the degree of institutional pressure.

This "intrinsic" quality of faculty motivation clearly is reflected as well in the patterns of faculty satisfaction with their work. Research on faculty mobility (Stecklein and Lathrop, 1960; Cammack, 1965; Brown, 1967; Nicholson and Miljus, 1972; McGee, 1971) and job and career satisfaction (Stecklein and Eckert, 1958; Whitlock, 1965; Swierenga, 1970; Avakian, 1971; Eckert and Williams, 1972; Leon, 1973; Moxley, 1977; Willie and Stecklein, 1982) suggests that faculty tend to find satisfaction in the nature of their work itself and in the autonomy with which it is pursued (Cares and Blackburn, 1978), whereas their dissatisfaction centers largely on extrinsic factors (such as facilities and administration). The distinctiveness of these findings becomes clearer when they are considered in the context of recent research on job satisfaction. Weaver (1978) completed a national study of the level and sources of job satisfaction among professional and nonprofessional workers. He reported the usual high correlation between overall level of job satisfaction and occupational status; that is, those in higher status, professional lines of work tend to express the highest overall level of job satisfaction. He did, however, uncover marked differences in the sources of job satisfaction. Among lower status workers and laborers, what job satisfaction they experienced was attributable to the nature of the work itself, and dissatisfaction tended to focus on extrinsic factors, such as money and the lower social status of their occupations. The higher overall level of job satisfaction among professional workers, on the other hand, was largely attributable to their satisfaction with the perquisites of professional work (high salary, social status); indeed, their major source of dissatisfaction seemed to rest with the nature of the work they performed. If Weaver is indeed correct, then faculty, as a group, appear to share with other professional workers the high overall level of job satisfaction and at the same time share with lower status workers and laborers their distinctive sources of job satisfaction.

The Professor as Everyman

If faculty emerge as a "distinct species" in their professional motivations and satisfactions, they appear, in certain other fundamental respects, to resemble closely other, less-exalted segments of the general population. This "commonality" is no more apparent than in professorial conduct in the social and political spheres of professional life. No less than the larger society, the professoriate employs ascriptive as well as meritocratic criteria in the allocation of status. How far an individual rises in the estimation of his or her professional colleagues may depend on the prestige and visibility afforded by institutional affiliation (Crane, 1970) or on the prominence and power of contacts (Cameron and Blackburn, 1981) and the prestige of one's doctoral institution (Hargens and Hagstrom, 1967; Crane, 1970; Lightfield, 1971; Youn, 1981) than on either the quality or the number of one's scholarly publications, and once there, one's promotion and salary increases may be tied more closely to longevity and seniority than to productivity (Astin and Bayer, 1973; Hargens and Farr, 1973).

As academic citizens, faculty respond to politically charged situations encountered in professional life much as any other citizens do—on the basis of their prior political socialization and their position within the academic stratification system rather than on the basis of the professional values of merit and academic freedom. Attitudes toward the prospect of unionization (McInnis, 1972; Ladd and Lipset, 1973) and toward student disruptions (Cole and Adamsons, 1969; Wences and Abramson, 1972) appear to hinge much more on a professor's general political leanings (relative political liberalism), institutional status, and situational factors than on an assessment of probable impacts on the functioning of the academic community. Moreover, professorial commitment to academic values and behavioral follow-through on value commitments vary as functions of available social support. Cole and Adamsons (1969, 1970) reported that faculty were significantly less likely to act out their ideological opposition to student demonstrations if their colleagues favored them. Both Lazarsfeld and Thielens (1958) and Goldblatt (1967) reported that the commitment of social scientists to the tenets of academic freedom appeared to fluctuate with the degree of social support for academic freedom among institutional colleagues. Indeed, they found that individuals vacillated in their commitment to academic freedom as they moved, over the course of their careers, to different institutions providing differential colleague support for that fundamental doctrine of the profession. To be sure, there are exceptions to these generalizations about academic citizenship—the ideal-typical professor, the productive scholar at the apex of the academic stratification system, has more fully operationalized academic values in the political and social life of his or her profession. Mandarin though he or she may be, this individual tends to be at once politically liberal and tolerant, though asserting academic values over political ones. The typical professor, however, appears to act out a citizenship role in the academic polity much as his or her neighbor does in the larger sociopolitical system.

Another fundamental respect in which faculty resemble "everyman" is that, like other adults, they grow and change over the course of their careers. Indeed, *age* emerges as the single most important source of individual change over the course of the academic career. It accounts for statistically significant variation in over half of the variables treated in the research literature, whereas changes in professional status (e.g., rank and tenure) significantly affect barely one-third. Most notably, age is associated with increased conservatism (Spaulding et al., 1968; Berger, 1973; Ladd and Lipset, 1975), decreased research orientation (Behymer, 1974; Fulton and Trow, 1974) and a heightened orientation toward teaching (Kelly and Hart, 1971; Klapper, 1969; Baldwin, 1979), but without any perceptible change in publication rate or in teaching effectiveness. In the absence of longitudinal data, it is, strictly speaking, impossible to disentangle the effects of aging per se from those attributable to generational differences among age cohorts studied cross-sectionally, let alone to specify precisely what it is about growing older that affects how faculty think and what they do. However, Baldwin's (1979) recent study of faculty at different career stages suggests that much of the impact of age is a function of the developmental changes that psychologists have shown to characterize growth during the adult years (Levinson, 1978).

In a more limited fashion, faculty may be seen to resemble that sector of the population engaged in professional occupations in the centrality of the work role. Academic work, like other professional work, tends to be preemptive and to overshadow the individual's family and personal life (Kistler, 1967; Lee, 1968; Parsons and Platt, 1968; Anderson and Murray, 1971; Gerstl, 1971; Friedman, 1971). A number of studies conclude that academic work, in contradistinction to that of other professions, tends to foster a distinctive species of lifestyle, but the relationship appears to be largely spurious. What differences are discernible between academics and other professionals—their relatively higher degree of ethnic and religious assimilation, their greater liberalism, and their predilection for "high culture"—seem to be more attributable to selection than to socialization factors. Available evidence on the timing of changes in religiosity (Thalheimer, 1965, 1973) and political orientation (Ladd and Lipset, 1975) suggests that faculty religious and political predilections were largely formed before entry into the academic profession. Changes occurring later are more likely attributable to adult socialization processes quite independent of the academic context (Mazur, 1971). Thus, academics tend to be very different types of people from other professionals, and these long-standing differences rather than the character of academic work and its environment account for any distinctiveness vis-à-vis other professionals.

Finally, academic life may be seen to mirror social life generally in the status of women and minorities. Ingrained sex role socialization and racial and ethnic cultural patterns appear to influence professional choices within the academy in much the same way that they influence life choices outside it. Professors, like everyone else, do sometimes discriminate overtly against individuals on the basis of their gender or their race. Moreover, like any "dominant" social group, white academic men have fashioned a "dominant" culture reflecting their values and activity preferences, in relation to which women and minorities remain at the periphery.

The Divided Academy

Thus far, we have discussed faculty almost *as if* they constituted a single, cohesive social group. But if the findings of research on college and university faculty suggest anything, it is that faculty are as different from each other as they are from the population at large. Indeed, the professoriate may be less a social *species* than a *genus* encompassing several distinct species. At the very least, both *institutional type and prestige* and *academic discipline* may be seen to differentiate among species of academics. Fulton and Trow (1974) suggest that the academic role itself, as a pattern of activities, may be a very different phenomenon at different types of institutions. At elite universities the role appears to be a more integrated one, combining nearly equal measures of teaching, research, adminstration, and service; at less prestigious undergraduate institutions, the role tends to be more lopsided, variously emphasizing one core function over another. Institutional type and prestige account for statistically significant variation in virtually every dependent variable that has come under investigative scrutiny. Among various disciplinary groupings, there are differential normative orientations to education (Gamson, 1966), differential commitments to traditional academic values, such as academic freedom (Lazarsfeld and Thielens, 1958; Lewis, 1966), and differential emphases on the components of the academic role (Biglan, 1973; Blau, 1973; Fulton and Trow, 1974). Research is a different kind of activity for natural scientists and for humanists or professional school faculty, as is teaching (Biglan, 1973; Morgan, 1970); and interaction with students takes very different forms and appears to have very different meanings among the three groups (Gamson, 1967; Wilson and Gaff, 1975). These differences appear as well to carry over into the broader personal and family life of faculty (Thalheimer, 1965; Kistler, 1967; Steinberg, 1974; Ladd and Lipset, 1975).

How can we account for this extraordinary internal differentiation among the professoriate? While the available evidence is meager, it does suggest that both selection and professional socialization factors are at work. Differential selection to institutional types and disciplinary groups may be more crucial since socialization appears to be "selective"—that is, insofar as the norms associated with professional socialization are congruent with the individual's pre-entry values and predilections, professional socialization appears to reinforce those values and predilections. However, insofar as professional norms and pre-entry values are not congruent, professional socialization appears to have very little effect indeed (Thalheimer, 1965, 1973; Spaulding et al., 1968; Ladd and Lipset, 1975).[1]

At the institutional level, the major socializing force appears to be "colleague climate" (Lazarsfeld and Thielens, 1958; Blau, 1973), that is, the qualifications and orientations of the individual's colleagues. At the disciplinary level, investigators have sought to locate the socializing influence of academic disciplines in the basic personality patterns that characterize their members (Smart and McLaughlin, 1978) as well as in their structural characteristics. The latter effort has yielded a series of bipolar continua upon which individual disciplines can be located: hard versus soft (methodological rigor), theoretical versus applied, high versus low level of paradigm development (degree of consensus on theoretical frameworks and research procedures). Although the location of a discipline on any one or all of these continua appears to have some predictive value, we are not even close to understanding how the various disciplinary groupings operate, independently of personality selection factors, to affect how faculty think and what they do. Whatever the explanations might be, one point is eminently clear: to attempt to generalize about faculty *as a group* except in the broadest possible way may be neither intellectually defensible nor operationally useful.

Taken together, these three sets of generalizations hardly provide a blueprint for working with contemporary faculty. They do, however, provide the most tested set of propositions we have for understanding the academic professions. And as such, they promise a more solid foundation for academic leadership in the 1980s and beyond.

---

1. Thus, the phenomenon of the reactionary sociologist and the radical agronomist or accountant.

Appendix A:
Search and Sampling Procedures

CRITERIA FOR SELECTION OF RESEARCH STUDIES

This inquiry was concerned with examining efforts thus far to build a verifiable body of knowledge that enhances our understanding of faculty as they actually think, feel, and behave. This concern suggested three *formal* criteria for selection of studies for examination: if a study is to contribute to a body of knowledge, then it must be systematic; if it is to contribute to understanding, then it must be explanatory; if it is to focus on how faculty actually think, feel, and behave, then it must be empirical.

A study is systematic and ipso facto contributes to the development of a body of knowledge to the extent that the data it presents and the inferences drawn from that data are *reproducible* (Cartwright, 1953). In order to be adjudged *systematic,* a study would have to demonstrate the following:

1. An explicit and methodologically defensible plan of procedure for making observations that can be replicated
2. An explicit and methodologically defensible framework for classifying and/or organizing the observations (via the use of a priori theoretical concepts or of conceptual categories empirically derived from the data)
3. An explicit and methodologically defensible plan for making inferences from the observations that can be replicated by other investigators.

Kaplan (1964) has identified two means by which we typically formulate an *explanation* of a given phenomenon: the pattern model and the deductive model. Under the pattern model, we enhance understanding of a phenomenon by fitting it into a known pattern or network of relations. These relations may be of various sorts, such as causal or purposive. Not all explanations, however, consist in fitting something into an already given pattern. The task of explanation is often to find or create a suitable pattern into which the phenomenon under investigation fits. Under the deductive model, we promote understanding of a phenomenon by exhibiting it as a special case of what is already known, that is, by referring it, as a particular instance, to a general principle. Thus, operationally, a study can be said to be explanatory if it:

1. Places the phenomenon under study into an already given pattern or network of relations or
2. Finds or creates a pattern of relations into which the phenomenon under study fits or
3. Shows that the phenomenon under study is either of necessity or, as is more likely the case, very probably, an instance subsumable under a more general principle (usually a theory).

In common parlance, an *empirical* study is considered to be one that makes observations of events in the phenomenal world. However, in order to provide an explanation, one need not always obtain new data; secondary analyses of other investigators' observations are also appropriate. Therefore, operationally, the empirical criterion was satisfied if a study either made observations in the phenomenal world or used observations that have been made by other investigators.

To these three formal criteria, were added two further *substantive* criteria, concerning, respectively, the dependent variable(s) examined in a study, and the time at which a study was completed.

Many studies collect data from samples of faculty in an effort to examine phenomena such as institutional goals, leadership and behavior of administrators, and so forth. This inquiry was concerned only with those research studies that take as their object of inquiry some aspect of faculty attitudes or behavior. Operationally, then, only those studies were selected for the sample whose dependent variable was some aspect of faculty attitudes or behavior.

Finally, it was decided to limit the purview of this inquiry to research studies published after 1942. The early forties were selected as an appropriate point of departure since the first genuine stirrings of the "academic revolution" in faculty careers date from that time (Jencks and Riesman, 1969; Light, 1972); and the year 1942, itself, was chosen because it represents a kind of benchmark in research on faculty—the publication of Logan Wilson's *The Academic Man*. Indeed, few research studies meeting our formal criteria were completed prior to 1942.

In sum, studies of faculty eligible for inclusion in our sample were empirical, systematic, explanatory studies, which were completed after 1942 and took as their dependent variable some aspect of the attitudes and/or behavior of faculty in four-year colleges and universities in the United States.

What are the concrete implications of employing the formal and substantive selection criteria we have outlined? First, because our focus is on the professoriate per se rather than on the several larger groups of which the professoriate may be a part, excluded from the sample were:

1. Studies in the sociology of occupations that treat faculty as one comparison group

2. Studies of intellectuals, except studies focused on academic intellectuals (since many intellectuals are not academics and many academics are not intellectuals)
3. Studies of discrete professional groups, such as economists, psychologists, engineers, except studies of academic economists, academic psychologists, and academic engineers (since in many professions, only a small proportion of practitioners are academics)
4. Studies of scientists, except studies of academic scientists.

Second, insofar as the inquiry focused on studies whose dependent variables are attitudes and/or behaviors of faculty, excluded were:

1. Studies of institutional goals whose focus is on determining what the goals are rather than explaining faculty perceptions of them
2. Studies of the determinants of student ratings of instruction whose concerns lie chiefly with determining what student-related or other extraneous factors affect the distribution of ratings, rather than pressing student ratings of instruction into service as a measure of teaching effectiveness and seeking to explain variations in teaching effectiveness.

Third, the systematic criterion clearly excluded fictional accounts of the professoriate as well as opinion pieces (while fictional accounts and opinion pieces generally involve observation, and may indeed weave a web of explanation, their methods and inferences clearly are not reproducible). The systematic criterion further excluded impressionistic studies such as Herbert Livesey's *The Professors,* or Professor X's *This Beats Working for a Living.* While these latter works may satisfy the empirical and explanatory criteria, they are clearly not systematic.

Finally, the explanatory criterion excluded purely descriptive and demographic studies. "Purely" is a critically important qualifier because descriptions can be explanatory—that is, they may not merely give us the "what" of a phenomenon but the "how" of the phenomenon; and the "how" may give us a clue to the "why." For example, Caplow and McGee's (1958) description of how the academic marketplace operates does indeed present us with a pattern of relations that is the mark of explanation. These sorts of descriptive studies, then, were included; those descriptive studies that exclusively focused on the "what" question were excluded. (Although the studies were excluded from the sample, the insights they provide are indeed called upon throughout in the interpretation of the findings generated from the study sample.)

BIBLIOGRAPHIC SOURCES

Three principal bibliographic sources were examined in order to compile studies on faculty from which the study sample might be drawn pursuant to the criteria outlined above. The first was Walter Eells's annotated bibliography entitled *College Teachers and College Teaching* (1957, 1959, 1962).

Eells compiled his bibliography by examining the *Education Index* from 1945 through 1961 under all pertinent headings and topics related to faculty, listing promising titles, and then examining those titles in the United States Office of Education Library and the Library of Congress. Further references provided by the titles were noted and followed up. In addition, he examined the complete files for the period 1945 through 1961 of about forty periodicals related to higher education as well as the annual proceedings, transactions, or yearbooks of national/regional organizations concerned with higher education. This prodigious effort yielded over five thousand references on college and university faculty over a seventeen-year period (1945 through 1961). The vast majority of these references are to opinion/hortatory pieces as well as purely descriptive studies. Eells did not distinguish between these and more systematic, empirical, explanatory research. He did, however, provide an abstract for each title entry which greatly facilitated the identification of those references which might be eligible for inclusion in the study sample.

Upon his death in 1962, Eells's compilation efforts were continued by Litton and Stickler (1967) for the period 1962–64, generating an additional thirteen hundred references. While the work of Eells and Litton and Stickler together does constitute the most comprehensive bibliography on faculty to date, it does suffer from two major limitations:

1. *Scope of substantive topics covered.* Eells and his colleagues were interested in faculty career choice and preparation, faculty status in their own institutions, and the teaching process. Their references thus do not include studies concerned with the more "professional" aspects of the faculty role (for example, faculty research productivity, disciplinary and other extra-institutional professional activity) or with the non-job related aspects of faculty lifestyles (for example, political and religious orientation).
2. *Nature of the sources drawn upon in compiling references.* References are mainly to the periodical literature. While approximately 150 periodicals are covered, most of these are education or education-related journals, with only a smattering of social science journals.[1] This selectively concentrated coverage of the periodical literature is supplemented only sparingly with dissertations and conference proceedings of organizations concerned with higher education.

The second major source of references to the literature on faculty was an extensive bibliography (more than fifteen hundred entries) compiled by Professor Robert T. Blackburn at the Center for the Study of Higher Education, University of Michigan. Blackburn's compilation efforts included five components.[2]

1. *Dissertations.* In 1968 Blackburn began what have become biennial *Dissertation Abstracts International* searches, going back as far as the forties. Using the key word index, he identified dissertation titles re-

lated to faculty. He then consulted the abstracts of these dissertations and selected those appearing to have objective data of high quality for inclusion in his bibliography. The dissertations listed thus have been prescreened on the basis of largely the same formal criteria adopted for sample selection in this inquiry. Specifically, Blackburn sought dissertations that used some kind of conceptual framework, that provided sophisticated treatment of the data, and that tested hypotheses; he excluded opinion surveys and other purely descriptive theses. While this procedure eliminated about 75 percent of all dissertations on faculty, it is assumed that the vast majority of these would not have met our own formal criteria.

2. *Topical bibliographies generated from bibliographies furnished by the dissertations.* Blackburn assumed that by carefully examining all citations made in the dissertations selected, good pieces of work would reappear even though they might have been completed during periods that he had not systematically searched.

3. *Psychological Abstracts and Sociological Abstracts searches.* Blackburn completed annual searches of *Psychological Abstracts* and *Sociological Abstracts,* going back as far as the late fifties. He assumed that these searches together with the citations generated by dissertations would pick up the "better" articles appearing in the social science journals.

4. *ERIC searches.* Blackburn has conducted biennial ERIC searches in an effort to pick up fugitive pieces, including institutional studies, papers presented at national conferences, reports to government agencies on funded research, and other unpublished material.

5. *Graduate student searches.* Blackburn also includes the fruits of student bibliographic searches, completed in the conduct of research studies for the graduate seminar he conducts on the college and university professor.

In comparison with Eells's, Blackburn's bibliography is clearly more comprehensive in the scope of sources upon which it draws. It covers social science as well as education periodicals, books, a larger number of dissertations, as well as fugitive, unpublished pieces. It is also more comprehensive in the scope of substantive topics covered. Blackburn includes references to studies of all aspects of the faculty role as well as of faculty lifestyles; indeed, his coverage extends to studies of scientists and other types of professionals (not necessarily in academic settings) as well as studies of faculty per se. While not as perfectly systematic as Eells, Blackburn's *prescreening* yields a bibliography which, from the point of view of this inquiry, is much richer and facilitates the task of sample selection by frequently including abstracts together with the entries themselves.

The third major source of references to research on faculty was the integrative reviews identified in chapter 1. Since Blackburn was wholly or partly responsible for fully half of these, it is not surprising that the character of references obtainable from them closely parallels that obtained from the Blackburn bibliography.

THE ACTUAL PROCESS OF STUDY SAMPLE SELECTION

From among the thousands of references furnished by these three sources, over four hundred items, which by virtue of their titles or the information contained in abstracts appeared eligible for inclusion in the study sample, were selected for further examination. With the exception of fourteen items that proved to be unavailable and dissertations (for which the abstracts only were consulted), this entire group of potentially eligible studies was procured and examined with two purposes in mind:

1. To determine whether each study fulfilled the three formal and two substantive criteria established for inclusion in the study sample
2. To examine references furnished by these studies in an effort to track down "overlooked" references until the number of new references discovered appeared to approach zero. New studies discovered by this procedure were then added to the pool and examined in terms of their eligibility for inclusion in the study sample.

This procedure yielded just over three hundred studies that met all formal and substantive criteria for inclusion in the study sample. Included in this group, however, were multiple reports of single studies as well as discrete reports of components of larger studies. This, then, raised the question of what was to be considered the appropriate sampling unit, that is, *a case,* for purposes of this inquiry. Was each individual research report to be considered a case, even if it represented a duplication of a report already published in another medium? Or was each individual data collection effort, irrespective of the number of research reports it generated, to be considered a case? In order to proceed, several decision rules were developed to determine whether a given research report indeed constituted a case. Implicit in these decision rules was the definition of a case as a discrete data collection effort, albeit with some notable exceptions. The decision rules adopted were as follows:

1. The same study (that is, a single data collection effort or a secondary analysis effort) reported two or more times in different formats or media was counted as a single case.
2. A large-scale study (that is, a single large-scale data collection or secondary analysis effort) that was reported in toto and then reported in part in a different format or in different media was counted as a single case, *except* when the part or parts reported were the results of secondary analyses of the original data or focused on data collected, but not reported on, in the original study.
3. A dissertation that generated one or more journal articles, books, monographs, or conference papers was counted as a single case.
4. A large-scale data collection/secondary analysis effort that was *not*

reported in toto but only reported in several parts was counted as several cases.

It was felt that this procedure increased the face validity of any conceptual map generated from the sample insofar as it

1. Provided a more accurate estimate of the actual distribution of effort in the study of college and university faculty (uncontaminated by the contemporary predilection for squeezing as many publications as possible out of a single study)
2. Recognized, at the same time, that a single data collection effort can be extended and reanalyzed to generate what amounts to a new study.

The application of these decision rules to the group of over three hundred studies yielded 236 cases, which constituted the original study sample. What do these 236 cases represent? Clearly, they constitute no more than a "chunk" of all extant studies that meet the formal and substantive criteria we have established. The difficulty is that the parameters of the population of all studies that meet these criteria are not known; and, therefore, the representativeness of this particular chunk of 236 cases cannot be determined. It was hoped that by obtaining bibliographical references from a wide variety of sources, it would be possible to discover less publicized research and avoid an overly biased collection of studies (for example, only those conducted by "mainstream" investigators). It was also assumed that the larger the number of studies tracked down, the more representative and trustworthy would be the study sample drawn from them. Although these 236 cases clearly do not exhaust all extant research that might meet our criteria (including undergraduate research reports, graduate student seminar research projects, master's theses, unpublished institutional studies), they would seem to represent a reasonably comprehensive sample.

1. Only six journals in psychology, four in sociology, one in economics, and one in political science are covered, and none in business or public administration.

2. These were described to the author in a personal communication.

Appendix B:
Data Collection and Analysis Procedures

DATA COLLECTION, CODING, AND RETRIEVAL

The amount of information available in the research studies themselves is overwhelming unless one develops a systematic schema for collecting, coding, and retrieving this information. As a first step, twenty-three variables for which data were collected from each case were identified. The variables were selected on the basis of their potential utility in describing the body of research and synthesizing the findings. Data on a fairly large number of variables were sought insofar as a greater number of variables would increase opportunities for achieving greater comparability among studies. The variables were:

1. Date of research publication
2. Position of the principal investigator
3. The disciplinary affiliation of the principal investigator
4. Extramural sources of support for the investigation (if any)
5. Basic vs. applied orientation[1]
6. Conceptual/theoretical framework employed (if any)
7. Deductive/exploratory orientation[2]
8. Dependent variable(s) examined
9. Operational definition(s)/measure(s) of dependent variable(s) examined
10. Dimensions of dependent variable(s) examined (if not unidimensional)
11. Independent/intervening variable(s) examined
12. Operational definition(s)/measure(s) of independent variable(s)
13. Dimensions of independent variable(s) (if not unidimensional)
14. Sampling procedure (for institutions and for faculty)
15. Sample composition: institutional type(s) represented
16. Sample composition: academic field(s) of faculty studied
17. Research strategy (for example, experiment, survey, secondary analysis, life history)

18. Data collection method(s) (for example, interview, paper and pencil questionnaire)
19. Data sources (for example, faculty, administrators, students, documents)
20. Data analysis procedure(s)
21. Unit of analysis employed (for example, the individual faculty member or the department)
22. Medium for reporting research results
23. The findings (descriptive statistics and significance test results).

For each case in the sample, data on the twenty-three variables were recorded directly on *Indecks* punch cards. Indecks is a manual information storage and retrieval system. It employs cards providing twenty-six alphanumeric fields on which enumeration and measurement data on up to twenty-six variables can be punched for retrieval via the use of sorting rods.

Once the data on all cases were recorded on punch cards, the process of developing a coding scheme was initiated for seventeen of the twenty-three variables (variables numbered 9, 10, 12, 13, 14, and 23 in the above list were not coded). A preliminary schema of coding categories was developed by drawing a random one-sixth sample of all punch cards (each punch card contained data on all seventeen variables for one case). For each of the seventeen codable variables, the data recorded on that variable across the sample of punch cards were arrayed and categories were empirically developed. This preliminary coding schema was then tested in two ways. A random one-sixth sample of all punch cards was again drawn (after replacement). A duplicate of each punch card/case was then punched for all seventeen variables, using the preliminary coding schema that had been developed. Each punch card was then examined to determine the "goodness of fit" between the data as recorded in writing and the data as punched. Several revisions in the coding schema were made on the basis of this trial run and it was decided to leave several variables open for establishing new categories. In addition, the preliminary coding schema had been sent to three members of the investigator's dissertation committee for their critique. Feedback from these individuals also contributed to revision of the coding scheme. The final coding scheme that emerged from these two tests is as follows:

Variable	Coding Categories
Date of research report	Decade (40s–70s)
	Year (0–9)
Position of principal investigator	Faculty member
	Institutional administrator
	Institutional researcher
	University-based institute research staff (for example, CRDHE, Berkeley; SRI, Michigan)

VARIABLE	CODING CATEGORIES
	Nonprofit educational organization staff (for example, ACE, ETS)
	Graduate student
	Do not know
Discipline of principal investigator	Sociology
	Social psychology
	Psychology
	Political science
	Economics
	Management/business administration
	Higher education
	Other education (for example, educational psychology)
	Other
	Do not know
Source of research support	Local (campus based)
	Professional association
	Private foundation
	Federal government agency
	Other, private nonprofit organization
	None
	Do not know
Basic vs. applied orientation	Basic (that is, concerned with the development, testing, and/or refinement of theory)
	Applied (all other)
	Both
	Do not know
Deductive vs. exploratory orientation	Deductive (that is, testing specific hypotheses)
	Exploratory
	Both
	Do not know
Conceptual/theoretical framework employed	*Organizational Theory*
	Structure, goals, decision frameworks
	Power and authority
	Bureaucratic vs. professional authority
	Organizational control systems
	Social influence theories (for example, French and Raven, 1960)
	Role theory
	Gouldner's cosmopolitan-local construct
	Open systems theory
	Organizations as political systems

VARIABLE	CODING CATEGORIES
	Human relations theory
	Leadership theories
	Unclassified
	Psychological Theory
	Clinical psychology
	Humanistic/self theory
	Cognitive-developmental
	Social psychology of attitudes
	Industrial/personnel psychology
	Unclassified
	Sociological Theory
	Symbolic interactionism
	Social systems theory (functionalist)
	Professional socialization (subculture theory)
	Theories of adult socialization
	Stratification theory/sociology of science
	Sociology of religion
	Sociology of work/professions
	Theories of political socialization
	Labor economic theory
	Other
	None
	Do not know
Dependent variable(s) examined	*Academic Career*
	Career choice
	Role orientation
	Educational and professional values
	Morale and satisfaction
	Rewards and recognition
	Mobility
	Career adjustment
	Perceptions of institutional functioning
	Faculty Performance
	Overall performance
	Teaching activity
	Research activity
	Administration and other work activities
	Faculty-student interaction
	Relations with colleagues
	Faculty-administrator relations
	Participation in governance
	Collective bargaining
	Response to student activism
	Role conflict

VARIABLE	CODING CATEGORIES
	Faculty Lifestyles
	Political orientation
	Religious-ethnic orientation
	Marriage and family life
	Personality and cognitive structure
Independent variable(s) examined	Institutional characteristics
	Departmental characteristics
	Individual professional characteristics (for example, discipline, rank)
	Individual nonprofessional characteristics (for example, age, sex)
	Situational factors (for example, stress, job satisfaction)
Sample composition: Institutional types	Single institution: University
	Single institution: 4-year college
	Denominational colleges and universities
	Liberal arts colleges
	Public 4-year colleges
	Public colleges and universities
	Universities (private and/or public)
	"Major" universities
	Mixed (that is, spanning at least 3 categories other than "single institution" and "major universities")
	Do not know
Sample composition: Academic fields	Single field: Social sciences
	Single field: Natural sciences
	Single field: Professional/applied
	Social sciences (several fields)
	Natural sciences (several fields)
	Professional/applied (several fields)
	Natural and social sciences
	Arts and sciences (natural and social sciences and humanities)
	All (arts and sciences and professional/applied)
	Do not know
Research strategy	Experiment[3]
	Social survey: One-shot case study[4]
	Social survey: Static group comparison[5]
	Secondary analysis of survey data
	Field strategy[6]
	Life history[7]
	Unobtrusive techniques[8]
	Do not know

VARIABLE	CODING CATEGORIES
Data collection method(s)	Self-administered questionnaire Interview Observation Examination of records/documents Clinical projective techniques (for example, Rorschach) No data collected Do not know
Data sources	Faculty Students Administrators Documents/records/files Do not know
Data analysis procedures	Content or other qualitative analysis Descriptive statistics *Bivariate* Bivariate contingency analysis Zero-order correlation One-way analysis of variance (including t-tests) *Multivariate*[9] Multivariate contingency analysis Multiple regression Do not know
Unit of analysis	Individual faculty member Department Institution Other Do not know
Form/medium of research report	*Publications* Book or book chapter Monograph Published conference proceedings General, comprehensive journal Sociology journal Psychology journal Political science journal Religion journal Public administration journal Higher education journal Other education journal Other journals *Nonpublished* Doctoral dissertation

Variable	Coding Categories
	Nonpublished
	ERIC document
	Report to government agency
	Unpublished manuscript

An examination of the coding schema reveals rather wide variation among variables in the number of coding categories generated. Depending on the number of coding categories, each variable was assigned one or more alpha-numeric fields, and each category for that variable was assigned a position in that alpha-numeric field. Each case was then punched for each variable, permitting easy retrieval via the use of the sorting rods.

DATA ANALYSIS PROCEDURES

The data analysis was undertaken in two phases, corresponding to the two purposes of the initial dissertation inquiry: the aggregate conceptual mapping of the sample of cases and the integration of findings. Although, in practice, the two phases of the analysis were interconnected, they are presented here, for purposes of clarify, as distinct stages.

Aggregate Conceptual Mapping of the Study Sample

This initial phase of the analysis constituted an analysis of the aggregate characteristics of the study sample. As a first step, a simple distribution of the cases over the categories of each of the seventeen coded variables was undertaken. Next, bivariate distributions of each of the seventeen coded variables with every other coded variable were completed.[10] This initial mapping was particularly directed toward answering the basic question of who studied what, when, and how. In these bivariate analyses, then, we were especially interested in trends in each of the seventeen coded variables over time (that is, date of publication × all other variables). In answering our basic question, these sorts of analyses provide a species of history of the effort to develop a body of knowledge on faculty at four-year colleges and universities, within the limitations of the variables and studies examined. The aggregate conceptual map is reported in chapter 4 of the original dissertation.

Integration of the Findings

The integration phase of the analysis focused on one of the seventeen coded variables on which data were gathered for each case: the dependent variable(s) examined. As a first step, all cases were clustered by dependent variable.[11] These dependent variable clusters provided a locus for intracluster conceptual mapping and a point of departure for the integration efforts that followed. Intracluster conceptual mapping proceeded in two stages:

1. A description, in tabular form, of all studies within the dependent variable cluster in terms of the twenty-two other variables on which data were collected (including both coded and noncoded variables)
2. The development of a typology of studies of the focal dependent variable, based on any one or more of the following:
   a. Operational definition/measure of the dependent variable
   b. Independent variable or classes of independent variables studied in relation to the focal dependent variable
   c. Conceptual frameworks employed
   d. Composition of the samples studied
   e. Unit of analysis employed or analytical procedures
   f. *Purpose* of the studies
   g. Research strategy employed
   h. Orientation of the investigation—deductive/inductive, basic/applied.

The integration process was initiated by further clustering cases within a given dependent variable cluster by independent variable(s) or by classes of independent variable(s) examined (to the extent this was not already achieved in the conceptual mapping phase). The findings within each independent variable subcluster were then arrayed across cases. As a rule, an insufficient number of cases was available within independent variable subclusters to permit meta-analysis. Meta-analysis refers to the statistical analysis of descriptive statistics (not original data) generated by several studies of the relationship of a given independent and dependent variable. Since each descriptive statistic is a measure of magnitude, meta-analysis permits inferences concerning the magnitude as well as the direction of a relationship over a large number of studies. Therefore, findings within independent variable subclusters were most often integrated by "taking a vote." In employing the "voting" method, the integrator assumes three possible outcomes for all studies of the relationship of a particular independent variable to the focal dependent variable: the relationship may be significantly positive, significantly negative, or nonsignificant. The findings of each individual study are assigned to the appropriate outcome category. The category with the highest number of studies is then assumed to provide the best estimate of the direction of the true relationship. However, several additional steps were taken to offset some of the weaknesses that inhere in the voting approach or that may attend its use.

In cases of inconsistent findings across cases within a given independent variable subcluster (especially in cases of a "close vote"), the following steps were taken:

1. Votes were weighed by sample size in an effort to interpret the real direction of the vote (insofar as the number of cases was always small, weighing was accomplished via the proverbial investigator's eyeball).
2. Further clustering by sample composition, etc., was initiated in order to discover whether any consistent patterns might be discerned under various conditions.

3. In cases where independent variable subclusters showed marked variations in the quality of studies (especially research design and data analysis procedures), the "eyeball" was used to weigh votes by quality of the case;

4. Where independent variable subclusters contained an insufficient number of cases to allow for the exercise of the preceding step or did not show marked variation in quality among studies, the dimensions along which cases differed were investigated as a means of suggesting likely explanations for the inconsistent findings.

Once any equivocality in the voting itself was addressed, if not always resolved, the following procedures were applied to each individual independent variable subcluster:

1. When provided in a given case, F-ratios and correlation coefficients were used to calculate the practical significance of a relationship, that is, the proportion of variance in the dependent variable explained by the given independent variable.[12]

2. The relationship suggested by the outcome of the voting was interpreted in terms of (a) the validity of the inferences made in light of the type of data on which they were based and the research methods employed (for example, those instances in which inferences were made from cross-sectional data *as if* they were longitudinal data are pointed out), (b) an assessment of possible explanations of the "why" of the relationship,[13] and (c) its generalizeability, that is, the conditions (sample composition, level of analysis, analytic procedure) under which the finding appears to hold.

Once the above procedures were carried out for each individual subcluster, the following procedures were applied to all independent variable subclusters within a dependent variable cluster:

1. An attempt was made to determine the relative impact of the several independent variables (defining their own subclusters) on the focal dependent variable via the ranking of independent variables within cases. That is, insofar as some sharing of independent variables was evident across cases, it was possible to juxtapose the within-case rankings of several common independent variables by performing an "eyeball" comparison across cases (simultaneously taking into account differences in magnitude between ranks within studies).

2. In order to get at the potential "interaction" effects of two independent variables that had heretofore been considered separately (as separate subclusters), cases within the larger dependent variable cluster were examined for incidences of pairing of independent variables within the same study; and all incidents of pairing were examined for clues of consistent interaction effects.

---

1. A case was classified as *basic* if it explicitly sought to develop or test a theory or conceptual framework.

2. A case was classified as *deductive* if it explicitly tested specific hypotheses derived from theory or previous research.

3. Includes *observation at two points in time* (pretreatment and posttreatment), use of at least one *control group,* and *random assignment* of subjects to observational groups.

4. Observations are collected via interview or self-administered questionnaire at *one point in time*—no "before" observations are made, and no control groups are constructed. A group of persons is observed at one point in time and questioned about their behaviors, attitudes, and beliefs with respect to a series of issues (Denzin, 1970).

5. The static group comparison adds to the one-shot case study the use of a *control group.* Two groups are chosen for study and each is observed at one point in time. An attempt is made to explain events occurring in the target sample by comparing them to the control group (Denzin, 1970).

6. The field strategy combines document analysis, respondent and informant interviewing, and/or direct participation or observation in an effort to develop, test, and revise hypotheses as the research is conducted (Denzin, 1970).

7. The life history approach employs records, documents, and/or in-depth interviews to present the experiences and definitions held by a person or group as they themselves interpret those experiences (Denzin, 1970). It may be oriented toward historical reconstruction or the wholistic reconstruction of the individual or group life experience at one point in time.

8. Unobtrusive techniques include any method of data collection that removes the investigator from interaction with the subjects being studied. Data for analysis are usually gleaned from institutional records and bibliographic sources (Denzin, 1970).

9. Strictly speaking, the term "multivariate" is often applied only to those analyses involving *both* multiple independent *and* multiple dependent variables. Following Kerlinger (1973), this inquiry construes the term more broadly to include analyses involving more than one independent variable *or* more than one dependent variable, or both. Thus, in our usage, "multivariate" would include multiple regression and contingency analysis with more than one independent variable.

10. Chi-square tests were not performed since the cases examined did not constitute a probability sample from a known population.

11. Since some cases examined more than one dependent variable, individual cases sometimes appeared in more than one cluster.

12. The correlation coefficient was simply squared, and the F-ratio was entered into the formula developed by McNamara (1979) for calculating omega squared on the basis of F.

13. Sometimes this involved an assessment of several alternative, speculative explanations proffered by the investigators themselves and sometimes an attempt to proffer an explanation in the absence of any other. In both cases, the explanation proffered is grounded in data presented by the studies or data available from other studies.

References

CHAPTER 1
Introduction

Bess, James L. *University Organization: A Matrix Analysis of the Academic Professions.* New York: Human Sciences Press, 1982.

Blackburn, Robert T. *The Professor's Role in a Changing Society.* ERIC Research Reports, No. 10. Washington, D.C.: ERIC Clearinghouse on Higher Education, 1971.

————. "Faculty Responsiveness and Faculty Productivity as Functions of Age, Rank, and Tenure: Some Inferences from the Empirical Literature." *Resources in Education* 7 (June 1972): 44.

Blackburn, Robert T. and Charles Aurand. "Mobility Studies on Academic Men: Some Methodological Concerns and Substantive Findings." *Resources in Education* 7 (November 1972): 76.

Blackburn, Robert T. and Charles Behymer. "A Paradigm for Academic Scholarly Productivity." Mimeographed. Ann Arbor: Center for the Study of Higher Education, University of Michigan, 1976.

Blau, Peter M. *The Organization of Academic Work.* New York: John Wiley and Sons, 1973.

Cohen, Arthur and Florence Brawer. *The Two-Year College Instructor Today.* New York: Praeger, 1977.

Faia, Michael A. "The Myth of the Liberal Professor." *Sociology of Education* 47 (Spring 1974): 171–202.

Feldman, Kenneth A. "Using the Work of Others: Some Observations on Reviewing and Integrating." *Sociology of Education* 44 (Winter 1971): 86–102.

Finkelstein, Martin J. "Three Decades of Research on American Academics: A Descriptive Portrait and Synthesis of Findings." Unpublished Ph.D. dissertation, State University of New York at Buffalo, 1978.

Glass, Gene V. "Primary, Secondary, and Meta-Analysis of Research." *Educational Researcher* 6 (November 1976): 3–8.

Glass, Gene V. et al. *Meta-Analysis in Social Research*. Beverley Hills: Sage Publications, 1981.

Hodgkinson, Harold L. "How to Evaluate Faculty When You Don't Know Much about Them." *The Research Reporter* 7 (1972): 5–8.

Jackson, Gregory. *Methods for Reviewing and Integrating Research in the Social Sciences*. Washington, D.C.: National Science Foundation, 1978.

Ladd, Everett C. and Seymour M. Lipset. *The Divided Academy*. New York: McGraw-Hill, 1975.

Leslie, David, Samuel Kellams, and Manuel Gunne. *Part-Time Faculty in American Higher Education*. New York: Praeger, 1982.

Lewis, Lionel. *Scaling the Ivory Tower*. Baltimore: The Johns Hopkins University Press, 1975.

Light, Donald et al. *The Impact of the Academic Revolution on Faculty Careers*. ERIC-AAHE Research Reports, No. 10. Washington, D.C.: American Association for Higher Education, 1972.

Light, Richard J. and Paul V. Smith. "Accumulating Evidence: Procedures for Resolving Contradictions among Different Research Studies." *Harvard Educational Review* 41 (1971): 429–71.

Livesey, Herbert. *The Professors*. New York: Charterhouse, 1975.

Mandell, Richard D. *The Professor Game*. Garden City, N.Y.: Doubleday, 1977.

Medalia, N. Z. *On Becoming a College Teacher: A Review of Three Variables*. SREB Research Monograph, No. 6. Atlanta: Southern Regional Education Board, 1963.

Newcomb, Theodore and Kenneth Feldman. *The Impact of College on Students*. San Francisco: Jossey-Bass, 1969.

Stecklein, John E. "Research on Faculty Recruitment and Motivation." In *Studies of College Faculty*. Boulder: Western Interstate Commission for Higher Education, 1961.

Steinberg, Stephen. *The Academic Melting Pot*. New York: McGraw-Hill, 1974.

Tuckman, Howard. *Publication, Teaching, and the Academic Reward Structure*. Lexington, Mass.: D.C. Heath, 1976.

──────. "Who is Part-Time in Academe?" *AAUP Bulletin* 64 (December 1978): 305–15.

Tuckman, Howard and Jaime Caldwell. "The Reward Structure for Part-Timers in Academe." *Journal of Higher Education* 50 (November/December 1979): 745–60.

Wilson, Logan. *American Academics: Then and Now*. New York: Oxford University Press, 1979.

Wilson, Robert C., Jerry G. Gaff, Evelyn Dienst, Lynn Wood, and James Bavry. *College Professors and Their Impact on Students.* New York: John Wiley and Sons, 1975.

CHAPTER 2
The Emergence of the Modern Academic Role

Berelson, Bernard. *Graduate Education in the United States.* New York: McGraw-Hill, 1960.

Bowen, Howard. *Faculty Compensation.* New York: Teacher's Insurance Annuity Association, 1978.

Brubacher, John and Willis Rudy. *Higher Education in Transition.* Rev. ed. New York: Harper and Row, 1968.

Calhoun, Daniel. *Professional Lives in America.* Cambridge, Mass.: Harvard University Press, 1965.

Carrell, William. "American College Professors: 1750–1800." *History of Education Quarterly* 8 (1968): 289–305.

Cowley, William. *Professors, Presidents, and Trustees,* edited by Donald T. Williams. San Francisco: Jossey-Bass, 1980.

Creutz, Alan. "From College Teacher to University Scholar: The Evolution and Professionalization of Academics at the University of Michigan, 1841–1900." Unpublished Ph.D. dissertation, University of Michigan, 1981.

Curti, Merle and Vernon Carstensen. *The University of Wisconsin: 1848–1925.* Madison: University of Wisconsin Press, 1949.

Dwight, Timothy. *Memories of Yale Life and Men, 1845–1899.* New York: Dodd, Mead and Co., 1903.

Eliot, Samuel. *A Sketch of the History of Harvard College.* Boston: Little and Brown, 1848.

The General Catalog of the University of Michigan, 1837–1911. Ann Arbor: University of Michigan, 1912.

Gruber, Marilyn. *Mars and Minerva.* Baton Rouge: Louisiana State University Press, 1976.

Haggerty, William and George Works. *Faculties of Colleges and Universities Accredited by the North Central Association of Colleges and Secondary Schools, 1930–37.* Commission on Institutions of Higher Education, Publication 12. Chicago: North Central Association of Colleges and Secondary Schools, 1939.

Historical Catalog of Brown University, 1764–1904. Providence: Brown University, 1905.

Historical Register of Yale University, 1701–1937. New Haven: Yale University Press, 1939.

Hofstadter, Richard and Walter Metzger. *The Development of Academic Freedom in the United States.* New York: Columbia University Press, 1955.

Kunkel, B. W. "A Survey of College Faculties." *American Association of University Professors Bulletin* 24 (March 1938): 249–62.

Light, Donald et al. *The Impact of the Academic Revolution on Faculty Careers.* ERIC-AAHE Research Reports No. 10. Washington: American Association of Higher Education, 1972.

Lipset, Seymour M. and Everett C. Ladd. "The Changing Social Origins of American Academics." In *Qualitative and Quantitative Social Research,* edited by Robert Merton, James Coleman, and Peter Rossi. New York: Free Press, 1979, pp. 319–38.

McCaughey, Robert. "The Transformation of American Academic Life: Harvard University 1821–1892." *Perspectives in American History* 8 (1974): 239–334.

Metzger, Walter P. "Academic Tenure in America: A Historical Essay." In *Faculty Tenure: A Report and Recommendations,* Commission on Academic Tenure in Higher Education. San Francisco: Jossey-Bass, 1973, pp. 93–159.

Morison, Samuel E. *Harvard College in the Seventeenth Century.* Cambridge, Mass.: Harvard University Press, 1936.

Oleson, Alexandra and Sanborn Brown (eds). *The Pursuit of Knowledge in the Early American Republic.* Baltimore: The Johns Hopkins University Press, 1976.

Oleson, Alexandra and John Voss (eds). *The Organization of Knowledge in Modern America, 1860–1920.* Baltimore: The Johns Hopkins University Press, 1979.

Orr, Kenneth. "The Impact of the Depression Years, 1929–39, on Faculty in American Colleges and Universities." Unpublished Ph.D. dissertation, University of Michigan, 1978.

Packard, Alpheus (ed.). *History of Bowdoin College.* Boston: James Ripley Osgood and Co., 1882.

Rudolph, Frederick. *Mark Hopkins and the Log.* New Haven: Yale University Press, 1956.

———. *The American College and University: A History.* New York: Vintage Books, 1962.

Smith, Wilson. "The Teacher in Puritan Culture." *Harvard Educational Review* 36 (1966): 394–411.

Tobias, Marilyn. *Old Dartmouth on Trial: The Transformation of the Academic Community in Nineteenth Century America.* New York: New York University Press, 1982.

Veysey, Laurence. *The Emergence of the American University.* Chicago: University of Chicago Press, 1965.

Wertenbaker, J. *Princeton, 1746–1896*. Princeton: Princeton University Press, 1946.

Wolfle, Dale. *The Home of Science*. New York: McGraw-Hill, 1972.

CHAPTER 3
A Demographic Portrait of the Contemporary Academic Profession

Atelsek, Frank J. and Irene Gomberg. *New Full-Time Faculty 1976–77: Hiring Patterns by Field and Educational Attainment*. Higher Education Panel Reports, No. 38. Washington, D.C.: American Council on Education, 1978.

Bayer, Alan E. *Teaching Faculty in Academe: 1972–73*. ACE Research Reports, Vol. 8, No. 2. Washington, D.C.: American Council on Education, 1973.

Cartter, Allan. *Ph.D.s and the Academic Marketplace*. New York: McGraw-Hill, 1976.

Gourman, John. *The Gourman Report*. Phoenix: The Continuing Education Institute, 1967.

Levine, Arthur. *Handbook of Undergraduate Curriculum*. San Francisco: Jossey-Bass, 1978.

Lipset, Seymour M. and Everett C. Ladd. "The Changing Social Origins of American Academics." In *Qualitative and Quantitative Social Research,* edited by Robert K. Merton et al. New York: Free Press, 1979.

National Center for Education Statistics. *Digest of Education Statistics— 1980*. Washington, D.C.: U.S. Government Printing Office, 1980.

National Education Association. *Higher Education Faculty: Characteristics and Opinions*. Washington, D.C.: NEA, 1979.

Rose, H. M. "An Appraisal of the Negro Educator's Situation in the Academic Marketplace." *Journal of Negro Education* 35 (1966): 18–26.

Stadtman, Verne A. *Academic Adaptations*. San Francisco: Jossey-Bass, 1980.

Trow, Martin (ed.). *Teachers and Students*. New York: McGraw-Hill, 1975.

U.S. Department of Health, Education, and Welfare. National Center for Educational Statistics. *The Condition of Education—1980*. Washington, D.C.: U.S. Government Printing Office, 1980.

CHAPTER 4
The Academic Career

Acuff, Gene and Donald Allen. "Hiatus in 'Meaning': Disengagement for Retired Professors." *Journal of Gerontology* 25 (April 1970): 126–28.

Acuff, Gene and Benjamin Gorman. "Emeritus Professors: The Effect of Professional Activity and Religion on 'Meaning.'" *Sociological Quarterly* 9 (Winter 1968): 112–66.

Allison, Paul David. "Processes of Stratification in Science." Unpublished Ph.D. dissertation, University of Wisconsin, Madison, 1976.

Astin, Helen S. and Alan E. Bayer. "Sex Discrimination in Academe." In *Academic Women on the Move,* edited by Alice Rossi and Ann Calderwood. New York: Russell Sage Foundation, 1973.

Atchley, Robert C. "Disengagement among Professors." *Journal of Gerontology* 26 (October 1971): 476–80.

Aurand, Charles H. and Robert T. Blackburn. "Career Patterns and Job Mobility of College and University Music Faculty." *Journal of Research in Music Education* 21 (Summer 1973): 162–68.

Baldridge, J. Victor, David V. Curtis, George Ecker, and Gary L. Riley. *Policy Making and Effective Leadership.* San Francisco: Jossey-Bass, 1978.

Baldwin, Roger. "Adult and Career Development: What are the Implications for Faculty?" *Current Issues in Higher Education.* No. 2. Washington, D.C.: American Association for Higher Education, 1979a.

————. "The Faculty Career Process—Continuity and Change: A Study of College Professors at Five Stages of the Academic Career." Unpublished Ph.D. dissertation, University of Michigan, 1979b.

Baldwin, Roger and Robert T. Blackburn. "The Academic Career as a Developmental Process." *Journal of Higher Education* 52 (November/December 1981): 598–614.

Baldwin, Roger, Louis Brakeman, Russell Edgerton, Janet Hagber, and Thomas Maher. *Expanding Faculty Options.* Washington, D.C.: American Association for Higher Education, 1981.

Bayer, Alan E. *Teaching Faculty in Academe: 1972–73.* ACE Research Reports, Vol. 8, No. 2. Washington, D.C.: American Council on Education, 1973.

Bayer, Alan E. and John Folger. "Some Correlates of a Citation Measure of Productivity in Science." *Sociology of Education* 59 (Fall 1966): 381–90.

Berdahl, Robert Oliver. *Statewide Coordination of Higher Education.* Washington: American Council on Education, 1971.

Blackburn, Robert T. Personal communication, August 13, 1982.

Blackburn, Robert T., C. E. Behymer, and D. E. Hall. "Correlates of Faculty Publication." *Sociology of Education* 51 (April 1978): 132–41.

Blackburn, Robert T. and Robert J. Havighurst. "Career Patterns of U.S. Male Academic Social Scientists." *Higher Education* 8 (September 1979): 553–72.

Bloom, Michael and Mervin Freedman. "Personal History and Professional Career." In *Facilitating Faculty Development,* edited by Mervin Freedman. New Directions for Higher Education, No. 1. San Francisco: Jossey-Bass, 1973.

Breneman, David. *Graduate School Adjustments to the "New Depression" in Higher Education.* Washington, D.C.: National Board on Graduate Education, 1975.

————. "Higher Education and the Economy." *Educational Record* 62 (Spring 1981): 18–21.

Brown, David G. *The Mobile Professors.* Washington, D.C.: The American Council on Education, 1967.

Brown, J. Wesley and Robert C. Shukraft. "Personal Development and Professional Practice in College and University Professors." Unpublished Ph.D. dissertation, Graduate Theological Union, 1974.

Cameron, Susan and Robert T. Blackburn. "Sponsorship and Academic Career Success." *Journal of Higher Education* 52 (July/August 1981): 369–77.

Caplow, Theodore and Reece J. McGee. *The Academic Marketplace.* New York: Basic Books, 1958.

Cares, Robert C. and Robert T. Blackburn. "Faculty Self-Actualization: Factors Affecting Career Success." *Research in Higher Education* 9 (1978): 123–36.

Cartter, Allan M. *Ph.D.s and the Academic Labor Market.* New York: McGraw-Hill, 1976.

Chronicle of Higher Education 23 (December 2, 1981): 3.

Clark, Stanley A. and Richard F. Larson. "Mobility, Productivity, and Inbreeding at Small Colleges: A Comparative Study." *Sociology of Education* 45 (Fall 1972): 426–34.

Cohn, Elchanan. "Factors Affecting Variations in Faculty Salaries and Compensation in Institutions of Higher Education." *Journal of Higher Education* 44 (February 1973): 124–35.

Cole, Jonathan R. "IQ and Achievement in American Science." Paper presented at the annual meeting of the American Sociological Association, Montreal, 1974.

————. *Fair Science: Women in the Scientific Community.* New York: Free Press, 1979.

Cole, Jonathan R. and Stephen Cole. *Social Stratification in Science.* Chicago: University of Chicago Press, 1973.

Cole, Stephen and Jonathan R. Cole. "Scientific Output and Recognition: A Study in the Operation of the Reward System in Science." *American Sociological Review* 32 (June 1967): 377–90.

Crane, Diana M. "The Academic Marketplace Revisited: A Study of Faculty Mobility Using the Cartter Ratings." *American Journal of Sociology* 75 (May 1970): 953–64.

———. "Scientists at Major and Minor Universities: A Study of Productivity and Recognition." *American Sociological Review* 30 (October 1965): 699–714.

———. "Social Class Origin and Academic Success: The Influence of Two Stratification Systems on Academic Careers." *Sociology of Education* 42 (Winter 1969): 1–17.

Cyphert, Frederick R. and Nancy L. Zimpher. "The Education Deanship: Who Is the Dean?" In *The Dilemma of the Deanship,* edited by Daniel E. Griffiths and Donald J. McCarty. Danville, Ill.: Interstate, 1980.

Danziger, Nina K. "Career Attainment Patterns of University Professors." Unpublished Ph.D. dissertation, University of Chicago, 1978.

Dorfman, Lorraine T. "Professors in Retirement: A Study of the Activities and Reactions to Retirement of University of Iowa Emeritus Faculty." Unpublished Ph.D. dissertation, University of Iowa, 1978.

Eckert, Ruth E. and John E. Stecklein. "Academic Woman." *Association of American Colleges Bulletin* 45 (October 1959): 390–97.

Eckert, Ruth E. and Howard Y. Williams. *College Faculty View Themselves and Their Jobs.* Minneapolis: College of Education, University of Minnesota, 1972.

El-Khawas, Elaine H. and W. Todd Furniss. *Faculty Tenure and Contract Systems, 1972 and 1974.* Higher Education Panel Reports, No. 22. Washington, D.C.: American Council on Education, 1974.

Espy, James A. "Factors Influencing the Choice of College Teaching as a Career: A Study of Faculties in Predominantly Negro Institutions." Unpublished Ph.D. dissertation, University of Minnesota, 1963.

Ferber, Marianne A. and Jane W. Loeb. "Performance, Rewards, and Perceptions of Sex Discrimination among Male and Female Faculty." *American Journal of Sociology* 78 (January 1973): 995–1002.

Fillenbaum, Gerda G. and George L. Maddox. "Work after Retirement: An Investigation into Some Psychologically Relevant Variables." *Gerontologist* 14 (October 1974): 418–24.

Fincher, Arvel. "Job Mobility of Academic Physicists in American Higher Education: A Preliminary Study." Unpublished Ph.D. dissertation, University of Michigan, 1969.

Freedman, Mervin et al. *Academic Culture and Faculty Development.* Berkeley: Montaigne Press, 1979.

Fulton, Oliver and Martin Trow. "Research Activity in American Higher Education." *Sociology of Education* 47 (Winter 1974): 29–73.

Goldblatt, Harold S. "Academic Mobility and Cross Pressures on College Teachers During the McCarthy Era." *Sociology of Education* 40 (Spring 1967): 132–44.

Gustad, John W. *The Career Decisions of College Teachers.* SREB Research Monograph, No. 2. Atlanta: Southern Regional Education Board, 1960.

Hargens, Lowell L. "Patterns of Mobility of New Ph.D.s among American Academic Institutions." *Sociology of Education* 42 (Winter 1969): 18–37.

Hargens, Lowell L. and Grant M. Farr. "An Examination of Recent Hypotheses about Institutional Inbreeding." *American Journal of Sociology* 78 (May 1973): 1381–402.

Hargens, Lowell L. and Warren O. Hagstrom. "Sponsored and Contest Mobility of American Academic Scientists." *Sociology of Education* 40 (Winter 1967): 24–38.

Jencks, Christopher and David Riesman. *The Academic Revolution*. Garden City, N.Y.: Doubleday, 1968.

Kanter, Rosabeth Moss. "Changing the Shape of Work: Reform in Academe." In *Current Issues in Higher Education*, No. 1. Washington, D.C.: American Association for Higher Education, 1979.

Katz, David A. "Faculty Salaries, Promotions, and Productivity at a Large University." *American Economic Review* 63 (June 1973): 469–77.

Koch, James V. and John F. Chizmar. "The Influence of Teaching and Other Factors upon Absolute Salary Increments at Illinois State University." *Journal of Economic Education* 5 (Fall 1973): 27–34.

Ladd, Everett C. and Seymour M. Lipset. *Survey of the Social, Political, and Educational Perspectives of American College and University Faculty*. Final Report. 2 Volumes. Storrs, Conn.: Connecticut University, 1976.

——. "The Faculty Mood: Pessimism is Predominant." *The Chronicle of Higher Education* 15 (October 3, 1977): 1, 14.

Lazarsfeld, Paul F. and Wagner Thielens. *The Academic Mind*. Glencoe, Ill.: The Free Press, 1958.

Lightfield, E. Timothy. "Output and Recognition of Sociologists." *American Sociologist* 6 (May 1971): 128–33.

Lipset, Seymour M. and Everett C. Ladd. "The Changing Social Origins of American Academics." In *Qualitative and Quantitative Social Research*, edited by Robert Merton, James Coleman, and Peter Rossi. New York: Free Press, 1979.

Lewis, Lionel S. "Faculty Support of Academic Freedom and Self-Government." *Social Problems* 13 (1966): 450–61.

——. *Scaling the Ivory Tower: Merit and Its Limits in Academic Careers*. Baltimore: Johns Hopkins University Press, 1975.

Lewis, Lionel S., Richard A. Wanner, and David I. Gregorio. "Performance and Salary Attainment in Academia." *American Sociologist* 14 (August 1979): 157–69.

List, Murray D. "An Intensive Life History Study of Pre- and Post-Retirement Personality Factors of Retired College Professors." Unpublished Ph.D. dissertation, New York University, 1956.

Long, John. "Productivity and Academic Position in the Scientific Career." *American Sociological Review* 43 (December 1978): 899–908.

Lovett, Clara M. "Difficult Journey: Senior Academics and Career Change." *AAHE Bulletin* 33 (September 1980): 8–10, 13.

McGee, Reece. *Academic Janus.* San Francisco: Jossey-Bass, 1971.

Marshall, Howard D. *The Mobility of College Faculties.* New York: Pageant Press, 1964.

Martin, Patricia Y. "Choice among Professions: A Comparative Study of Medicine, Law, and College Teaching." Unpublished Ph.D. dissertation, Florida State University, 1969.

Merton, Robert K. "The Matthew Effect in Science." *Science* 159 (January 1968): 56–63.

Metzger, Walter P. *Academic Freedom in the Age of the University.* New York: Columbia University Press, 1955.

Muffo, John. "Relationships between Colleague Ratings and Faculty Compensation." *Research in Higher Education* 10 (1979): 25–35.

Muffo, John and John R. Robinson. "Early Science Career Patterns of Recent Graduates from Leading Research Universities." *The Review of Higher Education* 5 (Fall 1981): 1–13.

Neff, Charles B. "Faculty Retraining: A Four State Perspective." Paper presented at the 1978 National Conference on Higher Education. Chicago: American Association for Higher Education, March 1978.

Neff, Charles B. and Thomas E. Nyquist. *Faculty Retraining: Final Report of the Faculty Retraining Project.* New York: State University of New York, 1979.

Nicholson, Edward A. and Robert C. Miljus. "Job Satisfaction and Turnover among Liberal Arts College Professors." *Personnel Journal* 51 (November 1972): 840–45.

Palmer, David C. and Carl V. Patton. "Mid-Career Change Options in Academe: Experience and Possibilities." *Journal of Higher Education* 52 (July/August 1981): 378–98.

Parsons, Talcott and Gerald M. Platt. *The American Academic Profession: A Pilot Study.* Cambridge, Mass.: Harvard University, 1968.

―――. *The American University.* Cambridge, Mass.: Harvard University Press, 1973.

Patton, Carl V. "Early Retirement in Academia: Making the Decision." *The Gerontologist* 17 (August 1977): 347–54.

Reskin, Barbara. "Academic Sponsorship and Scientists' Careers." *Sociology of Education* 52 (July 1979): 129–46.

―――. "Scientific Productivity and the Reward Structure of Science." *American Sociological Review* 42 (June 1977): 491–504.

Rice, Eugene. "A Study of Three Cohorts of Danforth Fellows." *AAHE Bulletin* 32 (April 1980): 4.

Roe, Anne. "A Psychological Study of Eminent Biologists." *Psychological Monographs 65,* No. 14 (1951a): 1–68.

———. "A Psychological Study of Physical Scientists." *Genetic Psychology Monographs* 43 (1951b): 121–239.

———. "A Psychological Study of Eminent Psychologists and Anthropologists, and a Comparison with Biological and Physical Scientists." *Psychological Monographs* 67, No. 2 (1953): 1–55.

Roman, P. B. and P. Taietz. "Organizational Structure and Disengagement: The Emeritus Professor." *Gerontologist* 7 (1967): 147–52.

Rowe, Alan R. "Retired Academics and Research Activity." *Journal of Gerontology* 31 (July 1976): 456–61.

Scott, W. Richard. "Professionals in Bureaucracies—Areas of Conflict." In *Professionalization,* edited by Vollmer and Mills. Englewood Cliffs, N.J.: Prentice-Hall, 1970.

Scully, Malcolm. "Academic Musical Chairs: Many Say the Game's Ending." *Chronicle of Higher Education* 17 (October 23, 1978): 1.

Siegfried, John J. and Kenneth J. White. "Teaching and Publishing as Determinants of Academic Salaries." *Journal of Economic Education* 5 (Spring 1973): 90–99.

Skrabench, R. L. "Adjustment of Former University Faculty Members to Retirement." *Proceedings of the Southwestern Sociological Association* (1969): 65–69.

Snyder, R. A., A. Howard, and T. L. Hammer. "Mid-Career Change in Academia: The Decision to Become an Administrator." *Journal of Vocational Behavior* 13 (1978): 229–41.

Stecklein, John E. and Ruth Eckert. *An Exploratory Study of the Factors Influencing the Choice of College Teaching as a Career.* Minneapolis: University of Minnesota, 1958.

Stecklein, John E. and Robert L. Lathrop. *Faculty Attraction and Retention: Factors Affecting Faculty Mobility at the University of Minnesota.* Minneapolis: Bureau of Institutional Research, University of Minnesota, 1960.

Steinberg, Stephen. *The Academic Melting Pot.* New York: McGraw-Hill, 1974.

Stewart, Michael O. "Correlates of Faculty Reward." Unpublished Ph.D. dissertation, Kansas State University, 1972.

Tuckman, Barbara H. and Howard P. Tuckman. "The Structure of Salaries at American Universities." *Journal of Higher Education* 47 (January/February 1976): 51–64.

Tuckman, Howard P. *Publication, Teaching, and the Academic Reward System.* Lexington, Mass.: Lexington Books, 1976.

Tuckman, Howard P. and Robert P. Hagemann. "An Analysis of the Reward Structure in Two Disciplines." *Journal of Higher Education* 47 (July/August 1976): 447–64.

Waltzer, Herbert. *The Job of Academic Department Chairman: Experience and Recommendations from Miami University.* Washington, D.C.: American Council on Education, 1975.

Watts, William. "Americans' Hopes and Fears: The Future Can Fend for Itself." *Psychology Today* 15 (September 1981): 36–48.

Wences, Rosalio and Harold J. Abramson. "Faculty Opinion on the Issues of Job Placement and Dissent in the University." *Social Problems* 18 (Summer 1971): 27–38.

West, Sara C. "Antecedents of Academic Motivation: A Descriptive Study of University Professors." Unpublished Ph.D. dissertation, Ohio State University, 1971.

Willie, Reynold and John E. Stecklein. "A Three Decade Comparison of College Faculty Characteristics, Activities, and Attitudes." *Research in Higher Education* 16 (1982): 81–93.

Wilson, Logan. *The Academic Man.* London: Oxford University Press, 1942.

———. *American Academics: Then and Now.* New York: Oxford University Press, 1979.

Yankelovich, Daniel. *New Rules: Searching for Self-Fulfillment in a World Turned Upside Down.* New York: Random House, 1981.

Youn, Ted I. "The Careers of Young Ph.D.s: Temporal Change and Institutional Effects." Unpublished Ph.D. dissertation, Yale University, 1981.

CHAPTER 5
Faculty at Work

Aleamoni, L. M. "The Usefulness of Student Evaluations in Improving College Teaching." *Instructional Science* 7 (January 1978): 95–105.

Avakian, A. Nancy. "An Analysis of Factors Relating to the Job Satisfaction and Dissatisfaction of Faculty Members in Institutions of Higher Education." Unpublished Ph.D. dissertation, State University of New York at Albany, 1971.

Bachman, Jerald G. "Faculty Satisfaction and the Dean's Influence: An Organizational Study of Twelve Liberal Arts Colleges." *Journal of Applied Psychology* 52 (1968): 55–61.

Baldridge, J. Victor, David V. Curtis, George Ecker, and Gary L. Riley. *Policy Making and Effective Leadership.* San Francisco: Jossey-Bass, 1978.

Baldridge, J. Victor et al. *Assessing the Impact of Faculty Collective Bargaining.* AAHE-ERIC Higher Education Research Report No. 8. Washington, D.C.: American Association for Higher Education, 1981.

Baldwin, Roger. "Adult and Career Development: What are the Implications for Faculty?" *Current Issues in Higher Education.* No. 2. Washington, D.C.: American Association for Higher Education, 1979.

Baldwin, Roger and Robert T. Blackburn. "The Academic Career as a Developmental Process: Implications for Higher Education." *Journal of Higher Education* 52 (November/December 1981): 598–614.

Barnard, William W. "Role Expectations and Role Conflict in University Work Activities." Unpublished Ph.D. dissertation, University of Michigan, 1971.

Barnard, William W. and Robert T. Blackburn. "Faculty Role Conflicts in a Rapidly Changing Environment." *Resources in Education* 7 (November 1972): 77.

Barnes, Carol P. "A Descriptive Study of the Questioning Behavior of College Instructors." Unpublished Ph.D. dissertation, Claremont Graduate School, 1976.

_____. "Questioning in College Classrooms." In *Studies of College Teaching,* by Carolyn Ellner et al. Lexington, Mass.: D.C. Heath, 1983.

Batchelder, Ann S. and Frank Keane. "An Analysis of Lecture in the College Classroom through Systematic Observation." *Journal of Classroom Interaction* 13 (1977): 33–43.

Bayer, Alan E. *Teaching Faculty in Academe: 1972–73.* ACE Research Reports, Vol. 8, No. 2. Washington, D.C.: American Council on Education, 1973.

Bayer, Alan E. and Jeffrey Dutton. "Career Age and Research-Professional Activities of Academic Scientists." *Journal of Higher Education* 48 (May/June 1977): 259–82.

Behymer, Charles E. "Institutional and Personal Correlates of Faculty Productivity." Unpublished Ph.D. dissertation, University of Michigan, 1974.

Bem, Daryl J. *Beliefs, Attitudes, and Human Affairs.* Belmont, Calif.: Brooks-Cole, 1970.

Bendig, A. W. "Ability and Personality Characteristics of Introductory Psychology Instructors Rated Competent and Empathetic by Students." *Journal of Educational Research* 48 (1955): 705–9.

Biglan, Anthony. "The Relationship of University Department Organization to the Characteristics of Academic Tasks." Unpublished Ph.D. dissertation, University of Illinois, 1971.

_____. "The Characteristics of Subject Matter in Different Academic Areas." *Journal of Applied Psychology* 57 (June 1973): 195–203.

Blackburn, Robert T. Personal communication, 1982.

Blackburn, Robert T. and John D. Lindquist. "Faculty Behavior in the Legislative Process: Professorial Attitudes vs. Behavior Concerning Inclusion of Students in Academic Decisionmaking." *Sociology of Education* 44 (Fall 1971): 398–421.

Blackburn, Robert T. and Mary Jo Clark. "An Assessment of Faculty Performance: Some Correlates between Administration, Colleague, Student, and Self-Ratings." *Sociology of Education* 48 (Spring 1975): 242–56.

Blackburn, Robert T., C. E. Behymer, and D. E. Hall. "Correlates of Faculty Publication." *Sociology of Education* 51 (April 1978): 132–41.

Blackburn, Robert T. et al. "Are Instructional Improvement Programs Off-Target?" *Current Issues in Higher Education 1980.* Washington, D.C.: American Association for Higher Education, 1980.

Blackburn, Robert T., David Chapman, and Susan Cameron. "Cloning in Academe: Mentorship and Academic Careers." *Research in Higher Education* 15 (1981): 315–27.

Blank, Rolf K. "An Organizational Model of Academic Institutions and the Teaching Goals of Faculty Members." Unpublished Ph.D. dissertation, Florida State University, 1976.

Blau, Peter M. *The Organization of Academic Work.* New York: John Wiley and Sons, 1973.

Bloland, Harland. "Opportunities, Traps, and Sanctuaries: A Frame Analysis of Learned Societies." *Urban Life* 11 (April 1982): 79–105.

Bloom, Michael and Mervin Freedman. "Personal History and Professional Career." In *Facilitating Faculty Development,* edited by Mervin Freedman. New Directions for Higher Education, No. 1. San Francisco: Jossey-Bass, 1973.

Borland, David. "The University as an Organization: An Analysis of the Faculty Rewards System." Unpublished Ed.D. dissertation, Indiana University, 1970.

Boyenga, Kirk W. "Job Stress and Coping Behavior of Married Male and Female University Faculty Members." Unpublished Ph.D. dissertation, Purdue University, 1978.

Bresler, Jack B. "Teaching Effectiveness and Government Awards." *Science* 12 (April 1968): 164–67.

Brown, David G. *The Mobile Professors.* Washington, D.C.: American Council on Education, 1967.

Bryant, Anne L. "Faculty Collective Bargaining in Higher Education: A Case Study of the University of Massachusetts, Amherst Election, November, 1973." Unpublished Ph.D. dissertation, University of Massachusetts, 1978.

Buerer, Jerrold B. "Professional Role Identification and Role Stress: The Case of the Church College Academician." Unpublished Ph.D. dissertation, University of Iowa, 1967.

Cameron, Susan W. "Women Faculty in Academia: Sponsorship, Informal Networks, and Career Success." Unpublished Ph.D. dissertation, University of Michigan, 1978.

Cameron, Susan W. and Robert T. Blackburn. "Sponsorship and Academic

Career Success." *Journal of Higher Education* 52 (July/August 1981): 369–77.

Cares, Robert C. and Robert T. Blackburn. "Faculty Self-actualization: Factors Affecting Career Success." *Research in Higher Education* 9 (1978): 123–36.

Carnegie Council on Policy Studies in Higher Education. *A Classification of Institutions of Higher Education*. Revised edition. Berkeley: Carnegie Council, 1976.

Centra, John A. "Effectiveness of Student Feedback in Modifying College Instruction." *Journal of Educational Psychology* 65 (1973): 395–401.

———. "College Teaching: Who Should Evaluate It?" *Findings* 1 (1974): 5–8.

Choy, Chunghoon. "The Relationship of College Teacher Effectiveness to Conceptual Systems Orientation and Perceptual Orientation." Unpublished Ed.D. dissertation, Colorado State College, 1969.

Clark, Mary Jo. "A Study of Organizational Stress and Professional Performance of Faculty Members in a Small Four-Year College." Unpublished Ph.D. dissertation, University of Michigan, 1973.

Clark, Mary Jo and Robert T. Blackburn. "Faculty Performance under Stress." In *Proceedings: The First Invitational Conference on Faculty Effectiveness as Evaluated by Students,* edited by Alan L. Sockloff. Philadelphia: Measurement and Research Center, Temple University, 1973.

Clemente, Frank. "Early Career Determinants of Research Productivity." *American Journal of Sociology* 79 (September 1973): 409–19.

Clemente, Frank and Richard B. Sturgis. "Quality of Department of Doctoral Training and Research Productivity." *Sociology of Education* 47 (Spring 1974): 287–99.

Cole, Jonathan R. *Fair Science: Women in the Scientific Community*. Glencoe, Ill.: Free Press, 1979.

Cole, Jonathan R. and Stephen Cole. *Social Stratification in Science*. Chicago: University of Chicago Press, 1973.

Cole, Stephen and Hannelore Adamsons. "Determinants of Faculty Support for Student Demonstrations." *Sociology of Education* 42 (Fall 1969): 315–29.

———. "Professional Status and Faculty Support of Student Demonstra-tions." *Public Opinion Quarterly* 34 (Fall 1970): 389–94.

Coltrin, Sally A. "Differential Characteristics of Effective Research Performance in a University Setting." Unpublished Ph.D. dissertation, University of Missouri, 1974.

Coltrin, Sally A. and William F. Glueck. "The Effect of Leadership Roles on the Satisfaction and Productivity of University Research Professors." *Academy of Management Journal* 20 (1977): 101–16.

Cope, Robert G. "Bases of Power, Administrative Preferences, and Job Satisfaction: A Situational Approach." *Journal of Vocational Behavior* 2 (October 1972): 457–65.

Crane, Diana M. "The Environment of Discovery: A Study of Academic Research Interests and Their Setting." Unpublished Ph.D. dissertation, Columbia University, 1964.

――――. "Scientists at Major and Minor Universities: A Study of Productivity and Recognition." *American Sociological Review* 30 (October 1965): 699–714.

Curtis, David. "Types of Faculty Participation in Academic Governance." Unpublished Ph.D. dissertation, Stanford University, 1972.

DeVries, David L. "The Relationship of Role Expectations to Faculty Behavior." *Research in Higher Education* 3 (1975): 111–29.

Delaney, Edward L. "The Influence of Teaching Experience and Instructional Development Activities on Student Ratings of Instruction Obtained by Beginning Professors at a Large University." Unpublished Ph.D. dissertation, New York University, 1977.

Donovan, John D. *The Academic Man in the Catholic College.* New York: Sheed and Ward, 1964.

Dykes, Marie D. "Organizational and Individual Influences on Faculty Participation in the Implementation of a University Innovation." Unpublished Ph.D. dissertation, University of Michigan, 1978.

Ecker, George P. "Pressure, Structure, and Attitude: Organizational Structure and Faculty Milieux." Unpublished Ph.D. dissertation, Stanford University, 1973.

Eckert, Ruth E. and Howard Y. Williams. *College Faculty View Themselves and Their Jobs.* Minneapolis: College of Education, University of Minnesota, 1972.

Elmore, Patricia B. and Karen LaPointe. "Effect of Teacher Sex, Student Sex, and Teacher Warmth on the Evaluation of College Instructors." *Journal of Educational Psychology* 67 (June 1975): 368–74.

Elmore, Patricia B. and John T. Pohlman. "Effect of Teacher, Student, and Class Characteristics on the Evaluation of College Instructors." *Journal of Educational Psychology* 70 (April 1978): 187–92.

Evans, Richard I. and P. K. Leepman. *Resistance to Innovation in Higher Education.* San Francisco: Jossey-Bass, 1968.

Fahrer, Robert F. "A Study of General Stress and its Impact upon Selected Faculty in Three Types of Public Higher Education Institutions." Unpublished Ph.D. dissertation, Washington State University, 1978.

Feldman, Kenneth E. "The Superior College Teacher from the Students' View." *Research in Higher Education* 5 (1976): 243–88.

Ferguson, John. "Job Satisfaction and Job Performance within a University Faculty." Unpublished Ph.D. dissertation, Cornell University, 1960.

Feuille, Peter and James Blandin. "University Faculty and Attitudinal

Militancy toward the Employment Relationship." *Sociology of Education* 49 (April 1976): 139–45.

Finkelstein, Martin J. "Faculty Colleagueship Patterns and Research Productivity." Paper presented at the Annual Meeting of the American Educational Research Association, New York, March 1982.

Fischer, Cheryl Givens and Grace Grant. "Intellectual Levels in College Classrooms." In *Studies of College Teaching,* by Carolyn Ellner et al. Lexington, Mass: D. C. Heath, 1983.

Fox, Thomas G. and Robert T. Blackburn. "Factors Influencing Medical School Faculty Disposition toward Collective Bargaining." *Journal of Medical Education* 50 (March 1975): 229–36.

Francis, John B., Martin Finkelstein, and Lisa Stratton. *The Recognition and Reward of Teaching Excellence: An Evaluation.* Albany, N.Y.: State University of New York, March 1978.

Freedman, Mervin et al. *Academic Culture and Faculty Development.* Berkeley: Montaigne Press, 1979.

French, J. R. and B. Raven. "The Bases of Social Power." In *Group Dynamics,* edited by D. Cartwright and A. Zander. Evanston, Ill.: Row, Peterson, and Company, 1960.

Fulton, Oliver and Martin Trow. "Research Activity in American Higher Education." *Sociology of Education* 47 (Winter 1974): 29–73.

Gaff, Jerry G. and Robert C. Wilson. "Faculty Impact on Students." In *College Professors and Their Impact on Students,* by Robert C. Wilson, Jerry G. Gaff, Evelyn R. Dienst, Lynn Wood, and James L. Bavry. New York: John Wiley and Sons, 1975.

Galiano, Russell P. "A Predictive Study of Faculty Attitudes toward Collective Bargaining in a Selected Institution of Higher Education." Unpublished Ph.D. dissertation, University of Southern Mississippi, 1977.

Gamson, Zelda. "Utilitarian and Normative Orientations toward Education." *Sociology of Education* 39 (1966): 46–73.

––––––. "Performance and Personalism in Student-Faculty Relations." *Sociology of Education* 40 (Fall 1967): 279–301.

Gardner, Carroll A. "Faculty Participation in Departmental Administrative Activities." Unpublished Ph.D. dissertation, University of Michigan, 1971.

Givens, Cheryl F. "A Descriptive Study of the Cognitive Level of Classroom Discourse of College Professors and Students." Unpublished Ph.D. dissertation, Claremont Graduate School, 1976.

Glueck, William F. and Lawrence Jauch. "Sources of Research Ideas among Productive Scholars." *Journal of Higher Education* 46 (January/February 1975): 103–14.

Glueck, William F. and Cary D. Thorp. "The Role of the Academic Administrator in Research Professors' Satisfaction and Productivity." *Educational Administration Quarterly* 10 (Winter 1974): 72–90.

Gress, James R. "Predicting Faculty Attitudes toward Collective Bargaining." *Research in Higher Education* 4 (1976): 247–56.

Hall, David E. "Determinants of Publication Productivity of Faculty at Four-Year Colleges." Unpublished Ph.D. dissertation, University of Michigan, 1975.

Hargens, Lowell L. and Grant M. Farr. "An Examination of Recent Hypotheses about Institutional Inbreeding." *American Journal of Sociology* 78 (May 1973): 1381–1402.

Harry, Joseph and Norman S. Goldner. "Null Relationship between Teaching and Research." *Sociology of Education* 45 (Winter 1972): 47–60.

Hayes, John R. "Research, Teaching, and Faculty Fate." *Science* 172 (April 1971): 227–30.

Herzberg, Frederick, Bernard Mausner, and Barbara B. Snyderman. *The Motivation to Work*. New York: John Wiley and Sons, 1959.

Hesseldenz, Jon S. "An Analysis of Predictors of Instruction Work Effort." *Research in Higher Education* 4 (1976): 219–34.

Hill, Winston W. and Wendell L. French. "Perceptions of the Power of Department Chairmen by Professors." *Administrative Science Quarterly* 11 (1967): 548–74.

Hind, Robert R., Sanford Dornbusch, and W. Richard Scott. "A Theory of Evaluation Applied to a University Faculty." *Sociology of Education* 47 (Winter 1974): 114–28.

Ittelson, John C. "Factors Influencing the Utilization of Instructional Media by College Faculty." Unpublished Ph.D. dissertation, Northwestern University, 1978.

Johnson, Lynn G. "Receptivity and Resistance: Faculty Response to the External Graduate Degree at the University Michigan." Unpublished Ph.D. dissertation, University of Michigan, 1978.

Kazlow, Carole. "Faculty Receptivity to Organizational Change: A Test of Two Explanations of Resistance to Innovation in Higher Education." *Journal of Research and Development in Education* 10 (Winter 1977): 87–98.

Kelly, Richard and B. Derrell Hart. "The Role Preferences of Faculty in Different Age Groups and Academic Disciplines." *Sociology of Education* 44 (Summer 1971): 351–57.

Kemmerer, Frank and J. Victor Baldridge. *Unions on Campus: A National Study of the Consequences of Faculty Bargaining*. San Francisco: Jossey-Bass, 1975.

Kenen, Peter B. and Regina H. Kenen. "Who Thinks Who's In Charge Here: Faculty Perceptions of Influence and Power in the University." *Sociology of Education* 51 (April 1978): 113–23.

Kenen, Regina H. "Professors' Academic Role Behavior and Attitudes, as Influenced by the Structural Effects and Community Context of the College or University." Unpublished Ph.D. dissertation, Columbia University, 1974.

Kerr, Clark. *The Uses of the University.* New York: Harper and Row, 1963.

King, Alma. "The Self-concept and Self-actualization of University Faculty in Relation to Student Perceptions of Effective Teaching." Unpublished Ph.D. dissertation, Utah State University, 1971.

Kintsfather, David P., Jr. "Administrative Factors and Faculty Use of Instructional Television in Higher Education." Unpublished Ph.D. dissertation, University of Mississippi, 1977.

Klapper, Hope L. "The Young College Faculty Member—A New Breed?" *Sociology of Education* 42 (Winter 1969): 38–49.

Koester, Lynne S. and Charles H. Clark. "Job Stress, Job Satisfaction." Paper presented at the Annual Meeting of the American Psychological Association, Montreal, September 1980. Cited by Cheryl Fields, "Faculty Stress is Found to be Highest among Married Women, Single Men." *Chronicle of Higher Education* 21 (September 8, 1980): 1.

Kozma, Robert B. "Faculty Development and the Adoption and Diffusion of Classroom Innovations." *Journal of Higher Education* 49 (September/October 1978): 438–49.

Kratcoski, Peter C. "A Study of Professorial Role Satisfaction among Faculty Members at Selected Catholic Colleges." Unpublished Ph.D. dissertation, Pennsylvania State University, 1969.

Ladd, Everett C. "The Work Experience of American College Professors: Some Data and an Argument." *Current Issues in Higher Education— 1979.* Washington, D.C.: American Association for Higher Education, 1979.

Ladd, Everett C. and Seymour M. Lipset. *Professors, Unions, and American Higher Education.* Berkeley: The Carnegie Commission, 1973.

————. "Faculty Members Note Both Positive and Negative Aspects of Campus Unions." *Chronicle of Higher Education* 11 (February 23, 1976): 11.

Lane, Robert E. "Faculty Unionism in a California State College—A Comparative Analysis of Union Members and Non-members." Unpublished Ph.D. dissertation, University of Iowa, 1967.

Lanning, Allan and Robert T. Blackburn. "Faculty Consulting and the Consultant." *Resources in Education* 14 (January 1979): 107. ED 160 024.

Leon, Julio. "An Investigation of the Applicability of the Two-Factor Theory of Job Satisfaction among College and University Professors." Unpublished Ph.D. dissertation, University of Arkansas, 1973.

Levine, Sue Ann. "The Professional-Bureaucratic Dilemma: Alienation from Work among University Faculty." Unpublished Ph.D. dissertation, Oklahoma State University, 1978.

Linsky, Arnold S. and Murray A. Straus. "Student Evaluations, Research Productivity, and Eminence of College Faculty." *Journal of Higher Education* 46 (January 1975): 89–102.

Lodahl, Janice B. and Gerald Gordon. "The Structure of Scientific Fields and the Functioning of University Graduate Departments." *American Sociological Review* 37 (February 1972): 57–72.

Long, John. "Productivity and Academic Position in the Scientific Career." *American Sociological Review* 43 (December 1978): 899–908.

Manis, J. G. "Some Academic Influences on Publication Productivity." *Social Forces* 29 (March 1950): 267–72.

Mann, Richard D. et al. *The College Classroom*. New York: John Wiley and Sons, 1970.

Marver, James D. and Carl V. Patton. "The Correlates of Consultation: American Academics in 'The Real World'." *Higher Education* 5 (August 1976): 319–35.

Maslow, A. H. and W. Zimmerman. "College Teaching Ability, Scholarly Activity, and Personality." *Journal of Educational Psychology* 47 (1956): 185–89.

McCord, Beverly. "A Study of the Relationship of the Influence of Deans of Schools of Nursing to the Personal Satisfaction and Professional Productivity of Faculty." Unpublished Ph.D. dissertation, University of Denver, 1970.

McDaniel, Ernest, D. and John F. Feldhusen. "Relationships between Faculty Ratings and Indexes of Service and Scholarship." *Proceedings of the 78th Annual American Psychological Association Convention*. Washington, D.C.: American Psychological Association, 1970.

McInnis, Malcolm Cleveland, Jr. "Demographic and Non-demographic Variables Associated with the Florida State University Faculty Members' Attitudes toward Collective Bargaining in Higher Education." Unpublished Ph.D. dissertation, Florida State University, 1972.

Michalak, Stanley and Robert Friedrich. "Research Productivity and Teaching Effectiveness at a Small Liberal Arts College." *Journal of Higher Education* 52 (November/December 1981): 578–97.

Miller, M. "Instructor Attitudes toward, and Their Use of, Student Ratings of Teachers." *Journal of Educational Psychology* 62 (1971): 235–39.

Minter, John and Howard R. Bowen. *Independent Higher Education: Sixth Annual Report on Financial and Educational Trends in the Independent Sector of American Higher Education*. Washington, D.C.: National Institute of Independent Colleges and Universities, 1982.

Montenegro, Zenia P. "Ideal and Actual Perceptions of College Instructors as Predictors of Teacher Effectiveness." Unpublished Ph.D. dissertation, University of Hawaii, 1978.

Morgan, Richard H. "The Conflict between Teaching and Research in the

Academic Role." Unpublished Ph.D. dissertation, Columbia University, 1970.

Morstain, Barry R. and John Smart. "Educational Orientations of Faculty: Assessing a Personality Model of the Academic Profession." *Psychological Reports* 39 (1976): 1199–1211.

Moxley, Linda S. "Job Satisfaction of Faculty Teaching Higher Education: An Examination of Herzberg's Dual-Factor Theory and Porter's Need Satisfaction Research." *Resources in Education* 12 (October 1977): 92. ED 139 349.

Neumann, Yoram. "Determinants of Faculty Attitudes toward Collective Bargaining in a University Graduate Department: An Organizational Approach." *Research in Higher Education* 10 (1979): 123–38.

Nixon, Howard L. "Faculty Support of University Authority." *Administrative Science Quarterly* 20 (March 1975): 114–23.

Oncken, Gerald R. "The Relationship of Control Structure to Faculty Productivity and Satisfaction in University Departments." Unpublished Ph.D. dissertation, University of Illinois, 1971.

Overall, J. V. and H. W. Marsh. "The Relationship between Students' Evaluations of Faculty and Instructional Improvement." Paper presented to the Third International Conference on Improving University Teaching, Newcastle-upon-Tyne, England, 1977.

Pambookian, H. S. "Initial Level of Student Evaluation of Instruction as a Source of Influence on Instructor Change after Feedback." *Journal of Educational Psychology* 66 (1974): 52–56.

––––––. "Feedback to Instructors on Their Teaching to Improve Instruction." Paper presented at the Third International Conference on Improving University Teaching, Newcastle-upon-Tyne, England, 1977.

Parsons, Talcott and Gerald M. Platt. *The American Academic Profession: A Pilot Study.* Cambridge, Mass.: Harvard University, 1968.

––––––. "Faculty Teaching Goals, 1968–1973." *Social Problems* 24 (December 1976): 298–307.

Pascarella, Ernest T. et al. "Student-Faculty Interactional Settings and Their Relationship to Predicted Academic Performance." *Journal of Higher Education* 49 (September/October 1978): 450–63.

Patton, Carl V. and James D. Marver. "Paid Consulting by American Academics." *Educational Record* 60 (Spring 1979): 175–84.

Pelz, Donald C. and Frank M. Andrews. *Scientists in Organizations.* New York: Wiley, 1966.

Perry, William G. *Forms of Intellectual and Ethical Development During the College Years.* New York: Holt, Rinehart, and Winston, 1970.

––––––. "Cognitive and Ethical Growth: The Making of Meaning." In *The Modern American College,* by Arthur Chickering and Associates. San Francisco: Jossey-Bass, 1981.

Plumley, Virginia D. "Relationship between Faculty Concerns and Their Attitude toward Collective Bargaining at Marshall University." Unpublished Ph.D. dissertation, Kent State University, 1978.

Poole, Darryl G. "Professional Orientations of University Professors and Their Behavior at Meetings of Learned Societies." Unpublished Ph.D. dissertation, University of Florida, 1974.

Ralph, Norbert. "Stages of Faculty Development." In *Facilitating Faculty Development,* edited by Mervin Freedman. New Directions in Higher Education, No. 1. San Francisco: Jossey-Bass, 1973.

Razak, Warren N. "Departmental Structure and Faculty Loyalty in a Major University." Unpublished Ph.D. dissertation, University of Kansas, 1969.

Reskin, Barbara. "Scientific Productivity and the Reward Structure of Science." *American Sociological Review* 42 (June 1977): 491–504.

––––––. "Academic Sponsorship and Scientists' Careers." *Sociology of Education* 52 (July 1979): 129–46.

Rice, Eugene. "A Study of Three Cohorts of Danforth Fellows." *AAHE Bulletin* 32 (April 1980): 4.

Riley, John F. "Attitudes of Faculty of Private Colleges towards Collective Bargaining in Higher Education." Unpublished Ph.D. dissertation, Lehigh University, 1976.

Roe, Anne. "A Psychological Study of Eminent Biologists." *Psychological Monographs* 65, No. 14 (1951a): 1–68.

––––––. "A Psychological Study of Physical Scientists." *Genetic Psychology Monographs* 43 (1951b): 121–239.

––––––. "A Psychological Study of Eminent Psychologists and Anthropologists, and a Comparison with Biological and Physical Scientists." *Psychological Monographs* 67 No. 2 (1953): 1–55.

––––––. "Patterns in Productivity of Scientists." *Science* 176 (May 1972): 940–41.

Schultz, Charles B. "Some Limits to the Validity and Usefulness of Student Ratings of Teachers: An Argument for Caution." *Educational Research Quarterly* 3 (Summer 1978): 12–27.

Sherman, Barbara R. and Robert T. Blackburn. "Personal Characteristics and Teaching Effectiveness of College Faculty." *Journal of Educational Psychology* 67 (1975): 124–31.

Sorey, Kenneth E. "A Study of the Distinguishing Personality Characteristics of College Faculty Who Are Superior in Regard to the Teaching Function." Unpublished Ed.D. dissertation, Oklahoma State University, 1967.

Stadtman, Verne. *Academic Adaptations.* San Francisco: Jossey-Bass, 1980.

Stark, Joan and Barry R. Morstain. "Educational Orientations of Faculty in

Liberal Arts Colleges: An Analysis of Disciplinary Differences." *Journal of Higher Education* 49 (September/October 1978): 420–37.

Stecklein, John E. and Ruth E. Eckert. *An Exploratory Study of Factors Influencing the Choice of College Teaching as a Career.* Minneapolis: University of Minnesota, 1958.

Stuntebeck, Susan. "Perceived Need Satisfaction and Teaching Effectiveness: A Study of University Faculty." Unpublished Ph.D. dissertation, University of Notre Dame, 1974.

Swierenga, Lloyd G. "Application of Herzberg's Dual-Factor Theory to Faculty Members in a University." Unpublished Ed.D. dissertation, Western Michigan University, 1970.

Theophilus, Donald K. "Professorial Attitudes toward Their Work Environment at the University of Michigan." In *The Instructional Process and Institutional Research,* edited by G. N. Drewry. Cortland, N.Y.: Association for Institutional Research, 1967.

Townsend, Clark W. "A Case Study: University of Washington Faculty Interest in Collective Bargaining." Unpublished Ph.D. dissertation, University of Washington, 1978.

Usher, Richard H. "The Relationship of Perception of Self, Others, and the Helping Task to Certain Measures of College Faculty Effectiveness." Unpublished Ed.D. dissertation, University of Florida, 1966.

Voeks, Virginia W. "Publications and Teaching Effectiveness." *Journal of Higher Education* 33 (April 1962): 212–18.

Wainstock, Susan. "Death of a Dream: The Variables Which Determine What Bargaining Agent Is Chosen at a Four-Year College." Unpublished Ph.D. dissertation, University of Michigan, 1971.

Ware, John E. and Reed G. Williams. "The Doctor Fox Effect: A Study of Lecturer Effectiveness and Ratings of Instruction." *Journal of Medical Education* 50 (February 1975): 149–56.

———. "Discriminant Analysis of Student Ratings as a Means for Identifying Lecturers Who Differ in Enthusiasm or Information Giving." *Educational and Psychological Measurement* 37 (Autumn 1977): 627–39.

Warriner, Charles K. and Linda D. Murai. "Factors in Faculty Role Performance: An Examination of the Latent Role Hypothesis." Mimeographed. Lawrence, Kans.: University of Kansas, 1973.

———. "Organizational Factors in Faculty Role Performance." Mimeographed. Lawrence, Kans.: University of Kansas, 1974.

Washington, Earl M. "The Relationship between College Department Chairpersons' Leadership Style as Perceived by Teaching Faculty and That Faculty's Feelings of Job Satisfaction." Unpublished Ed.D. dissertation, Western Michigan University, 1975.

Whitlock, Gerald H. "The Experiential Bases and Dimensions of Faculty Morale at a State University." Mimeographed. Knoxville: University of Tennessee, 1965.

Wieland, George F. and Jerald G. Bachman. "Faculty Satisfaction and the Department Chairmen: A Study of Academic Departments in Twelve Liberal Arts Colleges." Mimeographed. Ann Arbor: Survey Research Center, 1966.

Willie, Reynold and John E. Stecklein. "A Three-Decade Comparison of College Faculty Characteristics, Activities, and Attitudes." *Research in Higher Education* 16 (1982): 81–93.

Wilson, Robert C. and Jerry G. Gaff. "Faculty Views of Teaching." In *College Professors and Their Impact on Students,* by Robert C. Wilson, Jerry G. Gaff, Evelyn R. Dienst, Lynn Wood, and James L. Bavry. New York: John Wiley and Sons, 1975.

Wilson, Logan. *The Academic Man.* London: Oxford University Press, 1942.

———. "Prestige Patterns in Scholarship and Science." *Southwestern Social Science Quarterly* 23 (1943): 317–25.

Wispe, Lauren G. "The Bigger, the Better: Productivity, Size, and Turnover in a Sample of Psychology Departments." *American Psychologist* 24 (July 1969): 662–68.

Young, Robert E. "The Effect of Five Factors on University Faculty Members Participation in Instructional Improvement." Unpublished Ph.D. dissertation, Michigan State University, 1976.

Zirkel, Perry A. "In Search of the Meaning of Yeshiva." *AAHE Bulletin* 33 (April 1981). ED 198 788.

CHAPTER 6
Beyond the Work Role: Faculty as People and Citizens

Ali, Basharat. "Non-professional and Professional Variables, Political Orientation, and Faculty Support for the Critic Function as Primary for the University." Unpublished Ph.D. dissertation, University of New Mexico, 1972.

Anderson, Charles H. "The Intellectual Subsociety: An Empirical Test of the Intellectual Subsociety Hypothesis." Unpublished Ph.D. dissertation, University of Massachusetts, 1966.

———. "Religious Communality among Academics." *Journal of the Scientific Study of Religion* 7 (Spring 1968): 87–96.

Anderson, Charles H. and John Murray. "Kitsch and the Academic." *Sociology and Social Research* 51 (July 1967): 445–52.

———. (eds). *The Professors.* Cambridge, Mass.: Schenkman Publishing, 1971.

Armor, David J. et al. "Professors' Attitudes toward the Vietnam War." *Public Opinion Quarterly* 31 (Summer 1967): 159–75.

Baldwin, Roger. "Adult and Career Development: What Are the Implications for Faculty?" *Current Issues in Higher Education,* No. 2. Washington, D.C.: American Association for Higher Education, 1979.

Bayer, Alan E. *Teaching Faculty in Academe: 1972–73.* A.C.E. Research Reports, No. 8. Washington, D.C.: American Council on Education, 1973.

Berger, James. "Conservatism and the American Professoriate." Unpublished Ph.D. dissertation, University of Connecticut, 1973.

Crane, Diana M. "Social Class Origin and Academic Success: The Influence of Two Stratification Systems on Academic Careers." *Sociology of Education* 42 (Winter 1969): 1–17.

Doi, James I. (ed.) *Assessing Faculty Effort.* New Directions for Institutional Research, No. 2. San Francisco: Jossey-Bass, 1974.

Eaton, Travis E. "An Empirical Examination of Religiosity and Academic Discipline Based upon Two Variables, Scientism and Scholarly Distance." Unpublished Ph.D. dissertation, Indiana University, 1973.

Eckert, Ruth E. and Howard Y. Williams. *College Faculty View Themselves and Their Jobs.* Minneapolis: College of Education, University of Minnesota, 1972.

Eitzen, D. Stanley and Gary M. Maranell. "The Political Party Affiliation of College Professors." *Social Forces* 47 (December 1968): 145–53.

Espy, R. H. Edwin. "The Religion of College Teachers." *Christian Education* 33 (September 1950): 179–200.

———. *The Religion of College Teachers.* New York: Association Press, 1951.

Faia, Michael A. "The Myth of the Liberal Professor." *Sociology of Education* 47 (Spring 1974): 171–202.

Friedman, Norman L. "Jewish or Professorial Identity? The Priorization Process in Academic Situations." *Sociological Analysis* 32 (Fall 1971): 149–57.

Gappa, Judith M., Donald St. John-Parsons, and Jean O'Barr. "The Dual Careers of Faculty and Family: Can Both Prosper?" Paper presented at the annual meeting of the American Association of Higher Education, Washington, D.C. April, 1979. ED 196328

Gappa, Judith M. and Barbara S. Uehling. *Women in Academe: Steps to Greater Equality.* ERIC-AAHE Research Reports, No. 1. Washington, D.C.: American Association for Higher Education, 1979.

Gerstl, Joel. "Career Commitment and Style of Life in Three Middle Class Occupations." Unpublished Ph.D. dissertation, University of Minnesota, 1959.

———. "Leisure, Taste, and Occupational Milieu." In *The Professors,* edited by Charles Anderson and John Murray. Cambridge, Mass: Schenkman, 1971.

Glock, Charles Y. and Rodney Stark. *Religion and Society in Tension.* Chicago: Rand McNally and Co., 1965.

Gordon, Milton M. *Assimilation in American Life: The Role of Race, Religion, and National Origin.* New York: Oxford University Press, 1964.

Gustad, John W. *The Career Decisions of College Teachers.* SREB Research Monograph, No. 2. Atlanta: Southern Regional Education Board, 1960.

Harry, Joseph and Norman S. Goldner. "Null Relationship between Teaching and Research." *Sociology of Education* 45 (Winter 1972): 47–60.

Heckman, Norma A., Rebecca Bryson, and Jeff Bryson. "Problems of Professional Couples: A Content Analysis." *Journal of Marriage and Family* 39 (May 1977): 323–30.

Herman, Jeanne B. and Karen Gyllstrom. "Working Men and Women: Inter- and Intra-Role Conflict." *Psychology of Women Quarterly* 1 (Summer 1977): 319–33.

Hoge, Dean R. and Larry G. Keeter. "Determinants of College Teachers' Religious Beliefs and Participation." *Journal for the Scientific Study of Religion* 15 (September 1976): 221–35.

Kistler, Robert C. "The University Professor and His Family: A Study of the Duality in Roles." Unpublished Ph.D. dissertation, University of Maryland, 1967.

Ladd, Everett C. "Professors and Political Petitions." *Science* 163 (March 1969): 1425–30.

Ladd, Everett C. and Seymour M. Lipset. "The Academy: Politically Split." *Chronicle of Higher Education* 11 (October 28, 1975): 2. 1975a.

––––––. "Faculty Democrats Disagree with Party's Rank and File." *Chronicle of Higher Education* 11 (December 15, 1975): 11. 1975b.

––––––. "How Do Faculty Members Take Their Responsibilities as Citizens?" *Chronicle of Higher Education* 11 (December 22, 1975): 13. 1975c.

––––––. "War's Dramatic Impact on Faculty Behavior." *Chronicle of Higher Education* 11 (November 17, 1975): 14. 1975d.

––––––. "Professors' Religious and Ethnic Backgrounds." *Chronicle of Higher Education* 11 (September 22, 1975): 2. 1975e.

––––––. *The Divided Academy.* New York: McGraw-Hill, 1975f.

––––––. "The General Periodicals Professors Read." *Chronicle of Higher Education* 11 (January 19, 1976): 14.

––––––. "Professors Found to Be Liberal but Not Radical." *Chronicle of Higher Education* 15 (January 16, 1978): 9.

Lazarsfeld, Paul and Wagner Thielens. *The Academic Mind.* Glencoe, Ill.: The Free Press, 1958.

Lee, David. "Marital Disruption among University Physicians and Professors: An Empirical Study of the Relationship between Professorial Activities and Evaluations of Marital Disruption." Unpublished Ph.D. dissertation, University of Iowa, 1968.

Lehman, Edward C. "Academic Discipline and Faculty Religiosity in Secular and Church-related Colleges." *Journal for the Scientific Study of Religion* 13 (June 1974): 205–20.

Lehman, Edward C. and Donald W. Shriver. "Academic Discipline as Predictive of Faculty Religiosity." *Social Forces* 47 (December 1968): 171–182.

Leuba, James H. *The Belief in God and Immortality.* LaSalle, Illinois: The Open Court Publishing Company, 1921.

———. *The Reformation of the Churches.* Boston: Beacon Press, 1950.

Lipset, Seymour M. and Everett C. Ladd. "The Changing Social Origins of American Academics." In *Qualitative and Quantitative Social Research,* edited by Robert K. Merton et al. New York: Free Press, 1979.

Maranell, Gary M. and D. Stanley Eitzen. "The Effect of Discipline, Region, and Rank on the Political Attitudes of College Professors." *Sociological Quarterly* 11 (Winter 1970): 112–18.

Mazur, Allan C. "The Socialization of Jews into the Academic Subculture." In *The Professors,* edited by Charles Anderson and John Murray. Cambridge, Mass: Schenkman, 1971.

Murray, Dennis. "Catholic Academicians and the Intellectual Subsociety Hypothesis." In *The Professors,* edited by Charles Anderson and John Murray. Cambridge, Mass: Schenkman, 1971a.

———. "Religious Orthodoxy among Catholic Academicians." In *The Professors,* edited by Charles Anderson and John Murray. Cambridge, Mass: Schenkman, 1971b.

Parsons, Talcott and Gerald M. Platt. *The American Academic Profession: A Pilot Study.* Cambridge, Mass: Harvard University, 1968.

Schuman, Howard and Edward O. Laumann. "Do Most Professors Support the War?" *Trans-Action* 5 (November 1967): 32–35.

Shulman, Carol H. "Do Faculty Really Work That Hard?" *AAHE Bulletin* 33 (October, 1980): 5.

Spaulding, Charles and Henry A. Turner. "Political Orientation and Field of Specialization among College Professors." *Sociology of Education* 41 (Summer 1968): 245–62.

Steinberg, Stephen. *The Academic Melting Pot.* New York: McGraw-Hill, 1974.

Thalheimer, Fred. "Religiosity in the Academic Profession." Unpublished Ph.D. dissertation, University of California, Los Angeles, 1963.

———. "Continuity and Change in Religiosity: A Study of Academicians." *Pacific Sociological Review* 8 (Fall 1965): 101–8.

———. "Religiosity and Secularization in the Academic Professions." *Sociology of Education* 46 (Spring 1973): 183–202.

Turner, Henry A., Charles Spaulding, and Charles McClintock. "Political Orientations of Academically Affiliated Sociologists." *Sociology and Social Research* 47 (April 1963): 273–89.

Wilson, Logan. *American Academics: Then and Now.* New York: Oxford University Press, 1979.

Wilson, Robert C. and Jerry G. Gaff. *College Professors and Their Impact on Students.* New York: John Wiley and Sons, 1975.

CHAPTER 7
Women and Minority Faculty

Abramson, Joan. *The Invisible Woman: Discrimination in the Academic Profession.* San Francisco: Jossey-Bass, 1975.

Amsden, Celice H. and Collette Moser. "Job Search and Affirmative Action." *American Economic Review* 65 (May 1975): 83–91.

Anderson, William et al. "Black Survival in White Academe." *Journal of Negro Education* 48 (Winter 1979): 92–102.

Astin, Helen S. *The Woman Doctorate in America.* New York: Russell Sage, 1969.

Astin, Helen S. and Alan E. Bayer. "Sex Discrimination in Academe." *Educational Record* 53 (Spring 1972): 101–18.

Astin, Helen S., John A. Folger, and Alan E. Bayer. *Human Resources and Higher Education.* New York: Russell Sage, 1970.

Astin, Helen S. and Werner Hirsch (eds). *The Higher Education of Women.* New York: Praeger, 1978.

Baldridge, J. Victor et al. *Policy Making and Effective Leadership.* San Francisco: Jossey-Bass, 1978.

Barnett, Linda T. and Glenn Littlepage. "Course Preferences and Evaluations of Male and Female Professors by Male and Female Students." *Psychonomic Society Bulletin* 13 (January 1979): 44–46.

Bayer, Alan E. *Teaching Faculty in Academe: 1972–73.* A.C.E. Research Reports, No. 8. Washington, D. C.: American Council on Education, 1973.

Bayer, Alan E. and Helen S. Astin. "Sex Differentials in the Academic Reward System." *Science* 188 (May 1975): 796–802.

Berger, Michael, Martha Foster, Barbara Strubler Wallston, and Larry Wright. "You and Me Against the World: Dual-Career Couples and Joint Job Seeking." *Journal of Research and Development in Education* 10 (April 1977): 30–37.

Bernard, Jessie. *Academic Women.* University Park, Pa.: Pennsylvania State University Press, 1964.

———. *The Female World.* New York: Free Press, 1981.

Berwald, Helen. "Attitudes toward Women College Teachers in Institutions of Higher Education Accredited by the North Central Association." Unpublished Ph.D. dissertation, University of Minnesota, 1962.

Bickel, P. J., E. A. Hammel, J. W. O'Connell. "Sex Bias in Graduate Admissions: Data from Berkeley." *Science* 187 (February 7, 1975): 403.

Blackburn, Robert T., Charles Behymer, and David Hall. "Research Note: Correlates of Faculty Publication." *Sociology of Education* 51 (April 1978): 132–41.

Blackburn, Robert T., David Chapman, and Susan W. Cameron. "Cloning in Academe: Mentorship and Academic Careers." *Research in Higher Education* 15 (1981): 315–27.

Blau, Peter. *The Organization of Academic Work.* New York: John Wiley and Sons, 1973.

Bryant, James W. *Survey of Black American Doctorates.* New York: The Ford Foundation, 1970.

Cameron, Susan W. "Women Faculty in Academia: Sponsorship, Informal Networks, and Career Success." Unpublished Ph.D. dissertation, University of Michigan, 1978.

Cameron, Susan W. and Robert T. Blackburn. "Sponsorship and Academic Career Success." *Journal of Higher Education* 52 (July/August 1981): 369–77.

Cartter, Allan. *Ph.D.'s and the Academic Marketplace.* New York: McGraw-Hill, 1976.

Centra, John A. *Women, Men, and the Doctorate.* Princeton: Educational Testing Service, 1974.

Choy, Chunghoon. "The Relationship of College Teacher Effectiveness to Conceptual Systems Orientation and Perceptual Orientation." Unpublished Ed.D. dissertation, Colorado State College, 1969.

Chronicle of Higher Education 23 (November 15, 1981): 8.

Clemente, Frank. "Early Career Determinants of Research Productivity." *American Journal of Sociology* 79 (September 1973): 409–19.

Cole, Jonathan R. *Fair Science: Women in the Scientific Community.* Glencoe, Ill.: Free Press, 1979.

Cole, Jonathan R. and Stephen Cole. *Social Stratification in Science.* Chicago: University of Chicago Press, 1973.

Converse, Philip E. and Jean M. Converse. "The Status of Women as Students and Professionals in Political Science." *Political Science* 4 (Summer 1971): 328–48.

Crane, Diana M. "Scientists at Major and Minor Universities: A Study of Productivity and Recognition." *American Sociological Review* 30 (October 1965): 699–714.

———. "Social Class Origin and Academic Success: The Influence of Two Stratification Systems on Academic Careers." *Sociology of Education* 42 (Winter 1969): 1–17.

Crim, Roger D. "Expressed Attitudes of Faculty Men and Women toward

Faculty Women in Higher Education in New Hampshire." Unpublished Ph.D. dissertation, University of Mississippi, 1978.

Eckert, Ruth E. "Academic Women Revisited." *Liberal Education* 57 (December 1971): 479–87.

Educational Researcher 9 (October 1980): 4–20.

Elmore, Charles and Robert T. Blackburn. "Black and White Faculty in White Research Universities." *Journal of Higher Education* 54 (January/February 1983): 1–15.

Elmore, Patricia and Karen LaPointe. "Effect of Teacher Sex, Student Sex, and Teacher Warmth on the Evaluation of College Instructors." *Journal of Educational Psychology* 67 (June 1975): 368–74.

———. "Effects of Teacher Sex and Student Sex on the Evaluation of College Instructors." *Journal of Educational Psychology* 66 (June 1974): 386–89.

Ferber, M. A. and J. Loeb. "Performance, Rewards, and Perceptions of Sex Discrimination among Male and Female Faculty." *American Journal of Sociology* 78 (1973): 995–1002.

Ferber, M. A. and J. A. Huber. "Sex of Student and Instructor: A Study of Student Bias." *American Journal of Sociology* 80 (1975): 949–63.

Fidell, L. S. "Empirical Verification of Sex Discrimination in Hiring Practices in Psychology." *American Psychologist* 25 (Winter 1970): 1096–97.

Finkelstein, Martin J. "Three Decades of Research on American Academics: A Descriptive Portrait and Synthesis of Findings." Unpublished Ph.D. dissertation, S.U.N.Y. at Buffalo, 1978.

Fox, M. F. "Sex Segregation and Salary Structure in Academia." *Sociology of Work and Occupations* 8 (1981): 39–60.

Freeman, Bonnie Cook. "Faculty Women in the American University: Up the Down Staircase." *Higher Education* 6 (May 1977): 165–88.

Freeman, Richard B. "Discrimination in the Academic Marketplace." In *American Ethnic Groups,* edited by Thomas Sowell. Washington, D.C.,: The Urban Institute, 1978.

Fulton, Oliver. "Rewards and Fairness: Academic Women in the United States." In *Teachers and Students,* edited by Martin Trow. New York: McGraw-Hill, 1975.

Gappa, Judith M. and Barbara S. Uehling. *Women in Academe: Steps to Greater Equality.* AAHE-ERIC Higher Education Research Report, No. 1. Washington, D.C.: American Association for Higher Education, 1979.

Gappa, Judith M., Donald St. John-Parsons, and Jean O'Barr. "The Dual Careers of Faculty and Family: Can Both Prosper?" Paper presented at the annual meeting of the American Association for Higher Education, Washington, D.C., April, 1979. ED 196328

Goldberg, P. A. "Are Women Prejudiced against Women?" *Transaction* 5 (April 1968): 28–30.

Gordon, Nancy M., Thomas E. Morton, and Ina C. Braden. "Faculty Salaries: Is There Discrimination by Sex, Race, and Discipline?" *American Economic Review* 64 (June 1974): 419–27.

Guillemin, Jeanne, L. L. Holstrom, and M. Garvin. "Judging Competence: Letters of Recommendation for Men and Women Faculties." *School Review* 87 (February 1979): 157–70.

Hamovitch, William and Richard D. Morgenstern. "Children and the Productivity of Academic Women." *Journal of Higher Education* 48 (November/December 1977): 633–45.

Harvard Educational Review 49 (November 1979): 413–563.

———. 50 (February 1980): 1–128.

Hayden, Barbara L. "Purposes of Black Higher Education as Viewed by Black College Faculty and Black Studies Faculty." Unpublished Ph.D. dissertation, University of Pittsburgh, 1978.

Heckman, Norma A., Rebecca Bryson, and Jeff Bryson. "Problems of Professional Couples: A Content Analysis." *Journal of Marriage and Family* 39 (May 1977): 323–30.

Herman, Jeanne B. and Karen Gyllstrom. "Working Men and Women: Inter- and Intra-Role Conflict." *Psychology of Women Quarterly* 1 (Summer 1977): 319–33.

Hodge, Charles M. "An Analysis of the Attitudes Regarding Job Satisfaction Held by Negro Professors and White Professors in Selected Institutions of Higher Education Desegregated Since 1954." Unpublished Ph.D. dissertation, North Texas State University, 1976.

Hoffman, Nancy Jo. "Sexism in Letters of Recommendation: A Case for Consciousness Raising." *Modern Language Association Newsletter* 4 (Winter 1972): 4–5.

Howe, Florence. "Introduction: The First Decade of Women's Studies." *Harvard Educational Review* 49 (November 1979): 413–21.

Johnson, George E. and Frank P. Stafford. "The Earnings and Promotion of Women Faculty." *American Economic Review* 64 (December 1974): 888–903.

Kajander, Cheryl A. "The Effects of Instructor and Student Sex on Verbal Behavior in College Classrooms." Unpublished Ph.D. dissertation, University of Texas at Austin, 1976.

Kane, Roslyn D. *Sex Discrimination in Education: A Study of Employment Practices Affecting Professional Personnel.* 3 vols. Arlington, Va: ERIC Document Reproduction Service, 1976. ED 132 744.

Kanter, Rosabeth Moss. "Some Effects of Proportions on Group Life: Skewed Sex Ratios and Responses to Token Women." *American Journal of Sociology* 82 (March 1977): 965–90.

Katz, David. "Faculty Salaries Promotions and Productivity at a Large University." *American Economic Review* 63 (June 1973): 469–77.

Kaufman, Debra R. "Associational Ties in Academe: Some Male and Female Differences." *Sex Roles* 4 (1978): 9–21.

Koester, Lynne S. and Charles H. Clark. "Job Stress, Job Satisfaction." Paper presented at the annual meeting of the American Psychological Association, Montreal, September 1980, cited by Cheryl Fields, "Faculty Stress Is Found to Be Highest among Married Women, Single Men." *Chronicle of Higher Education* 21 (September 8, 1980): 1.

Ladd, Everett C. and Seymour M. Lipset. *Survey of the Social, Political, and Educational Perspectives of American College and University Faculty.* Final Report. 2 vols. Storrs, Conn.: University of Connecticut, 1976.

LaSorte, Michael A. "Academic Women's Salaries: Equal Pay for Equal Work?" *Journal of Higher Education* 42 (April 1971): 265–78.

Levin, Arie and Linda Duchin. "Women in Academia." *Science* 173 (September 1971): 892–95.

Lipset, Seymour M. and Everett C. Ladd. "The Changing Social Origins of American Academics." In *Qualitative and Quantitative Social Research,* edited by Robert K. Merton et al. New York: Free Press, 1979.

Mackie, Marlene. "Student's Perceptions of Female Professors." *Journal of Vocational Behavior* 8 (1976): 337–48.

Marwell, Gerald, Rachel Rosenfeld, and Seymour Spilerman. "Geographic Constraints on Women's Careers in Academia." *Science* 205 (September 21, 1979): 1225–31.

Mayfield, Betty and William Nash. "Career Attitudes of Female Professors." *Psychological Reports* 39 (October 1976): 631–34.

Menninger, Sally and Clare Rose. "Women Scientists in Academe: The Numbers and What the Numbers Don't Say." Paper presented at the annual conference on Women in Education, Madison, Wisconsin, October, 1978. ED 174 396

Middleton, Lorenzo. "Black Professors on White Campuses." *Chronicle of Higher Education* 17 (October 1978): 8–12.

Modern Language Association. "The Status of Women in Modern Language Departments: A Report of the MLA Commission on the Status of Women." *PMLA* 86 (May 1971): 459–68.

Mommsen, Kent G. "Black Ph.D.'s in the Academic Marketplace." *Journal of Higher Education* 45 (April 1974): 253–67.

Moore, William and Lonnie Wagstaff. *Black Educators in White Colleges.* San Francisco: Jossey-Bass, 1974.

Morlock, Laura. "Disciplinary Variation in the Status of Academic Women." In *Academic Women on the Move,* edited by Alice S. Rossi and Ann Calderwood. New York: Russell Sage Foundation, 1973.

National Center for Education Statistics. *Digest of Education Statistics 1979.* Washington, D.C.: Government Printing Office, 1979.

————. *The Condition of Education, 1980.* Washington, D.C.: Government Printing Office, 1980.

————. *Digest of Education Statistics, 1982.* Washington, D.C.: Government Printing Office, 1982.

Nielson, Linda L. "Sexism and Self-healing in the University." *Harvard Educational Review* 49 (November 1979): 467–76.

Oltman, Ruth M. "Campus 1970—Where Do Women Stand?" *American Association of University Women Journal* 64 (November 1970): 14–15.

Patterson, Michelle. "Alice in Wonderland: A Study of Women Faculty in Graduate Departments of Sociology." *American Sociologist* 6 (August 1971): 226–34.

Patterson, Patricia L. "A Description and Analysis of the Women Faculty in Pennsylvania's State-owned Colleges and Universities." Unpublished Ph.D. dissertation, University of Pittsburgh, 1974.

Rafky, David M. "The Black Scholar in the Academic Marketplace." *Teachers College Record* 74 (December 1972): 225–60.

Reagan, Barbara R. "Report of the Committee on the Status of Women in the Economics Profession." *American Economic Review* 65 (May 1975): 490–501.

Robinson, Lora H. "Institutional Variation in the Status of Academic Women." In *Academic Women on the Move,* edited by Alice S. Rossi and Ann Calderwood. New York: Russell Sage Foundation, 1973.

Rose, H. M. "An Appraisal of the Negro Educator's Situation in the Academic Marketplace." *Journal of Negro Education* 35 (1966): 18–26.

Rose, Clare et al. "Responsiveness vs. Resources: The Implementation and Impact of Affirmative Action Programs for Women Scientists in Postsecondary Education." Paper presented at the annual meeting of the Association for Institutional Research, May, 1978. ED 161 389.

Rossi, Alice S. "Status of Women in Graduate Departments of Sociology." *American Sociologist* 5 (February 1970): 1–12.

Sell, Lucy W. *Towards Affirmative Action.* New Directions for Institutional Research, No. 3. San Francisco: Jossey-Bass, 1974.

Shoemaker, Elwood A. and Ronald L. McKeen. "Affirmative Action and Hiring Practices in Higher Education." *Research in Higher Education* 3 (December 1975): 359–64.

Simon, R. J., S. M. Clark, and K. Galway. "The Woman Ph.D.: A Recent Profile." *Social Problems* 15 (Fall 1967): 221–36.

Simon, Rita J. and Ethel Rosenthal. "Profile of the Woman Ph.D. in Economics, History, and Sociology." *Journal of American Association of University Women* 60 (March 1967): 127–29.

Simpson, Lawrence A. "Attitudes of Employing Agents toward Women." *Graduate Comment* 12 (December 1969): 41–46.

Steele, Claude and Stephen Green. "Affirmative Action and Academic Hiring." *Journal of Higher Education* 47 (July/August 1976): 413–35.

Strober, Myra H. "Women Economists: Career Aspirations, Education, and Training." *American Economic Review* 65 (May 1975): 92–99.

Thompson, David. "The Teacher in the Negro College: A Scoiological Analysis." Unpublished Ph.D. dissertation, Columbia University, 1956.

Thornberry, Mary. "Unexpected Benefits, Expected Defeats: Affirmative Action for Women." *Resources in Education* 14 (April 1979): 80.

Tidball, M. Elizabeth. "Of Men and Research." *Journal of Higher Education* 47 (July/August 1976): 373–89.

Tuckman, Howard. *Publication, Teaching, and the Academic Reward System.* Lexington, Mass.: Lexington Books, 1976.

Walker, Gloria P. "Effective and Ineffective Images as Perceived by the Male Afroamerican University Professor." Unpublished Ph.D. dissertation, University of Pittsburgh, 1973.

Weidman, Carla S. and John C. Weidman. "The Woman Professor of Education: Social and Occupational Characteristics." Paper presented at the annual meeting of the American Educational Research Association, April, 1975. ED 104 893.

Wilkie, Jane R. and Irving L. Allen. "Women Sociologists and Co-authorship with Men." *American Sociologist* 10 (February 1975): 19–24.

Wilson, Deborah and Kenneth O. Doyle. "Student Ratings of Instruction: Student and Instructor Sex Interactions." *Journal of Higher Education* 47 (July/August 1976): 465–70.

CHAPTER 8
Summing Up

Anderson, Charles and John Murray (eds). *The Professors.* Cambridge, Mass.: Schenkman, 1971.

Astin, Helen S. and Alan E. Bayer. "Sex Discrimination in Academe." In *Academic Women on the Move,* edited by Alice Rossi and Ann Calderwood. New York: Russell Sage Foundation, 1973.

Avakian, A. Nancy. "An Analysis of Factors Relating to the Job Satisfaction and Dissatisfaction of Faculty Members in Institutions of Higher Education." Unpublished Ph.D. dissertation, State University of New York at Albany, 1971.

Baldwin, Roger. "Adult and Career Development: What Are the Implications for Faculty?" *Current Issues in Higher Education,* No. 2. Washington, D.C.: American Association for Higher Education, 1979.

Behymer, Charles E. "Institutional and Personal Correlates of Faculty Productivity." Unpublished Ph.D. dissertation, University of Michigan, 1974.

Berger, James. "Conservatism and the American Professoriate." Unpublished Ph.D. dissertation, University of Connecticut, 1973.

Biglan, Anthony. "The Characteristics of Subject Matter in Different Academic Areas." *Journal of Applied Psychology* 57 (June 1973): 195–203.

Blau, Peter. *The Organization of Academic Work.* New York: John Wiley and Sons, 1973.

Brown, David G. *The Mobile Professors.* Washington, D.C.: American Council on Education, 1967.

Cameron, Susan W. and Robert T. Blackburn. "Sponsorship and Academic Career Success." *Journal of Higher Education* 52 (July/August 1981): 369–77.

Cammack, E. F. "A Study of Factors Related to Mobility and Faculty Productivity and Achievement at Michigan State University." Unpublished Ph.D. dissertation, Michigan State, 1965.

Cares, Robert C. and Robert T. Blackburn. "Faculty Self-actualization: Factors Affecting Career Success." *Research in Higher Education* 9 (1978): 123–36.

Cole, Stephen and Hannelore Adamsons. "Determinants of Faculty Support for Student Demonstrations." *Sociology of Education* 42 (Fall 1969): 315–29.

———. "Professional Status and Faculty Support of Student Demonstrations." *Public Opinion Quarterly* 34 (Fall 1970): 389–94.

Crane, Diana M. "Social Class Origin and Academic Success: The Influence of Two Stratification Systems on Academic Careers." *Sociology of Education* 42 (Winter 1969): 1–17.

———. "The Academic Marketplace Revisited: A Study of Faculty Mobility Using the Cartter Ratings." *American Journal of Sociology* 75 (May 1970): 953–64.

Eckert, Ruth E. and Howard T. Williams. *College Faculty View Themselves and Their Jobs.* Minneapolis: College of Education, University of Minnesota, 1972.

Friedman, Norman L. "Jewish or Professorial Identity? The Priorization Process in Academic Situations." *Sociological Analysis* 32 (Fall 1971): 149–57.

Fulton, Oliver and Martin Trow. "Research Activity in American Higher Education." *Sociology of Education* 47 (Winter 1974): 29–73.

Gamson, Zelda. "Utilitarian and Normative Orientations toward Education." *Sociology of Education* 39 (1966): 46–73.

———. "Performance and Personalism in Student-Faculty Relations." *Sociology of Education* 40 (Fall 1967): 279–301.

Gerstl, Joel E. "Leisure, Taste, and Occupational Milieu." In *The Professors*, edited by Charles Anderson and John Murray. Cambridge, Mass.: Schenkman, 1971.

Goldblatt, Harold S. "Academic Mobility and Cross Pressures on College Teachers During the McCarthy Era." *Sociology of Education* 40 (Spring 1967): 132–44.

Hargens, Lowell L. and Grant M. Farr. "An Examination of Recent Hypotheses about Institutional Inbreeding." *American Journal of Sociology* 78 (May 1973): 1381–1402.

Hargens, Lowell L. and Warren O. Hagstrom. "Sponsored and Contest Mobility of American Academic Scientists." *Sociology of Education* 40 (Winter 1967): 24–38.

Kelly, Richard and B. Derrell Hart. "The Role Preferences of Faculty in Different Age Groups and Academic Disciplines." *Sociology of Education* 44 (Summer 1971): 351–57.

Kistler, Robert C. "The University Professor and His Family: A Study of the Duality in Roles." Unpublished Ph.D. dissertation, University of Maryland, 1967.

Klapper, Hope L. "The Young College Faculty Member—A New Breed?" *Sociology of Education* 42 (Winter 1969): 38–49.

Ladd, Everett C. and Seymour M. Lipset. *Professors, Unions, and American Higher Education.* Berkeley: The Carnegie Commission, 1973.

———. *The Divided Academy.* New York: McGraw-Hill, 1975.

Lazarsfeld, Paul F. and Wagner Thielens. *The Academic Mind.* Glencoe, Ill.: The Free Press, 1958.

Lee, David. "Marital Disruptions among University Physicians and Professors: An Empirical Study of the Relationship between Professional Activities and Evaluations of Marital Disruptions." Unpublished Ph.D. dissertation, University of Iowa, 1968.

Leon, Julio. "An Investigation of the Applicability of the Two-Factor Theory of Job Satisfaction among College and University Professors." Unpublished Ph.D. dissertation, University of Arkansas, 1973.

Levinson, Daniel J. *The Seasons of a Man's Life.* New York: Knopf, 1978.

Lewis, Lionel. "Faculty Support of Academic Freedom and Self-government." *Social Problems* 13 (1966): 450–61.

Lightfield, Timothy. "Output and Recognition of Sociologists." *American Sociologist* 6 (May 1971): 128–33.

McGee, Reece. *Academic Janus.* San Francisco: Jossey-Bass, 1971.

McInnis, Malcolm C. "Demographic and Non-Demographic Variables Associated with the Florida State University Faculty Members' Attitudes toward Collective Bargaining in Higher Education." Unpublished Ph.D. dissertation, Florida State University, 1972.

Mazur, Allan C. "The Socialization of Jews into the Academic Subculture."

In *The Professors,* edited by Charles Anderson and John Murray. Cambridge, Mass.: Schenkman, 1971.

Morgan, Richard H. "The Conflict between Teaching and Research in the Academic Role." Unpublished Ph.D. dissertation, Columbia University, 1970.

Moxley, Linda S. "Job Satisfaction of Faculty Teaching Higher Education: An Examination of Herzberg's Dual-Factor Theory and Porter's Need Satisfaction Research." *Resources in Education* 12 (October 1977): 92. ED 139 349.

Nicholson, Edward A. and Robert C. Miljus. "Job Satisfaction and Turnover among Liberal Arts College Professors." *Personnel Journal* 51 (November 1972): 840–45.

Parsons, Talcott and Gerald M. Platt. *The American Academic Profession: A Pilot Study.* Cambridge, Mass.: Harvard University, 1968.

Smart, John C. and Gerald W. McLaughlin. "Reward Structures of Academic Disciplines." *Research in Higher Education* 8 (1978): 39–55.

Spaulding, Charles B. and Henry Turner. "Political Orientation and Field of Specialization among College Professors." *Sociology of Education* 41 (Summer 1968): 245–62.

Stecklein, John E. and Ruth E. Eckert. *An Exploratory Study of Factors Influencing the Choice of College Teaching as a Career.* Minneapolis: University of Minnesota, 1958.

Stecklein, John E. and Robert L. Lathrop. *Faculty Attraction and Retention: Factors Affecting Faculty Mobility at the University of Minnesota.* Minneapolis: Bureau of Institutional Research, University of Minnesota, 1960.

Steinberg, Stephen. *The Academic Melting Pot.* New York: McGraw-Hill, 1974.

Swierenga, Lloyd G. "Application of Herzberg's Dual-Factor Theory to Faculty Members in a University." Unpublished Ed.D. dissertation, Western Michigan University, 1970.

Thalheimer, Fred. "Continuity and Change in Religiosity: A Study of Academicians." *Pacific Sociological Review* 8 (Fall 1965): 101–8.

————. "Religiosity and Secularization in the Academic Professions." *Sociology of Education* 46 (Spring 1973): 183–202.

Weaver, Charles. "Job Satisfaction as a Component of Happiness among Males and Females." *Personnel Psychology* 31 (Winter 1978): 831–40.

Wences, Rosalio and Harold J. Abramson. "Campus Dissent and Academic Punishment: The Response of College Professors to Local Political Activism." *Sociology of Education* 45 (Winter 1972): 61–75.

Whitlock, Gerald H. "The Experiential Bases and Dimensions of Faculty Morale at a State University." Mimeographed. Knoxville: University of Tennessee, 1965.

Willie, Reynold and John E. Stecklein. "A Three-Decade Comparison of College Faculty Characteristics, Satisfactions, Activities, and Attitudes." *Research in Higher Education* 16 (1982): 81–93.

Wilson, Robert C. and Jerry G. Gaff. *College Professors and Their Impact on Students.* New York: John Wiley and Sons, 1975.

Youn, Ted I. "The Careers of Young Ph.D.s: Temporal Change and Institutional Effects." Unpublished Ph.D. dissertation, Yale University, 1981.

APPENDIX A
Search and Sampling Procedures

Caplow, Theodore and Reece J. McGee. *The Academic Marketplace.* New York: Basic Books, 1958.

Cartwright, Dorwin P. "Analysis of Qualitative Material." In *Research Methods in the Behavioral Sciences,* edited by Leon Festinger and Daniel Katz. New York: The Dryden Press, 1953.

Eells, Walter C. *College Teachers and College Teaching.* Atlanta: Southern Regional Education Board, 1957.

———. *College Teachers and College Teaching.* 1st Supplement. Atlanta: Southern Regional Education Board, 1959.

———. *College Teachers and College Teaching.* 2nd Supplement. Atlanta: Southern Regional Education Board, 1962.

Jencks, Christopher and David Riesman. *The Academic Revolution.* Garden City, N.Y.: Doubleday Anchor, 1969.

Kaplan, Abraham. *The Conduct of Inquiry.* San Francisco: Chandler Publishing Company, 1964.

Light, Donald et al. *The Impact of the Academic Revolution on Faculty Careers.* ERIC-AAHE Research Reports, No. 10. Washington, D.C.: American Association for Higher Education, 1972.

Litton, Maurice L. and W. Hugh Stickler. *College Teachers and College Teaching.* 3rd Supplement. Atlanta: Southern Regional Education Board, 1967.

Livesey, Herbert. *The Professors.* New York: Charterhouse, 1975.

Professor X. *This Beats Working for a Living.* New Rochelle, N.Y.: Arlington House, 1973.

Wilson, Logan. *The Academic Man.* London: Oxford University Press, 1942.

APPENDIX B
Data Collection and Analysis Procedures

Denzin, Norman K. *The Research Act.* Chicago: Aldine, 1970.

French, J. R. and B. Raven. "The Bases of Social Power." In *Group Dynamics,* edited by D. Cartwright and A. Zander. Evanston, Ill.: Row, Peterson, and Co., 1960.

Kerlinger, Frederick N. *Foundations of Behavioral Research.* New York: Holt, Rinehart and Winston, 1973.

McNamara, James F. "Practical Significance and Mathematical Models in Administrative Research." In *Problem Finding in Educational Administration,* edited by Glenn Immegart and William Boyd. Lexington, Mass.: D. C. Heath, 1979.

Index

201–2; research productivity and marriage, 213–14; salary, 84 n. 7, 184–85; socioeconomic origins, 208; status, current, 181–86; student levels taught, 198; success, self-perceptions of, 107–8; teaching

effectiveness ratings, 203–4; teaching load, 198; tenure, 183

Women's movement, 179–81

World Wars I and II, academic roles in, 26